God of God, Light of Light, true God of true God. *

I ... , not made, *

... Father. *

I ... de. *

... salvation came

And He became flesh by the Holy Spirit of the Virgin Mary: *
  and was made Man. *
He was also crucified for us, *
  suffered under Pontius Pilate, and was buried. *
And on the third day He rose again, according to the Scriptures. *
He ascended into heaven and sits at the right hand of the Father. *
He will come again in glory to judge the living and the dead. *
And of His kingdom there will be no end. *
And I believe in the Holy Spirit, the Lord and Giver of life, *
  Who proceeds from the Father and the Son. *
Who together with the Father and the Son is adored and glorified, *
  and Who spoke through the prophets. *
And one holy, Catholic, and Apostolic Church. *
I confess one baptism for the forgiveness of sins. *
And I await the resurrection of the dead. *
  And the life of the world to come. Amen.

Page	Sunday or Feast	1969	1970	1971	1972	1973	1974
75	Holy Name of Jesus.	5 Jan.	4 Jan.	3 Jan.	2 Jan.	2 Jan.	2 Jan.
84	Feast of Holy Family	12 Jan.	11 Jan.	10 Jan.	9 Jan.	7 Jan.	13 Jan.
89	2nd Sun. after Epiph.	19 Jan.	18 Jan.	17 Jan.	16 Jan.	14 Jan.	20 Jan.
94	3rd Sun. after Epiph.	26 Jan.	....	24 Jan.	23 Jan.	21 Jan.	27 Jan.
98	4th Sun. after Epiph..	....	....	31 Jan.	.. --.	28 Jan.	3 Feb.
102	5th Sun. after Epiph..	....	....	....	....	4 Feb.	....
106	6th Sun. after Epiph..	....	....	....	....	11 Feb.	....
111	Septuagesima........	2 Feb.	25 Jan.	7 Feb.	30 Jan.	18 Feb.	10 Feb.
116	Sexagesima........	9 Feb.	1 Feb.	14 Feb.	6 Feb.	25 Feb.	17 Feb.
122	Quinquagesima ...	16 Feb.	8 Feb.	21 Feb.	13 Feb.	4 Mar.	24 Feb.
127	1st Sun. of Lent....	23 Feb.	15 Feb.	28 Feb.	20 Feb.	11 Mar.	3 Mar.
133	2nd Sun. of Lent....	2 Mar.	22 Feb.	7 Mar.	27 Feb.	18 Mar.	10 Mar.
137	3rd Sun. of Lent....	9 Mar.	1 Mar.	14 Mar.	5 Mar.	25 Mar.	17 Mar.
142	4th Sun. of Lent....	16 Mar.	8 Mar.	21 Mar.	12 Mar.	1 Apr.	24 Mar.
147	Passion Sunday.....	23 Mar.	15 Mar.	28 Mar.	19 Mar.	8 Apr.	31 Mar.
153	Palm Sunday......	30 Mar.	22 Mar.	4 Apr.	26 Mar	15 Apr.	7 Apr.
167	Easter Sunday.....	6 Apr.	29 Mar.	11 Apr.	2 Apr.	22 Apr.	14 Apr.
172	1st Sun. after Easter	13 Apr.	5 Apr.	18 Apr.	9 Apr.	29 Apr.	21 Apr.
176	2nd Sun. after Easter	20 Apr.	12 Apr.	25 Apr.	16 Apr.	6 May	28 Apr.
180	3rd Sun. after Easter	27 Apr.	19 Apr.	2 May	23 Apr.	13 May	5 May
184	4th Sun. after Easter	4 May	26 Apr.	9 May	30 Apr.	20 May	12 May
188	5th Sun. after Easter	11 May	3 May	16 May	7 May	27 May	19 May
192	Ascension Day.....	15 May	7 May	20 May	11 May	31 May	23 May
197	Sun. after Ascension.	18 May	10 May	23 May	14 May	3 June	26 May
201	Pentecost Sunday...	25 May	17 May	30 May	21 May	10 June	2 June
207	Trinity Sunday.....	1 June	24 May	6 June	28 May	17 June	9 June
211	Corpus Christi.....	5 June	28 May	10 June	1 June	21 June	13 June
218	2nd Sun. after Pent..	8 June	31 May	13 June	4 June	24 June	16 June
222	Sacred Heart.......	13 June	5 June	18 June	9 June	29 June	21 June
228	3rd Sun. after Pent..	15 June	7 June	20 June	11 June	1 July	23 June
232	4th Sun. after Pent..	22 June	14 June	27 June	18 June	8 July	30 June
236	5th Sun. after Pent..	29 June	21 June	4 July	25 June	15 July	7 July
240	6th Sun. after Pent..	6 July	28 June	11 July	2 July	22 July	14 July
244	7th Sun. after Pent..	13 July	5 July	18 July	9 July	29 July	21 July
248	8th Sun. after Pent..	20 July	12 July	25 July	16 July	5 Aug.	28 July
252	9th Sun. after Pent..	27 July	19 July	1 Aug.	23 July	12 Aug.	4 Aug.
256	10th Sun. after Pent.	3 Aug.	26 July	8 Aug.	30 July	19 Aug.	11 Aug.
260	11th Sun. after Pent.	10 Aug.	2 Aug.	15 Aug.	6 Aug.	26 Aug.	18 Aug.
264	12th Sun. after Pent.	17 Aug.	9 Aug.	22 Aug.	13 Aug.	2 Sept.	25 Aug.
269	13th Sun. after Pent.	24 Aug.	16 Aug.	29 Aug.	20 Aug.	9 Sept.	1 Sept
273	14th Sun. after Pent.	31 Aug.	23 Aug.	5 Sept	27 Aug.	16 Sept.	8 Sept.
277	15th Sun. after Pent.	7 Sept	30 Aug.	12 Sept	3 Sept	23 Sept.	15 Sept.
281	16th Sun. after Pent.	14 Sept.	6 Sept.	19 Sept	10 Sept	30 Sept.	22 Sept.
285	17th Sun. after Pent.	21 Sept.	13 Sept.	26 Sept	17 Sept	7 Oct. U	29 Sept
289	18th Sun. after Pent.	28 Sept	20 Sept.	3 Oct.	24 Sept	14 Oct.	6 Oct.
293	19th Sun. after Pent.	5 Oct.	27 Sept.	10 Oct.	1 Oct.	21 Oct.	13 Oct.
297	20th Sun. after Pent.	12 Oct.	4 Oct.	17 Oct.	8 Oct.	....	20 Oct.
306	21st Sun. after Pent.	19 Oct.	11 Oct.	24 Oct.	15 Oct.	4 Nov.	....
301	Christ the King.....	26 Oct.	25 Oct.	31 Oct.	29 Oct.	28 Oct.	27 Oct.
311	22nd Sun. after Pent.	....	18 Oct.	....	22 Oct.	11 Nov.	3 Nov
315	23rd Sun. after Pent.	2 Nov.	....	7 Nov.	....	18 Nov.	10 Nov
319	24th Sun. after Pent.	**9 Nov	*1 Nov.	14 Nov.	*5 Nov.	....	17 Nov.
319	25th Sun. after Pent.	16 Nov.	**8 Nov.	....	12 Nov.	....	....
319	26th Sun. after Pent.	....	15 Nov.	....	19 Nov.	....	....
319	27th Sun. after Pent.	....	....	....	....	....	....
322	Last Sun. after Pent.	23 Nov.	22 Nov.	21 Nov.	26 Nov.	25 Nov.	24 Nov.
46	1st Sun. of Advent..	30 Nov.	29 Nov.	28 Nov.	3 Dec.	2 Dec.	1 Dec.
50	2nd Sun. of Advent..	7 Dec.	6 Dec.	5 Dec.	10 Dec.	9 Dec.	8 Dec.
54	3rd Sun. of Advent..	14 Dec.	13 Dec.	12 Dec.	17 Dec.	16 Dec.	15 Dec.
58	4th Sun. of Advent..	21 Dec.	20 Dec.	19 Dec.	24 Dec.	23 Dec.	22 Dec.
68	Sun. after Christmas	28 Dec	27 Dec.	26 Dec.	31 Dec.	30 Dec.	29 Dec.

** Page 320.   * Page 321.

The People of God
together with Christ
worship the heavenly Father

Saint Joseph

SUNDAY MISSAL

APPROVED CANADIAN EDITION

**With all Mass prayers recited by the people
printed in BOLDFACE and arranged in SENSE LINES
for easy congregational recitation.**

	Page
• How to Use this Mass Book	4
• Ordinary of the Mass	10
• Proper of the Time	45
• Hymn Section	372
• English Sung Masses	436
• Treasury of Prayers	463

921-1-C

"He is the true Lamb Who has taken away the sins of the world. By dying He destroyed our death and by rising He gave us life remade."

(Easter Preface)

NEW
SAINT JOSEPH
SUNDAY MISSAL
AND HYMNAL

THE COMPLETE MASSES FOR SUNDAYS AND HOLYDAYS

**With the People's Parts of Holy Mass
Printed in Boldface Type
and Arranged for Parish Participation**

**In accordance with the
New Revised Liturgy**

•

APPROVED CANADIAN EDITION

CATHOLIC BOOK PUBLISHING CO.
"St. Joseph Editions: Bibles, Missals, and Prayer Books"

NIHIL OBSTAT:

L. Flynn
Censor Librorum

IMPRIMATUR: ✠ G. Emmett Carter, D.D.
Bishop of London

This new Missal has been diligently prepared with the invaluable assistance of a special Board of Editors, including specialists in Liturgy, Sacred Scripture, Catechetics, Sacred Music and Art.

The Official texts of the Ordinary and the Proper are reproduced with permission from the Roman Missal with English translations approved for liturgical use in Canada by the Canadian Hierarchy. © 1964 by the National Catholic Welfare Conference, Inc. Scriptural Verses adapted from the Book of Psalms © 1950 and 1955 by the Confraternity of Christian Doctrine. Prayers, Secrets and Postcommunions © 1964 by Benziger Bros. Inc., New York, N.Y.—International Copyright secured—All rights reserved.

All other texts, illustrations and special "sense-line arrangement" for congregational recitation (based on poetic structure) Copyright 1965 by Catholic Book Publishing Co., N.Y.

Music acknowledgments on p. 462.

How to use this Missal

1. Refer to Liturgical Calendar for the "Mass for Today."

2. Mass begins ("Ordinary") on p. 10.

3. **Boldface** type always indicates the **people's parts** that are to be recited aloud.

4. This arrow (**Ɐ**) means continue to read. This arrow (**➤**) indicates a reference to the "Ordinary" or the "Proper."

New Eucharistic Prayers and Prefaces © 1968, International Committee on English in the Liturgy, Inc. All rights reserved. Reproduced with permission.

(T-921)

INTRODUCTION

In the Constitution on the Sacred Liturgy of the Second Vatican Council, Holy Mother Church comments on the Eucharistic Sacrifice of the Altar as follows:

"At the Last Supper, on the night when He was betrayed, our Savior instituted the Eucharistic sacrifice of His Body and Blood. He did this in order to perpetuate the sacrifice of the Cross throughout the centuries until He should come again, and so to entrust to His beloved spouse, the Church, a memorial of His Death and Resurrection: a Sacrament of love, a sign of unity, a bond of charity, a Paschal banquet in which Christ is eaten, the mind is filled with grace, and a pledge of future glory is given to us.

"The Church, therefore, earnestly desires that Christ's faithful, when present at this Mystery of Faith, should not be there as strangers or silent spectators; on the contrary, through a good understanding of the rites and prayers they should take part in the sacred action conscious of what they are doing, with devotion and full collaboration. They should be instructed by God's word and be nourished at the table of the Lord's Body; they should give thanks to God; by offering the Immaculate Victim, not only through the hands of the priest, but also with him, they should learn also to offer themselves; through Christ the Mediator, they should be drawn day by day into ever more perfect union with God and with each other, so that finally God may be all in all" (Nos. 47. 48).

Accordingly, this new Sunday Missal has been edited, in conformity with the latest findings of modern liturgists, especially to enable the people to attain the most active participation.

To insure that "each . . . layman who has an office to perform [will] do all of, but only, those parts which pertain to his office" (No. 28), a simple method of instant identification of the various parts of the Mass, has been designed, utilizing different type faces:

(1) **boldface type** — clearly identifies all people's parts for each Mass.

(2) lightface type — indicates the priest's or lector's parts.

(a) lightface roman type — indicates the priest's parts, as well as the Scripture Readings proclaimed to the people by the priest, or lector.

(b) *lightface italic type* — indicates the parts said by the priest in the name of the people (Prayer, Secret, Postcommunion).

Because of its importance and dignity, the great Eucharistic Prayer of the Canon (which is said by the priest in the name of the people) is printed in a clear format—in sense lines and lightface roman type.

The people's parts are all arranged in sense-line format based on the poetic structure of the original chants, with pauses indicated by asterisks for easier understanding and congregational recitation.

In their desire to make this Missal completely serviceable under all conditions, the editors have also included a large selection of Popular Hymns and Antiphons, a few sung Masses, and a Treasury of Prayers.

The "Ordinary of the Mass" contains not only the complete English text but also the Latin Responses for dialogue Mass, to facilitate the fulfillment of the Church's desire that "steps should be taken so that the faithful may also be able to say . . . together in Latin those parts of the Ordinary of the Mass which pertain to them" (No. 54). For greater convenience, these are clearly marked and printed at the bottom of each page. In addition, each is broken up into phrases by pause marks (/) and the Latin words are separated into syllables for easier pronunciation.

Many other special features such as the "Thought for Today," concise notes on "Bible and Liturgy" and the capsule summaries of the prayers, as well as the modern liturgical drawings, are intended to enable all the faithful, in keeping with the desire of the Church, to "be led to that full, conscious, and active participation in liturgical celebrations which is demanded by the very nature of the liturgy. Such participation by the Christian people as a chosen race, a royal priesthood, a holy nation, a redeemed people (1 Pet. 2, 9; cf. 2, 4-5), is their right and duty by reason of their baptism" (No. 14).

PLAN OF THE MASS

The people's parts are in **bold type.**

LITURGY OF THE WORD OF GOD

—Entrance Rite—

1. Introit   **2. Kyrie**
3. Gloria   4. Prayer

— The Word of God —

5. Epistle   **6. Gradual**   **7. Alleluia**
8. Gospel   9. Homily   **10. Creed**
11. Prayer of the Faithful

LITURGY OF THE EUCHARIST

— Preparation of the Gifts —

12. Offertory Verse   13. Prayer over the Gifts

— The Eucharistic Prayer —

14. Introduction to the Preface
15. Acclamation - "Holy, holy, holy."
16. Sacred Canon
17. The Great Amen

— The Eucharistic Banquet —

18. Our Father   **19. Lamb of God**
20. Communion Verse
21. The Postcommunion   22. The Dismissal Rite

PRAYER BEFORE MASS

RECEIVE, O Holy Trinity, One God, this Holy Sacrifice of the Body and Blood of our Lord Jesus Christ, which I, Your unworthy servant, desire now to offer to Your Divine Majesty by the hands of this Your minister, with all the Sacrifices which have ever been or will be offered to You, in union with that most Holy Sacrifice offered by the same Christ our Lord at the Last Supper, and on the Altar of the Cross.

I offer it to You with the utmost affection of devotion, out of pure love for Your infinite goodness, and according to the most holy intention of the same Christ our Lord, and of our Holy Mother the Church.

O GOD, almighty and merciful, grant us through this Holy Sacrifice, joy and peace, a holier life, time to do penance, grace and consolation of the Holy Spirit, and perseverance in good works. Amen.

I. LITURGY of the WORD of GOD

II. LITURGY of the EUCHARIST

ORDINARY OF THE MASS
Entrance Rite

STAND

[If Hymn is omitted—KNEEL up to ★ on page 12]

The Prayers at the Foot of the Altar are the Priest's private preparation for Mass. The people usually recite or sing the Introit or an Entrance Hymn at this time.

On Sundays the opening prayer may take the form of the Asperges Rite or the blessing of the people with Holy Water as the Priest enters. This is a sacramental reminder of the Sacrament of Baptism by which we are constituted God's People. When this blessing is given the Priest omits the *Confiteor*.

IN THE NAME of the Father, ✠ and of the Son, and of the Holy Spirit. Amen.

PRIEST: I will go in to the altar of God.

SERVER: *The God of my gladness and joy.*

PRIEST: Our help is in the name of the Lord.

SERVER: *Who made heaven and earth.*

In nómine Patris, et Fílii, ✠ et Spíritus Sancti. Amen.

PRIEST: Introíbo ad altáre Dei.

SERVER: Ad De-um qui læ-tí-fi-cat iu-ven-tú-tem me-am.

PRIEST: Adiutórium nostrum in nómine Dómini.

SERVER: Qui fe-cit cæ-lum et ter-ram.

THE CONFITEOR

PRIEST: I confess to Almighty God, etc.

SERVER: *May Almighty God have mercy on you, forgive you your sins, and bring you to life everlasting.*

PRIEST: Amen.

SERVER: *I confess to Almighty God, to Blessed Mary, ever Virgin, to Blessed Michael the Archangel, to Blessed John the Baptist, to the Holy Apostles Peter and Paul, to all the Saints, and to you, Father, that I have sinned exceedingly in thought, word and deed,* (strike breast three times:) *through my fault, through my fault, through my most grievous fault. Therefore I beseech Blessed Mary, ever Virgin, Blessed Michael the Archangel, Blessed John the Baptist, the Holy Apostles Peter and Paul, all the Saints, and you, Father, to pray to the Lord our God for me.*

PRIEST: Confíteor Deo, etc.

SERVER: Mi-se-re-á-tur tu-i o-mní-po-tens De-us, / et di-mís-sis pec-cá-tis tu-is, / per-dú-cat te ad vi-tam æ-tér-nam.

PRIEST: Amen.

SERVER: Con-fí-te-or De-o o-mni-po-tén-ti, / be-á-tæ Ma-rí-æ sem-per Vír-gi-ni, / be-á-to Mi-cha-é-li Arch-án-ge-lo, / be-á-to Io-án-ni Bap-tí-stæ, / san-ctis A-pó-sto-lis Pe-tro et Pau-lo, / ó-mni-bus San-ctis, et ti-bi, Pa-ter: / qui-a pec-cá-vi ni-mis co-gi-ta-ti-ó-ne, ver-bo, et ó-pe-re: / (strike breast three times) me-a cul-pa, / me-a cul-pa, / me-a má-xi-ma cul-pa. / I-de-o pre-cor be-á-tam Ma-rí-am sem-per Vír-gi-nem, / be-á-tum Mi-cha-é-lem Arch-án-ge-lum, / be-á-tum Io-án-nem Bap-tí-stam, / san-ctos A-pó-sto-los Pe-trum et Pau-lum, / o-mnes San-ctos, et te, Pa-ter, / o-rá-re pro me ad Dó-mi-num De-um no-strum.

PETITION FOR REMISSION OF SINS

PRIEST: May Almighty God have mercy on you, forgive you your sins, and bring you to life everlasting.

SERVER: *Amen.*

PRIEST: May the Almighty and Merciful Lord grant us pardon, ✠ absolution, and remission of our sins.

SERVER: *Amen.*

PRIEST: Will You not, O God, give us life?

SERVER: *And shall not Your people rejoice in You?*

PRIEST: Show us, O Lord, Your kindness.

SERVER: *And grant us Your salvation.*

PRIEST: O Lord, hear my prayer.

SERVER: *And let my cry come to You.*

PRIEST: The Lord be with you.

SERVER: *And with your spirit.*

PRIEST: Let us pray. ★   *STAND*

PRIEST: Misereátur vestri omnípotens Deus, et dimíssis peccátis vestris, perdúcat vos ad vitam ætérnam.

SERVER: A-men.

PRIEST: Indulgéntiam, ✠ absolutiónem, et remissiónem peccatórum nostrórum, tríbuat nobis omnípotens et miséricors **Dóminus.**

SERVER: A-men.

PRIEST: Deus, tu convérsus vivificábis nos.

SERVER: Et plebs tu-a læ-tá-bi-tur in te.

PRIEST: Osténde nobis, Dómine, misericórdiam tuam.

SERVER: Et sa-lu-tá-re tu-um da no-bis.

PRIEST: Dómine, exáudi oratiónem meam.

SERVER: Et cla-mor me-us ad te vé-ni-at.

PRIEST: Dóminus vobíscum.

SERVER: Et cum spí-ri-tu tu-o.

PRIEST: Orémus.

PRAYER FOR PURITY

Going up to the Altar, the priest prays silently:

TAKE away from us our sins, O Lord, we beseech You, that we may enter with pure minds into the Holy of Holies. Through Christ our Lord. Amen.

Bowing down and kissing the Altar, the Priest prays:

WE BESEECH You, O Lord, by the merits of Your Saints whose relics lie here, and of all the Saints: deign in Your mercy to pardon me all my sins. Amen.

THE INTROIT

WE PRAISE GOD

The Lector and/or the people pray the Introit aloud. The Priest listens.

Turn to ➤ INTROIT — Today's Mass

STAND

THE KYRIE WE BEG GOD FOR MERCY

PRIEST: Lord, have mercy. (Kýrie, eléison.)

PEOPLE: Lord, have mercy. (Ký-ri-e, e-lé-i-son.)

PRIEST: Lord, have mercy. (Kýrie, eléison.)

PEOPLE: Christ, have mercy. (Chri-ste, e-lé-i-son.)

PRIEST: Christ, have mercy. (Christe, eléison.)

PEOPLE: Christ, have mercy. (Chri-ste, e-lé-i-son.)

PRIEST: Lord, have mercy. (Kýrie, eléison.)

PEOPLE: Lord, have mercy. (Ký-ri-e, e-lé-i-son.)

PRIEST: Lord, have mercy. (Kýrie, eléison.)

THE GLORIA *OUR HYMN OF PRAISE*

PRIEST: Glory to God in the highest.

PEOPLE: **And on earth peace to men of good will.** *

We praise You. We bless You. We worship You. We glorify You. *

We give You thanks for Your great glory. *

Lord God, heavenly King, God the Father almighty. *

Lord Jesus Christ, the Only-begotten Son. *

Lord God, Lamb of God, Son of the Father. *

You, Who take away the sins of the world, *
have mercy on us. *

You, Who take away the sins of the world, *
receive our prayer. *

PRIEST: Glória in excélsis Deo.

PEOPLE:

Et in ter-ra pax ho-mí-ni-bus bo-næ vo-lun-tá-tis. / Lau-dá-mus te. / Be-ne-dí-ci-mus te. / A-do-rá-mus te. / Glo-ri-fi-cá-mus te. / Grá-ti-as á-gi-mus ti-bi / pro-pter ma-gnam gló-ri-am tu-am. / Dó-mi-ne De-us, / Rex cæ-lé-stis, / De-us Pa-ter o-mní-po-tens. / Dó-mi-ne Fi-li u-nI-gé-ni-te, / Ie-su Chri-ste. / Dó-mi-ne De-us, / A-gnus De-i, / Fí-li-us Pa-tris. / Qui tol-lIs pec-cá-ta mun-di, / mi-se-ré-re no-bis. / Qui tol-lis pec-cá-ta mun-di, / sú-sci-pe de-pre-ca-ti-ó-nem no-stram. /

You, Who sit at the right hand of the Father, *

have mercy on us. *

For You alone are holy. *

You alone are Lord. *

You alone, O Jesus Christ, are most high, *

With the Holy Spirit, in the glory of God the Father. Amen.

PRIEST: The Lord be with you.

PEOPLE: And with your spirit.

PRIEST: Let us pray.

The Priest pauses while the people formulate their own intentions. He continues bringing these together, in the Prayer.

THE PRAYER *OUR PRAYER OF PETITION TO GOD*

Turn to ➤ PRAYER — *Today's Mass*

At the end of the Prayer the Priest prays aloud:

World without end.

We give our assent to this part of the Mass:

PEOPLE: Amen.

Qui se-des ad déx-te-ram Pa-tris, / mi-se-ré-re no-bis. / Quó-ni-am tu so-lus San-ctus. / Tu so-lus Dó-mi-nus. / Tu so-lus Al-tís-si-mus, / Ie-su Chri-ste. / Cum San-cto Spí-ri-tu in gló-ri-a De-i Pa-tris. / A-men.

At the Prayer

PRIEST: Dóminus vobíscum.   PEOPLE: Et cum spí-ri-tu tu-o.

PRIEST: Per ómnia sǽcula sæculórum.   PEOPLE: A-men

The Word of God

THE EPISTLE SIT

WE LISTEN TO GOD'S WORD

The Lector or Priest proclaims the Word of God.

PEOPLE: (at Low Mass): **Thanks be to God.**

THE GRADUAL AND ALLELUIA

WE RESPOND TO GOD'S WORD

The Lector and/or the people pray the Gradual, Alleluia or Tract aloud. The Priest listens.

Priest's Prayer before the Gospel

CLEANSE my heart and my lips, O Almighty God, Who cleansed the lips of the Prophet Isaia with a burning coal. In Your gracious mercy deign so to purify me that I may worthily proclaim Your holy Gospel. Through Christ our Lord. Amen.

The following prayer is omitted in Requiem Masses.

Lord, grant Your blessing.

The Lord be in my heart and on my lips, that I may worthily and fittingly proclaim His holy Gospel. Amen.

THE GOSPEL STAND

DEACON (OR PRIEST): The Lord be with you.

PEOPLE: And with your spirit.

DEACON (OR PRIEST): ✠ A reading from the holy Gospel according to N . . .

PEOPLE: Glory to You, O Lord.

THE WORD OF GOD

We listen to the Word of God proclaimed by the Priest or Deacon. The Gospel brings Jesus in our midst once again as our Master and Model. It is an invitation to a faithful following of Christ.

PEOPLE: (at Low Mass): **Praise to You, O Christ.**

The Priest (except in Requiem Masses) kisses the book, saying:

By the words of the Gospel may our sins be taken away.

THE SERMON OR HOMILY

THE PRIEST EXPLAINS THE WORD OF GOD FOR US
SIT

At the end of the Epistle
PEOPLE: De-o grá-ti-as.
Before the Gospel
PRIEST: Dóminus vobíscum.   PEOPLE: Et cum spí-ri-tu tu-o.
PRIEST: ✠ Sequéntia (vel Inítium) sancti Evangélii secúndum N . . .
PEOPLE: Gló-ri-a ti-bi, Dó-mi-ne.
After the Gospel
PEOPLE: Laus ti-bi, Chri-ste.

THE NICENE CREED   STAND

WE PROFESS OUR FAITH

We now tell God that we believe all that He has taught us. We sum up all that God has revealed and publicly proclaim our faith in it. We should repeat this Profession of Faith fervently and often.

PRIEST: I believe in one God.

PEOPLE: The Father almighty, Maker of heaven and earth, *

and of all things visible and invisible. *

And I believe in one Lord, Jesus Christ, *
the Only-begotten Son of God. *

Born of the Father before all ages. *

God of God, Light of Light, true God of true God. *

Begotten, not made, *
of one substance with the Father. *

By Whom all things were made. *

PRIEST: Credo in unum Deum.

PEOPLE:

Pa-trem o-mni-po-tén-tem, / fa-ctó-rem cæ-li et ter-ræ, / vi-si-bí-li-um ó-mni-um et in-vi-si-bí-li um. / Et in u-num Dó-mi-num Ie-sum Chri-stum, / Fí-li-um De-i u-ni-gé-ni-tum. / Et ex Pa-tre na-tum / an-te ó-mni-a sǽ-cu-la. / De-um de De-o, / lu-men de lú-mi-ne, / De-um ve-rum de De-o ve-ro. / Gé-nl-tum, non fa-ctum, / con-sub-stan-ti-á-lem Pa-tri: / per quem ó-mni-a fa-cta sunt. / Qui pro-pter nos hó-mi-nes, / et

Who for us men and for our salvation came down from heaven. *

And He became flesh by the Holy Spirit of the Virgin Mary; *
and was made man. *

He was also crucified for us, *
suffered under Pontius Pilate, and was buried. *

And on the third day He rose again, according to the Scriptures. *

He ascended into heaven and sits at the right hand of the Father. *

He will come again in glory to judge the living and the dead. *

And of His kingdom there will be no end. *

And I believe in the Holy Spirit, the Lord and Giver of life, *
Who proceeds from the Father and the Son. *

---

pro-pter no-stram sa-lú-tem / de-scén-dit de cæ-lis / et in-car-na-tus est de Spi-ri-tu San-cto / ex Ma-rí-a Vir-gi-ne: / et ho-mo fa-ctus est. / Cru-ci-fí-xus é-ti-am pro no-bis; / sub Pón-ti-o Pi-lá-to pas-sus, et se-púl-tus est. / Et re-sur-réx-it tér-ti-a di-e, / se-cún-dum Scri-ptú-ras. / Et a-scén-dit in cæ-lum: / se-det ad déx-te-ram Pa-tris. / Et í-te-rum ven-tú-rus est cum gló-ri-a iu-di-cá-re vi-vos, et mór-tu-os: / cu-ius re-gni non erit fi-nis. / Et in Spí-ri-tum San-ctum, / Dó-mi-num et vi-vi-fi-cán-tem: / qui ex Pa-tre Fi-li-ó-que pro-cé-dit. / Qui

Who together with the Father and the Son
    is adored and glorified, *
and Who spoke through the prophets. *

And one holy, Catholic, and Apostolic
    Church. *

I confess one baptism for the forgiveness
    of sins. *

And I await the resurrection of the dead. *

And the life of the world to come. Amen.

PRAYER OF THE FAITHFUL

STAND

PRIEST: The Lord be with you.

PEOPLE: And with your spirit.

PRIEST: Let us pray.

Now the Priest or Lector announces a series of petitions in which we make intercession for the needs of
the whole People of God, and for those of the local
community. We respond according to local usage.

The Priest leads the final prayer. People respond: Amen.

---

cum Pa-tre, et Fí-li-o / si-mul a-do-rá-tur, / et con-glo-ri-
fi-cá-tur: / qui lo-cú-tus est per Pro-phé-tas. / Et u-nam,
san-ctam, ca-thó-li-cam / et a-po-stó-li-cam Ec-clé-si-am.
/ Con-fí-te-or u-nam bap-tís-ma / in re-mis-si-ó-nem pec-ca-
tó-rum. / Et ex-spé-cto re-sur-re-cti-ó-nem mor-tu-ó-rum. / Et
vi-tam ven-tú-ri sǽ-cu-li. / A-men.

PRIEST: Dóminus vobíscum.   PEOPLE: Et cum spí-ri-tu tu-o.
PRIEST: Orémus.

Liturgy of 🕊️ the EUCHARIST

The Preparation of the Gifts

So far, the Mass has been a service of prayers and lessons preparing us inwardly for the sacrifice itself— a matter of words, the sacred words of prayer and revelation, but only a preliminary to the Holy Sacrifice which is an offering to God. Now we come to the preparation of the gifts of bread and wine, the materials to be used for Christ's sacrifice.

SIT

Turn to ➤ OFFERTORY VERSE — Today's Mass

Formerly, the complete psalm was sung while the people brought their gifts to the Altar. Now only a verse or two are read by the people as a reminder of the ceremony.

OFFERTORY PRAYERS

While we sing or recite the Offertory or a Hymn, the Priest begins preparing the gifts of the Sacrifice.

WE OFFER OURSELVES

The Priest offers bread. It is a sign of our offering of ourselves to God. We give ourselves through Jesus. In Holy Communion, God will give Himself to us through the true Bread that came down from heaven.

ACCEPT, O Holy Father, Almighty and Eternal God, this spotless host, which I, Your unworthy servant, offer to You, my living and true God, to atone for my numberless sins, offenses, and negligences; on behalf of all here present and likewise for all faithful Christians living and dead, that it may profit me and them as a means of salvation to life everlasting. Amen.

OUR UNION WITH CHRIST

O GOD, Who established the nature of man in wondrous dignity, and still more admirably restored it, grant that through the mystery of this water and wine, we may be made partakers of His Divinity, Who has condescended to become partaker of our humanity, Jesus Christ, Your Son, our Lord: Who with You lives and reigns in the unity of the Holy Spirit, God, world without end. Amen.

OUR PRAYER FOR THE WORLD

WE OFFER You, O Lord, the chalice of salvation, humbly begging of Your mercy that it may arise before Your divine Majesty, with a pleasing fragrance, for our salvation and for that of the whole world. Amen.

WE ASK GOD TO ACCEPT OUR SELF-OFFERING

IN A humble spirit and with a contrite heart, may we be accepted by You, O Lord, and may our sacrifice so be offered in Your sight this day as to please You, O Lord God.

OUR INVOCATION TO THE HOLY SPIRIT

COME, O Sanctifier, Almighty and Eternal God, and bless ✠ this sacrifice prepared for the glory of Your holy name.

WE PRAY FOR PURITY OF HEART AND MIND

I WASH my hands in innocence,
and I go around Your altar, O Lord,
Giving voice to my thanks,
and recounting all Your wondrous deeds.
O Lord, I love the house in which You dwell,
the tenting-place of Your glory.
Gather not my soul with those of sinners,
nor with men of blood my life.
On their hands are crimes,
and their right hands are full of bribes.
But I walk in integrity;
redeem me, and have pity on me.
My foot stands on level ground;
in the assemblies I will bless You, O Lord.

Glory be to the Father, and to the Son,
and to the Holy Spirit.
As it was in the beginning, is now, and ever
shall be,
world without end. Amen.

Omitted during Passion Time and in Requiem Masses.

OUR OFFERING TO THE BLESSED TRINITY

ACCEPT, most Holy Trinity, this offering which we are making to You in remembrance of the passion, resurrection, and ascension of Jesus Christ, our Lord; and in honor of Blessed Mary, ever Virgin, Blessed John the Baptist, the Holy Apostles Peter and Paul, and of these *(Saints whose relics are on the Altar)*, and of all the Saints; that it may add to their honor and aid our salvation; and may they deign to intercede in heaven for us who honor their memory here on earth. Through the same Christ our Lord. Amen.

THE ORATE FRATRES

PRIEST: Pray, brethren, that my Sacrifice and yours may become acceptable to God the Father Almighty.

SERVER: *May the Lord accept this Sacrifice from your hands, to the praise and glory of His name, for our advantage, and that of all His holy Church.*

At the Orate Fratres (Pray Brethren)

PRIEST: Oráte, fratres, ut meum ac vestrum sacrifícium acceptábile fiat apud Deum Patrem omnipoténtem.

SERVER: Su-scí-pi-at Dó-mi-nus sa-cri-fí-ci-um de má-ni-bus tu-ls / ad lau-dem et gló-ri-am nó-mi-nis su-i, / ad u-ti-li-tá-tem quo-que no-stram, / to-ti-ús-que Ec-clé-si-æ su-æ san-ctæ.

PRAYER OVER THE GIFTS (SECRET)

> **Turn to ➤ SECRET — Today's Mass**

The Offertory of bread and wine now comes to an end with the Secret, the climax and chief of the offering prayers. Although it varies from Mass to Mass, generally, it is a petition to God that He will accept the gift we have to offer and bless us in return. **STAND**

The Priest concludes the Secret, saying:

World without end.

We give our assent to all that has been said and done in this part of the Holy Sacrifice.

PEOPLE: Amen.

Now we approach the Sacrifice itself—not the presentation of the bread and wine, but the offering of Christ Himself. The *Preface* of Mass begins the long series of prayers surrounding the Consecration, called the *Canon* of the Mass.

The *Preface* is solemnly introduced by a kind of dialogue between the Priest and the people.

The *Preface* is a "eucharist," that is, an act of thanksgiving. Just as we enshrine the Sacred Host in the golden Ostensorium, so do we surround the Consecration with a Solemn Prayer of Thanksgiving.

At the end of the Secret

PRIEST: Per ómnia sǽcula sæculórum.

PEOPLE: A-men.

The Eucharistic Prayer

(For optional Eucharistic Prayers, see p. 447.)

PREFACE — CANON

PRIEST: The Lord be with you.

PEOPLE: And with your spirit.

PRIEST: Lift up your hearts.

PEOPLE: We have lifted them up to the Lord.

PRIEST: Let us give thanks to the Lord our God.

PEOPLE: It is right and just.

THE PREFACE FOR SUNDAYS

OUR PRAYER OF THANKSGIVING

RIGHT AND worthy it is,
fitting and for our good
that in every time and place
our thanks should rise to You,
O Lord, holy Father,
almighty and eternal God.

Together with Your only Son
and Holy Spirit,
You are one God, one Lord:
not one as a single person,
but as a Trinity of Persons
one in substance.

PRIEST: Dóminus vobíscum.   PEOPLE: Et cum spí-ri-tu tu-o.

PRIEST: Sursum corda.   PEOPLE: Ha-bé-mus ad Dó-mi-num.

PRIEST: Grátias agámus Dómino Deo nostro.

PEOPLE: Di-gnum et iu-stum est.

By the light of Your holy Word,
　what we believe of Your glory,
　we also hold of Your Son,
　we also hold of Your Holy Spirit,
　professing no difference or separation.

Therefore, when we proclaim
　Your true and eternal Godhead,
　we adore the Persons as distinct,
　their Essence as one
　and their Majesty as equal.

In praise of which
　the Angels and Archangels,
　the Cherubim, too,
　and the Seraphim,
　day by day with one voice
　chant their endless hymn:

THE SANCTUS　*OUR HYMN OF PRAISE*

PEOPLE:　　　　　　　*[First Acclamation of the People]*

Holy, holy, holy Lord God of Hosts. *

**Heaven and earth are filled with Your
　　glory.** *

Hosanna in the highest. *

**Blessed is He Who comes in the name
　　of the Lord.** *

Hosanna in the highest.　　　　　*KNEEL*

At the Sanctus
PEOPLE:
San-ctus, San-ctus, San-ctus, / Dó-mi-nus De-us Sá-ba-oth. /
Ple-ni sunt cæ-li et ter-ra gló-ri-a tu-a. / Ho-sán-na in ex-
cél-sis. / Be-ne-dí-ctus qui ve-nit in nó-mi-ne Dó-mi-ni. /
Ho-sán-na in ex-cél-sis.

THE CANON

[Praise to the Father]

We come to you, Father,
with praise and thanksgiving,
through Jesus Christ your Son.
Through him we ask you to accept and
  bless
these gifts we offer you in sacrifice.

[Intercessions: For the Church]

We offer them for your holy catholic
  Church,
watch over it, Lord, and guide it;
grant it peace and unity throughout the
  world.

We offer them for N. our Pope,

for N. our bishop,

and for all who hold and teach the catholic
   faith

that comes to us from the apostles.

[For the Living]

Remember, Lord, your people,

especially those for whom we now pray,
   N. and N.

Remember all of us gathered here before
   you.

You know how firmly we believe in you

and dedicate ourselves to you.

We offer you this sacrifice of praise

for ourselves and those who are dear to us.

We pray to you, our living and true God,

for our well-being and redemption.

[In Communion with the Saints]

In union with the whole Church

we honor Mary,

the ever-virgin mother of Jesus Christ our
   Lord and God.

We honor Joseph, her husband,

the apostles and martyrs Peter and Paul,

Andrew, James, John,
Thomas, James, Philip,
Bartholomew, Matthew, Simon and Jude;
we honor Linus, Cletus, Clement, Sixtus,
Cornelius, Cyprian, Lawrence, Chrysogonus,
John and Paul, Cosmas and Damian,
and all the saints.
May their merits and prayers
gain us your constant help and protection.
Through Christ our Lord. Amen.

Father, accept this offering
from your whole family.
Grant us your peace in this life,
save us from final damnation,
and count us among those you have chosen.
Through Christ our Lord. Amen.

Bless and approve our offering;
make it acceptable to you,
an offering in spirit and in truth.
Let it become for us
the body and blood of Jesus Christ,
your only Son, our Lord.

[The Lord's Supper]

The day before he suffered
he took bread in his sacred hands
and looking up to heaven,
to you, his almighty Father,
he gave you thanks and praise.
He broke the bread,
gave it to his disciples, and said:
Take this, all of you, and eat it:
this is my body.

When supper was ended,
he took the cup.
Again he gave you thanks and praise,
gave the cup to his disciples, and said:
Take this, all of you, and drink from it:
this is the cup of my blood,
the blood of the new and everlasting
covenant—
the mystery of faith.
It will be shed for you and for all men
so that sins may be forgiven.
Whenever you do this,
you will do it in memory of me.

[The Memorial Prayer]

Father, we celebrate the memory of
   Christ, your Son.
We, your people and your ministers,
recall his passion,
his resurrection from the dead,
and his ascension into glory;
and from the many gifts you have given us
we offer to you, God of glory and majesty,
this holy and perfect sacrifice:
the bread of life
and the cup of eternal salvation.

Look with favor on these offerings
and accept them as once you accepted
the gifts of your servant Abel,
the sacrifice of Abraham, our father in
   faith,
and the bread and wine offered by your
   priest Melchisedech.

Almighty God,
we pray that your angel may take this
   sacrifice

to your altar in heaven.
Then, as we receive from this altar
the sacred body and blood of your Son,
let us be filled with every grace and blessing.
Through Christ our Lord. Amen.

[For the Dead]

Remember, Lord, those who have died
and have gone before us marked with the
sign of faith,
especially those for whom we now pray,
N. and N.
May these, and all who sleep in Christ,
find in your presence
light, happiness, and peace.
Through Christ our Lord. Amen.

For ourselves, too, we ask
some share in the fellowship of your apostles and martyrs,
with John the Baptist, Stephen, Matthias,
Barnabas,
Ignatius, Alexander, Marcellinus, Peter,
Felicity, Perpetua, Agatha, Lucy,

Agnes, Cecilia, Anastasia,
and all the saints.
Though we are sinners,
we trust in your mercy and love.
Do not consider what we truly deserve,
but grant us your forgiveness,
through Christ our Lord.

Through him you give us all these gifts.
You fill them with life and goodness,
you bless them and make them holy.

[Concluding Doxology]

Through him,
with him,
in him,
in the unity of the Holy Spirit,
all glory and honor is yours,
almighty Father,
for ever and ever.
All reply: **Amen.**

At the end of the Canon

PRIEST: Per ómnia saécula saeculórum.   PEOPLE: A-men.

The Eucharistic Banquet

THE LORD'S PRAYER   STAND

In the Lord's Prayer, we, the children of a Divine Father, ask that His Will be done and that He may give us bread for the body and the Heavenly Bread of Holy Communion.

PRIEST: Let us pray: Taught by our Savior's command and formed by the word of God, we dare to say:

PEOPLE:

OUR Father, Who art in heaven, * hallowed be Thy name; * Thy kingdom come; * Thy will be done on earth as it is in heaven. * Give us this day our daily bread; * and forgive us our trespasses * as we forgive those who trespass against us; * and lead us not into temptation, * but deliver us from evil.

At the Our Father

Pa-ter no-ster, qui es in cæ-lis: / san-cti-fi-cé-tur no-men tu-um: / ad-vé-ni-at re-gnum tu-um: / fi-at vo-lún-tas tu-a, sic-ut in cæ-lo, et in ter-ra. / Pa-nem no-strum co-ti-di-á-num da no-bis hó-di-e, / et di-mít-te no-bis dé-bit-ta no-stra, / sic-ut et nos di-mít-ti-mus de-bi-tó-ri-bus no-stris. / Et ne nos in-dú-cas in ten-ta-ti-ó-nem. / Sed lí-be-ra nos a ma-lo.

or

PRIEST: Et ne nos indúcas in tentatiónem.

PEOPLE: Sed lí-be-ra nos a ma-lo.

OUR FATHER

PRIEST:

Let us pray: Taught by our Sav-iour's com-mand
and formed by the word of God, we dare to say:

PEOPLE:

Our Fa-ther, who art in hea-ven, hal-lowed
be thy name; thy king-dom come, thy will be done
on earth as it is in hea-ven. Give us this day
our dai-ly bread; and for-give us our tres-pas-ses,
as we for-give those who tres-pass a-gainst us;
And lead us not in-to temp-ta-tion,
but de-li-ver us from e-vil.

Optional "Our Father," pp. 432-433.

PRAYER FOR DELIVERANCE AND PEACE

DELIVER us, Lord from every evil, past, present and to come, and at the intercession of the Blessed and glorious everVirgin Mother of God, Mary, of Your Blessed Apostles, Peter, Paul, Andrew, and all the Saints, be pleased to grant peace in our time: so that through the help of Your loving kindness, we may be ever free from sin and safe from all turmoil.

Breaking of the Host

THROUGH the same Jesus Christ, Your Son, our Lord, Who is God, living and reigning with You in the unity of the Holy Spirit.

PRIEST: For ever and ever.

PEOPLE: Amen.

PRIEST: May the peace of the Lord be always with you.

PEOPLE: And with your spirit.

MAY this mingling and consecration of the Body and Blood of our Lord Jesus Christ help us who receive it to life everlasting. Amen.

At the Prayer for Peace

PRIEST: Per ómnia saécula saeculórum.   PEOPLE: A-men.

PRIEST: Pax Dómini sit semper vobíscum.

PEOPLE: Et cum spí-ri-tu tu-o.

THE AGNUS DEI

PEOPLE: *WE PRAY FOR PEACE*

Lamb of God, Who take away the sins of the world, * have mercy on us. *

Lamb of God, Who take away the sins of the world, * have mercy on us. *

Lamb of God, Who take away the sins of the world, * grant us peace.

In Requiem Masses he says twice, grant them rest; and lastly, grant them eternal rest.

Priest's Prayers BEFORE COMMUNION

PRAYER FOR UNITY AND PEACE   **KNEEL**

The following Prayer is omitted in Requiem Masses.

O LORD Jesus Christ, Who said to Your Apostles: "Peace I leave with you, My peace I give to you," regard not my sins but the faith of Your Church, and deign to give her peace and unity according to Your will: Who live and reign God, world without end. Amen.

PEOPLE: **At the Agnus Dei**

A-gnus De-i, qui tol-lis pec-cá-ta mun-di, / mi-se-ré-re no-bis.
(In Requiem Masses: do-na e-is ré-qui-em.)

A-gnus De-i, qui tol-lis pec-cá-ta mun-di, / mi-se-ré-re no-bis.
(In Requiem Masses: do-na e-is ré-qui-em.)

A-gnus De-i, qui tol-lis pec-cá-ta mun-di, / do-na no-bis pa-cem.
(In Requiem Masses: do-na e-is ré-qui-em sem-pi-tér-nam.)

PRAYER FOR HOLINESS

O LORD Jesus Christ, Son of the living God, Who, by the will of the Father, with the co-operation of the Holy Spirit, have by Your death given life to the world, deliver me by this Your most sacred Body and Blood from all my sins and from every evil. Make me always cling to Your commandments, and never permit me to be separated from You. Who with the same God the Father and the Holy Spirit, live and reign, God, world without end. Amen.

PRAYER FOR A WORTHY COMMUNION

L ET not the partaking of Your Body, O Lord, Jesus Christ, which I, though unworthy, presume to receive, turn to my judgment and condemnation; but through Your goodness, may it become a safeguard and an effective remedy, both of soul and body. Who live and reign with God the Father, in the unity of the Holy Spirit, God, world without end. Amen.

COMMUNION OF PRIEST AND PEOPLE

HUMILITY AND PEACE

I WILL take the Bread of heaven, and call upon the name of the Lord.

The Priest holds up a Sacred Host and says:

PRIEST: Behold the Lamb of God,   behold Him Who takes away the sins of the world.

PRIEST: Ecce Agnus Dei, ecce qui tollit peccáta mundi.

WE HUMBLY CONFESS OUR UNWORTHINESS

PEOPLE: (said 3 times):

LORD, I am not worthy that You should come under my roof. * Speak but the word and my soul will be healed.

THE LIVING BREAD OF HEAVEN

MAY the Body of our Lord Jesus Christ preserve my soul to life everlasting. Amen.

He reverently consumes the Host.

SHORT ACT OF THANKSGIVING

WHAT return shall I make to the Lord for all He has given me? I will take the chalice of salvation, and I will call upon the name of the Lord. Praising will I call upon the Lord and I shall be saved from my enemies.

SHORT ACT OF FAITH

MAY the Blood of our Lord Jesus Christ preserve my soul to life everlasting. Amen.

The Priest reverently consumes the Precious Blood.

THE COMMUNION VERSE

Meanwhile, the people say the Communion Verse.

| **Turn to → COMMUNION — Today's Mass** |

PEOPLE (3 times):

Dó-mi-ne, non sum di-gnus / ut in-tres sub te-ctum me-um; / sed tan-tum dic ver-bo, / et sa-ná-bi-tur á-ni-ma me-a.

The Priest administers Communion, saying to each person:

PRIEST: The Body of Christ.

Communicant: **Amen.**

While Communion is distributed the people may sing a Communion Hymn.

THE ABLUTIONS   SIT
PRAYER FOR HOLINESS

While the Server pours a little wine into the chalice, the Priest prays:

W HAT has passed our lips as food, O Lord, may we possess in purity of heart, that what is given to us in time, be our healing for eternity.

PRAYER FOR THE GRACE OF HOLY COMMUNION

M AY Your Body, O Lord, which I have eaten, and Your Blood which I have drunk, cleave to my very soul, and grant that no trace of sin be found in me, whom these pure and holy mysteries have renewed. Who live and reign, world without end. Amen.

Here a period of silence may be observed or a psalm of praise may be sung. (If not previously said, the Priest says the Communion Verse.) Then the Priest says:

PRIEST: The Lord be with you.

PEOPLE: **And with your spirit.**

PRIEST: Let us pray.

THE POSTCOMMUNION   STAND

THANKSGIVING AFTER COMMUNION

> *Turn to* ➤ **POSTCOMMUNION —** *Today's Mass*

At the end of the Postcommunion, the Priest prays aloud:

World without end.

We give our assent to this part of the Mass:

PEOPLE: **Amen.**

THE DISMISSAL

PRIEST: The Lord be with you.

PEOPLE: **And with your spirit.**

MAY Almighty God bless you, the Father, and the Son, ✠ and the Holy Spirit.

PEOPLE: **Amen.**

PRIEST: Dóminus vobíscum.   PEOPLE: Et cum spí-ri-tu tu-o.

PRIEST: Per ómnia saécula saeculórum.   PEOPLE: A-men.

At the Final Prayers

PRIEST: Dóminus vobíscum.   PEOPLE: Et cum spí-ri-tu tu-o.

PRIEST: Benedícat vos omnípotens Deus, Pater, ✠ et Fílius, et Spíritus Sanctus.   PEOPLE: A-men.

DEACON (OR PRIEST): Go in the peace of Christ.

PEOPLE: Thanks be to God.

In Masses to be followed by a procession:

PRIEST: Let us bless the Lord.

PEOPLE: Thanks be to God.

A Recessional Hymn may be sung.

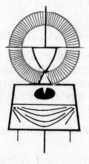

PRIEST: Ite, missa est.   PEOPLE: De-o grá-ti-as.

PRAYER CONCLUSIONS

Throughout the Missal the first few words of the prayer conclusions are indicated. When three Prayers, Secrets and Postcommunions are to be said, the conclusions of the 2nd Prayer, Secret and Postcommunion are omitted. The complete texts of these conclusions which should be memorized are as follows:

For Prayers addressed to God the Father:

Through our Lord Jesus Christ, Your Son, Who lives and reigns with You in the unity of the Holy Spirit, God, world without end. People: **Amen.**

When our Lord is mentioned at the beginning or body of the Prayer:

Through the same Jesus Christ, Your Son, our Lord, Who lives and reigns with You in the unity of the Holy Spirit, God, world without end. People: **Amen.**

For Prayers mentioning the Holy Spirit:

Through . . . in the unity of the same. Through our Lord Jesus Christ, Your Son, Who lives and reigns with You in the unity of the same Holy Spirit, God, world without end. People: **Amen.**

For Prayers whose final clause mentions our Blessed Lord:

Who with You lives and reigns in the unity of the Holy Spirit, world without end. People: **Amen.**

When the Prayer is addressed to God the Son:

Who live and reign with God the Father, in the unity of the Holy Spirit, God, world without end. People: **Amen.**

THE CHRISTMAS CYCLE (I)
ADVENT — The Preparation

Creation, including ourselves, is submitted to a master-plan, which is in a process of being realized by the Creator. All creation groans and travails in pain till it will be delivered from its slavery to corruption into the freedom of the glory of the sons of God (*see* Rom. 8, 21-22).

But when after millions of years man, created in innocence, finally appeared on the scene—one of the highlights of this Divinely-intended evolution—he chose not to cooperate with this process of mysterious growth into the image of the Creator (Gen. 1, 27). Consequently man's state of incompleteness became a sinful deficiency.

Advent is the time of waiting for Christ's coming in grace on Christmas to us (*see* John 14, 23) and for His final coming, when God's master-plan of creation will be fully realized in all who have put on Christ by Faith and Baptism (Gal. 3, 27).

THE CHRISTMAS CYCLE (II)
CHRISTMAS — EPIPHANY — CANDLEMAS
The Festive Celebrations

The Feasts of the Liturgical year place before our minds the sign of some hidden sacred reality which must be applied to all of us. During the Christmas season this hidden sacred reality is the light, the life and the joy, beaming from Christ, the "Sun of Justice," upon mankind in the darkness of ignorance and sin (Mal. 4, 2).

This mystery of our Salvation is to be honored not as something that happened 2000 years ago, but as something present, for while the act itself (Christ's birth and manifestation) is past, its effects are present. The hidden reality in this mystery is ultimately Christ and His saving action.

The Sundays after Epiphany are an after-glow, repeating and elaborating themes of this cycle.

"It is now the hour for you to wake up from sleep."

FIRST SUNDAY OF ADVENT

THOUGHT FOR TODAY: It is now the hour for us to rise from the sleep of sin and of religious indifference. Let us start our preparation for the blessing of Christmas with great confidence in Jesus, for "no one who waits for (Him) shall be put to shame."

BIBLE AND LITURGY: The Church sees Christ's coming to us at Christmas and at the end of the world in one perspective. What matters is Christ's coming in Grace. READ: Gen. 12, 1-9; 17, 1-8; Ex. 19, 1-8; Jer. 31, 31-33; Gal. 3, 7-9; 16, 26-29.

INTROIT Ps. 24, 1 3   [*Hope*]

To You I lift up my soul; *
  in You, O my God, I trust; *
Let me not be put to shame; *
  let not my enemies exult over me. *
No one who waits for You shall be put to shame. *
(Ps.) Your ways, O Lord, make known to me; *
  teach me Your paths. *

Glory be to the Father, and to the Son, *
   and to the Holy Spirit. *

As it was in the beginning, is now, and ever
      shall be, *
   world without end. Amen. *

To You I lift up my soul; *
   in You, O my God, I trust; *

Let me not be put to shame; *
   let not my enemies exult over me. *

No one who waits for You shall be put to
   shame.

→ *Kyrie, p. 13. Omit Gloria.*

PRAYER   [Protection from Sin]

*Put forth Your power, O Lord, we beseech You,
and come, that with You as our Protector we
may be rescued from the impending danger of
our sins; and with You as our Deliverer, may
we obtain our salvation. Who live, etc.* † People: **Amen.** ⍱

EPISTLE Rom. 13, 11-14   [Live in the Light]

Brethren: It is now the hour for you to wake
up from sleep, because our salvation is
closer than when we first accepted the faith.
The night is far gone; the day is drawing near.
Let us cast aside deeds of darkness and put on
the armor of light. Let us live honorably, as in
daylight: not in carousing and drunkenness, not
in sexual excess and lust, not in quarreling and
jealousy. Instead, put on the Lord Jesus Christ. ⍱

† The different endings of the Prayers are on p. 44.

GRADUAL　Ps. 24, 3. 4　　　*[Hopes Fulfilled]*

No one who waits for You shall be put to shame. *
Your ways, O Lord, make known to me; *
teach me Your paths.

Alleluia, alleluia. *　　　*[Mercy for All]*
Show us, O Lord, Your kindness, *
and grant us Your salvation. Alleluia.

➤ *Prayer before the Gospel, p.* 16.

GOSPEL　Luke 21, 25-33　　　*[Christ's Next Coming]*

At that time Jesus said to His disciples: "There will be signs in the sun, the moon, and the stars. On the earth nations will be in anguish, distraught at the roaring of the sea and the waves. Men will die of fright in anticipation of what is coming over the earth; for the hosts of heaven will be shaken loose. And then men will see the Son of Man coming on a cloud with great power and glory. When these things begin to happen stand up straight and raise your heads, for your redemption is near at hand."

Then He told them a parable: "Notice the fig-tree and trees in general. When they are budding, you see them and know for yourselves that summer is near. Likewise, when you see these things happening, you know that the kingdom of God is near. Let me tell you this: the present generation will not pass away until all these things happen. Heaven and earth will pass away; My words will never pass away."

➤ *Creed, p.* 18.

OFFERTORY   Ps. 24, 1-3   [*Trust in God*]

To You I lift up my soul; *
  in You, O my God, I trust; *
Let me not be put to shame; *
  let not my enemies exult over me. *
No one who waits for You shall be put to
    shame.

➤ *Offertory Prayers, p. 21.*

SECRET   [*Our Coming to God*]

May these offerings, O Lord, cleanse us by their
mighty power and thus make us come purer
before You Who are their Author. Through our
Lord, etc. People: **Amen.**

➤ *Preface, p. 61.*

COMMUNION   Ps. 84, 13   [*A New World*]

The Lord will give His benefits: *
  and our land shall yield its increase.

POSTCOMMUNION   [*True Preparation*]

May we receive Your mercy, O Lord, in the midst
of Your temple, and thus prepare with due ob-
servance for the coming festal season of our
redemption. Through our Lord, etc. People:
Amen.

➤ *Dismissal, p. 42.*

"John in prison heard about Christ's achievements and sent a message through his disciples."

SECOND SUNDAY OF ADVENT

THOUGHT FOR TODAY: We need not wait for another Savior. We are certain that Jesus is the Son of God become Man, the Anointed Priest-Victim, Redeemer of all mankind. We want to show our love for Him by purifying our hearts.

BIBLE AND LITURGY: The History of our Salvation began with God's revelation to Abraham and reached its peak in Christ's coming. Christian Hope stems from Christ, Who came and will come ever more to save us. **READ:** Jer. 17, 13-18; Heb. 6, 9-20; Eph. 1, 3-23; 2, 1-22; Tit. 2, 11-14; Acts 26, 1-32.

INTROIT Isa. 30, 30; Ps. 79, 2 [*Lord of Salvation*]

People of Sion, *
> behold the Lord shall come to save the nations; *

And the Lord shall make the glory of His voice to be heard, *
> in the joy of your heart. *

(Ps.) **O Shepherd of Israel, hearken,** *
> **O Guide of the flock of Joseph!** *

Glory be to the Father, etc.

People of Sion, *
   behold the Lord shall come to save the
      nations; *
And the Lord shall make the glory of His voice
   to be heard, *
   in the joy of your heart.

➤ *Kyrie, p. 13. Omit Gloria.*

PRAYER   [Interior Preparation]

*Stir up our hearts, O Lord, to prepare the ways
of Your Only-begotten Son, so that through
His coming we may be able to serve You with
purified minds. Who live, etc.* People: **Amen.** ↓

EPISTLE   Rom. 15, 4-13   [Christ, Center of Glory]

Brethren: Everything that was written in
times past was written for our instruction,
that through the patience and encouragement
afforded by the Scriptures we might have hope.
May the God of patience and encouragement
enable you to live in harmony with one another
according to the example of Christ Jesus, so
that with one heart and voice you may glorify
God, the Father of our Lord Jesus Christ. So
accept one another as Christ accepted you,
for the glory of God. I say that Christ ex-
ercised His ministry to the circumcised to
show God's fidelity in fulfilling His promises
to the fathers, whereas the Gentiles glorify God
for His mercy, as it is written: "Therefore will
I proclaim You among the nations, and I will
sing praise to Your name." And again it says:
"Exult, you nations, with His people"; and
again: "Praise the Lord, all you nations; glorify
Him, all you peoples!" And again Isaia says:

"The root of Jesse will appear, the One Who will rise up to rule the nations; in Him the Gentiles will hope." Now may the God of hope fill you with all joy and peace in your faith, so that through the power of the Holy Spirit you may have hope in abundance. ↓

GRADUAL   Ps. 49, 2-3. 5   [Beauty of God]

From Sion, perfect in beauty, *
  God shines forth. *

Gather His faithful ones before Him, *
  those who have made a covenant with Him
    by sacrifice.

Ps. 121, 1

Alleluia, alleluia. *   [Beauty of God's House]

I rejoiced because they said to me: *
  "We will go up to the house of the Lord."
    Alleluia.

→ *Prayer before the Gospel, p. 16.*

GOSPEL   Matt. 11, 2-10   [John, Herald of Christ]

A t that time, John in prison heard about Christ's achievements and sent a message through his disciples to ask Him, "Are You 'He-Who-is-to-come,' or are we to expect someone else?" In reply, Jesus said to them, "Go back and report to John what you hear and see: the blind recovering their sight, cripples walking, lepers being cleansed, the deaf hearing, dead men being raised to life, the poor hearing the good news. And happy the man who does not falter because of Me." As the messengers were setting off, Jesus began to speak to the crowds about John, "What did you go out to see in the desert—a reed swayed by the wind? Really, what did you go out to see—someone luxuriously clad? Remember, those who dress luxuriously are to be found in royal palaces. Then why did you go out—to see a prophet? Of course it was!—in fact something more than a prophet. It is about this man that Scripture says, 'Look, I am sending My messenger ahead of You, who will prepare Your way before You.'" ➤ *Creed, p. 18.*

OFFERTORY   Ps. 84, 7-8   [Joy in God]

Will You not, O God, give us life; *
   and shall not Your people rejoice in You? *
Show us, O Lord, Your kindness, *
   and grant us Your salvation.

➤ *Offertory Prayers, p. 21.*

SECRET   [Help Us]

Be appeased, we beseech You, O Lord, by the prayers and offerings of our human frailty, and where the support of our own merits is lacking, come to our assistance with Your protection. Through our Lord, etc. People: **Amen.**

➤ *Preface, p. 61.*

Bar. 5, 5; 4, 36

COMMUNION   [A New Jerusalem]

Up, Jerusalem! stand upon the heights; *
   and behold the joy that comes to you from your God.

POSTCOMMUNION   [Heaven]

We who have been refreshed by the food of spiritual nourishment, humbly beseech You, O Lord, that through partaking of this sacrament You will teach us to disdain the things of earth and love those of heaven. Through our Lord, etc. People: **Amen.** ➤ *Dismissal, p. 42.*

"I am — 'a herald's voice in the desert.'"

THIRD SUNDAY OF ADVENT

THOUGHT FOR TODAY: While we are rejoicing for "the Lord is near," there are millions who do not know the One Who should stand in the midst of them. The unbelievers must find a guiding beacon in the shining light of our Christian life.

BIBLE AND LITURGY: God is near and goes along with us on the path of life in Christ, Whose coming we will celebrate on Christmas Eve. That is the reason why we are invited to spiritual joy. READ: Prov. 10, 28; Ex. 33, 12-19; Rom. 13, 11-14; Isa. 40, 1-11; Ps. 84.

INTROIT   Phil. 4, 4-6; Ps. 84, 2   [The Lord Is Near]

Rejoice in the Lord always: *
   again I say, rejoice. *
Let your moderation be known to all men: *
   for the Lord is near. *
Have no anxiety, *
   but in everything by prayer *
     let your petitions be made known to God. *

(Ps.) You have favored, O Lord, Your land; *
   You have restored the well-being of Jacob. *

Glory be to the Father, etc.

Rejoice in the Lord always: *
  again I say, rejoice. *
Let your moderation be known to all men: *
  for the Lord is near. *
Have no anxiety, *
  but in everything by prayer *
  let your petitions be made known to God.

→ *Kyrie, p. 13. Omit Gloria.*

PRAYER   [Enlighten Our Minds]

Lend Your ear to our prayers, O Lord, we be-
seech You; and brighten the darkness of our
minds by the grace of Your coming. Who live,
etc. People: **Amen.** ↓

EPISTLE   Phil. 4, 4-7   [Joy and Peace]

Brethren: Rejoice in the Lord always; I say
it again, rejoice! All men should notice
how kind you are. The Lord is near. Put all
anxiety away from your minds. Present your
needs to God in every form of prayer and in
petitions full of gratitude. Then will God's own
peace, which goes beyond all comprehension,
stand guard over your hearts and minds, in
Christ Jesus, our Lord. ↓

GRADUAL   Ps. 79, 2. 3. 2   [Save Us with Power]

From Your throne, O Lord, upon the Cherubim, *
  rouse Your power, and come. *
O Shepherd of Israel, hearken, *
  O Guide of the flock of Joseph.

Alleluia, alleluia. *   [The Lord's Salvation]
Rouse, O Lord, Your power, *
  and come to save us. Alleluia.

➤ *Prayer before the Gospel, p. 16.*

GOSPEL   John 1, 19-28   [John's Mission]

A t that time (when the Jews sent priests and
  Levites from Jerusalem to ask John, "Who
are you?"), he declared without any qualifica-
tion, "I am not the Messiah." They questioned
him further, "Well, who are you? Elia?" "I am
not," he answered. "Are you the Prophet?"
"No!" was his reply. Then they said to him,
"Just who are you?—so that we can give some
answer to those who sent us. What do you have
to say for yourself?" He said, quoting the
prophet Isaia, "I am—'a herald's voice in the
desert, "Make the Lord's way straight!"'" Now
the envoys, who were of the Pharisees' party,
questioned him further, "If you are not the
Messiah, nor Elia, nor the Prophet, why then
are you baptizing?" John answered them, "I
am only baptizing with water, but there is One
among you Whom you do not recognize, the
One Who is to come after me, and Whose san-
dal straps I am not even worthy to unfasten."
It was in Bethany that this happened, across
the Jordan where John used to baptize.

➤ *Creed, p. 18.*

OFFERTORY   Ps. 84, 2   [Renewal]

You have favored, O Lord, Your land: *
   You have restored the well-being of Jacob. *
You have forgiven the guilt of Your people.

➤ *Offertory Prayers, p. 21.*

SECRET   [Salvation through the Mass]

*We beseech You, O Lord, that the gift we
dedicate to You, may be sacrificed continually,
so that the sacramental rite You have ordained
may be fully observed, and the work of Your
salvation may be wonderfully effective within
us. Through our Lord, etc.* People: **Amen.**

➤ *Preface, p. 61.*

COMMUNION   Isa. 35, 4   [Have No Fear]

Say to those who are frightened: *
   Be strong, fear not! *
Here is our God, *
   He comes to save us.

POSTCOMMUNION   [Cléansing of Soul]

*We entreat You, merciful Lord, that these divine
helps may cleanse us from our sins and prepare
us for the coming festal season. Through our
Lord, etc.* People: **Amen.**

➤ *Dismissal, p. 42.*

"And he went into the whole region of the Jordan preaching a baptism of repentance."

FOURTH SUNDAY OF ADVENT

THOUGHT FOR TODAY: As Mary is about to give her Divine Son to the world and to us, we cleanse our hearts in sincere confession to prepare the way of the Lord. The most precious Christmas gift is Christ Himself, Whom we receive in Holy Communion.

BIBLE AND LITURGY: During Advent we yearn for an ever more perfect coming of Christ in Grace. **READ:** Mich. 4, 1-5; 5, 2-4; 1 Cor. 1, 1-9; Eph. 4, 11-16; Ps. 144.

INTROIT   Isa. 45, 8; Ps. 18, 2   [*The Advent Plea*]

Drop down dew, you heavens, from above, *
and let the clouds rain the Just: *
let the earth be opened and bud forth a
Savior. *

(Ps.) The heavens declare the glory of God, *
and the firmament proclaims His handiwork. *

Glory be to the Father, etc.

Drop down dew, you heavens, from above, *
and let the clouds rain the Just: *
let the earth be opened and bud forth a
Savior.

→ *Kyrie, p. 13. Omit Gloria.*

PRAYER   [*The Mercy of Christ's Coming*]

Put forth Your power, O Lord, we beseech You, and delay not: and with Your great might come to our aid, so that what is hindered by our sins may be hastened by Your merciful goodness. Who live, etc. People: **Amen.** ↓

EPISTLE   1 Cor. 4, 1-5   [*The Coming of the Judge*]

Brethren: This is how men should regard us: as servants of Christ and stewards of the mysteries of God. The first requirement of a steward is that he prove trustworthy. With me it matters very little that you or any "Day of Man" pass judgment on me. I do not even pass judgment on myself. I have nothing on my conscience; but that does not mean that I have been acquitted. It is the Lord who passes judgment on me. Therefore stop making judgments before the time when the Lord comes. He will bring to light what is hidden in darkness and will manifest the intentions of men's hearts. Then everyone will receive his praise from God. ↓

GRADUAL   Ps. 144, 18. 21

[*Praise the Lord Who Is Near*]

The Lord is near to all who call upon Him, *
  to all who call upon Him in truth. *
May my mouth speak the praise of the Lord, *
  and may all flesh bless His holy Name.

Alleluia, alleluia. *   [*Do Not Delay*]
Come, O Lord, and delay not; *

forgive the sins of Your people Israel. Alleluia.

> ➤ *Prayer before the Gospel, p. 16.*

GOSPEL Luke 3, 1-6 [*The Preaching of Preparation*]

In the fifteenth year of the reign of Tiberius Cæsar, when Pontius Pilate was governor of Judea, Herod tetrarch of Galilee, Philip, his brother, tetrarch of the land of Iturea and Trachonitis, and Lysanias tetrarch of Abilene, during the high-priesthood of Annas and Caiaphas, the word of God was spoken to John, the son of Zachary, in the desert. And he went into the whole region of the Jordan preaching a baptism of repentance leading to remission of sins; as it is written in the book of the words of Isaia the prophet: "A herald's voice in the desert, 'Make ready the way of the Lord, make His paths straight. Every valley shall be filled and every mountain and hill shall be leveled; the windings shall be made straight and the rough ways smooth, and all mankind shall see the salvation of God.'" ➤ *Creed, p. 18.*

OFFERTORY Luke 1, 28 [*Christ's New Paradise*]

Hail, Mary full of grace, *
   the Lord is with you, *
Blessed are you among women, *
   and blessed is the fruit of your womb.

> ➤ *Offertory Prayers, p. 21.*

SECRET [*Fuller Devotion*]

Look with favor, O Lord, we beseech You, upon the offerings here present, that they may be profitable for our devotion and for our salvation. Through our Lord, etc. People: **Amen.**

PREFACE FOR ADVENT

[*Our Prayer of Thanksgiving*]

Right and worthy it is, fitting and for our good that in every time and place our thanks should rise to You, O Lord, holy Father, almighty and eternal God: through Christ our Lord. Merciful, and true to Your word, You promised Him as Saviour to the lost race of man: His truth to be the light of the ignorant, His holiness to be the sanctity of the sinful, His power to be the strength of the weak. And now, since the One Whom You are to send is at hand, and the day of our great release is dawning, our trust in Your pledges arouses us to holy joy. And therefore, with the Angels and Archangels, with the Thrones and Dominations, and all the forces of heaven, we chant the endless hymn of Your glory:

➤ *Sanctus, p.* 27.

COMMUNION Isa. 7, 14 [*The Virgin-Mother*]

Behold, the virgin shall be with child and bear a Son. *

and shall name Him Emmanuel.

POSTCOMMUNION [*Increase of Holiness*]

Having received Your gifts, we beseech You, O Lord, that each partaking of this Sacrament may increase within us its saving effect. Through our Lord, etc. People: **Amen.**

➤ *Dismissal, p.* 42.

"Today, in the city of David, a Savior has been born to you."

CHRISTMAS DAY

FIRST MASS AT MIDNIGHT

THOUGHT FOR TODAY: May our hearts express our love and gratitude and our resolve to belong entirely to Jesus, as we contemplate this manifestation that God is Love, and that He so loved the world as to give us His Only-begotten Son.

BIBLE AND LITURGY: The Son of God became Man to "cleanse for Himself a people of His very Own." He is their Lord. This people, the Church, is the spiritualized Israel. Indeed Christ took over the throne of His ancestor David in a transcending and mysterious way. READ: 2 Kgs. 5, 1-5; Isa. 2, 6-7; Luke 1 (esp. 1, 30-33); 2, 1-20; Ps. 109.

INTROIT Ps. 2, 7. 1 [*The Deep Mystery*]

The Lord said to Me, "You are My Son; *
   this day I have begotten You." *

(Ps.) Why do the nations rage *
   and the people utter folly? *

Glory be to the Father, etc.

The Lord said to Me, "You are My Son; *
this day I have begotten You. "

➤ *Kyrie and Gloria, pp.* 13-14.

PRAYER   [*The Light Has Come*]

*O God, Who have brightened this most holy
night with the splendor of the True Light, grant,
we beseech You, that we may know in heaven
the joy of that Light which we have known
mystically on earth. Who with You, etc.* People:
Amen. ↓

EPISTLE   Tit. 2, 11-15   [*God Our Savior*]

Beloved: God's favor has appeared, bringing
salvation to all men. It trains us, once we
have rejected godlessness and worldly lusts,
to live a life of self-control, holiness, and piety
in the present age while waiting for the blessed
object of our hope, the glorious appearance of
our great God and Savior Christ Jesus. He
gave Himself up for us to redeem us from all
iniquity and to cleanse for Himself a people
of His very own, enthusiastic for noble deeds.
Speak with insistence about these things, in
Christ Jesus, our Lord. ↓

GRADUAL   Ps. 109, 3. 1   [*The Eternal Ruler*]

Yours is princely power in the day of Your
birth in holy splendor; *
before the daystar I have begotten You. *

**The Lord said to my Lord: "Sit at My right
     hand, ***
till I make Your enemies Your footstool."

Alleluia, alleluia. *   Ps. 2, 7   [*Begotten of God*]
The Lord said to Me, "You are My Son; *
this day I have begotten You. " Alleluia.

→ *Prayer before the Gospel, p. 16.*

GOSPEL   Luke 2, 1-14   [*Story of Christ's Birth*]

At that time Cæsar Augustus published a
decree ordering a census of the whole
world. This first census took place while
Cyrinus was governor of Syria. And all went
to register, each to his own town. Joseph also
went from the town of Nazareth in Galilee to
Judea to the town of David, which is called
Bethlehem—because he was of the house and
family of David—to register with Mary, his
engaged wife, who was with Child. But while
they were there the time came for the Child
to be born, and she gave birth to her firstborn
Son, and wrapped Him in swaddling clothes,
and laid Him in a crib because there was no
place for them in the inn. And there were
shepherds in the locality living in the fields and
keeping night watch by turns over their flock.
And the angel of the Lord appeared to them
and the glory of the Lord shone around them,
and they were very much afraid. And the angel
said to them: "Do not be afraid! I proclaim
good news to you of a great joy which will be
shared by the whole people: today, in the city

of David, a Savior has been born to you, who is Messiah and Lord. And this will be a sign for you: you will find an infant wrapped in swaddling clothes and laid in a crib."

And suddenly a multitude of the heavenly host was with the angel, praising God and saying:

"Glory to God in high heaven, and on earth peace among men of good will."

➤ *Creed, p.* 18.

OFFERTORY   Ps. 95, 11. 13   [*Universal Rejoicing*]

Let the heavens be glad and the earth rejoice * before the Lord, for He comes.

➤ *Offertory Prayers, p.* 21.

SECRET   [*Make Us Christlike*]

May the offerings of this day's festivity, we beseech You, O Lord, find acceptance with You; that, by the bounty of Your grace, we may, through these sacred dealings, be made like unto Him in Whom our nature is united with You. Who with You, etc. People: **Amen.** ↓

PREFACE FOR CHRISTMAS

[*Our Prayer of Thanksgiving*]

Right and worthy it is, fitting and for our good that in every time and place our thanks should rise to You, O Lord, holy Father, almighty and eternal God: because, through the mystery of the Word made flesh, our minds see Your glory in new splendour. And so, when we acknowledge God made visible, we are inspired by Him with a longing for what is invisible. And therefore, with the Angels and Archangels, with the Thrones and Dominations, and all the forces of heaven, we chant the endless hymn of Your glory:

➤ *Sanctus, p. 27.*

COMMUNION Ps. 109, 3   [*Eternal Son*]

In holy splendor, before the daystar I have begotten You.

POSTCOMMUNION   [*Union by a Holy Life*]

Grant, we beseech You, O Lord our God, that we who joyfully celebrate the birth of our Lord Jesus Christ, in this Sacrament may gain His companionship by worthy living. Who with You, etc. People: **Amen.**

➤ *Dismissal, p. 42.*

SECOND MASS AT DAWN

INTROIT Isa. 9, 3. 6; Ps. 92,1   [*The Hero's Arrival*]

A light shall shine upon us this day: *
    for the Lord is born to us: *
And He shall be called wonderful, God, *
    Prince of peace, Father of the world to come: *
    of Whose reign there shall be no end. *
(Ps.) The Lord is King, in splendor robed; *
    robed is the Lord and girt about with strength. *
Glory be to the Father, etc.
Repeat: **A light,** etc., *as far as* (Ps.).

GRADUAL Ps. 117, 26. 27. 23 [Light of the World]

Blessed is He Who comes in the Name of the
    Lord; *
  the Lord is God, and He has given us light. *
By the Lord has this been done; *
  it is wonderful in our eyes.

Alleluia, alleluia. * Ps. 92, 1 [Glory of the New King]
The Lord is King, in splendor robed; *
  robed is the Lord and girt about with strength.
    Alleluia.

OFFERTORY Ps. 92, 1-2 [God's Eternal Throne]

God has made the world firm, *
  not to be moved. *
Your throne, O God, stands firm from of old; *
  from everlasting You are.

COMMUNION Zach. 9, 9 [The Shout of Joy]

Rejoice heartily, O daughter Sion, *
  shout for joy, O daughter Jerusalem! *
See, your King shall come, *
  a just Savior of the world is He.

THIRD MASS DURING THE DAY

*Mass: Same as on Jan. 1, p. 72, substituting the follow-
ing Alleluia after the Gradual:*

Alleluia, alleluia. * [The Holy Light]
A sanctified day has shone upon us; *
  come, you nations, and adore the Lord: *
    for this day a great light has descended upon the
    earth. Alleluia.

Simeon said, "This Child is destined for the fall and the rise of many in Israel."

SUNDAY WITHIN OCTAVE OF CHRISTMAS

THOUGHT FOR TODAY: Mary and Joseph were wondering at the things which were spoken about Jesus. They realized better that their hearts would be pierced with the sword of sorrow because they were so closely associated with the "Man of Sorrows."

BIBLE AND LITURGY: By His ready obedience first to God His Father and then to His parents, Jesus teaches us the value of obedience in our daily lives. By being obedient, He grew in wisdom and grace, and His obedience unto death was rewarded by His Father with the glory of the Resurrection. READ: Rom. 6, 15-26; Deut. 27f; Sir. 3, 1-16; Eph. 6, 1-10; Phil. 2, 5-11; Heb. 5, 7-10; 1 Pet. 2, 13-25.

INTROIT   Wis. 18, 14. 15; Ps. 92, 1

[The Mystery of the Night]

When a profound stillness compassed everything *

    and the night in its swift course was half spent, *

Your all-powerful Word, O Lord, *

    bounded from heaven's royal throne. *

(Ps.) **The Lord is King, in splendor robed; ***
robed is the Lord, and girt about with strength. *

Glory be to the Father, etc.

When a profound stillness compassed everything *
and the night in its swift course was half spent, *

Your all-powerful Word, O Lord, *
bounded from heaven's royal throne. *

→ *Kyrie and Gloria, pp. 13-14.*

PRAYER [Good Works]

O almighty and eternal God, direct our actions in conformity with Your will, that in the name of Your beloved Son we may be worthy to do good works in abundance. Who with You, etc.
People: **Amen.** ↓

EPISTLE Gal. 4, 1-7 [Freedom of God's Sons]

Brethren: As long as a designated heir is not of age, his condition is no different from that of a slave, though he is titular master of all his possessions; for he is under the supervision of guardians and administrators until the time set by his father. In the same way we also, while still not yet of age, were like slaves subordinated to the elements of the world. But when the established time had come, God sent forth His Son, born of a woman and born under the Law—for the purpose of buying release from the Law for those who were subject to it, so that we might receive our status of adopted sons. What proves that you are sons is the fact that God has sent forth into our hearts the Spirit of His Son, which cries out "Abba!" (that is, "Father!"). Therefore you are no longer a slave; you are a son! And by the very fact of being a son you are also an heir, by God's will. ↓

GRADUAL   Ps. 44, 3. 2   [*Beauty of the Word*]

Fairer in beauty are You than the sons of men; *
    grace is poured out upon Your lips. *
My heart overflows with a goodly theme; *
    as I sing my ode to the King, *
     my tongue is nimble as the pen of a skillful
       scribe.

Alleluia, alleluia. *   Ps. 92, 1 [*Splendor of the King*]

The Lord is King, in splendor robed; *
    robed is the Lord and girt about with
       strength. Alleluia.

→ *Prayer before the Gospel, p.* 16.

GOSPEL   Luke 2, 33-40   [*The Sword in Mary's Heart*]

A^t that time the father and mother of Jesus were marveling at what was being said about Him. Simeon blessed them and said to Mary His mother, "This Child is destined for the fall and rise of many in Israel and for a sign that will be contradicted—and your soul, too, will be pierced with a sword—so that the thoughts of many hearts will be revealed."

Now there was a prophetess, Anna, daughter of Phanuel, of the tribe of Aser. She was quite old, having lived seven years with her husband after her marriage, and then as a widow until she was eighty-four. She was constantly in the temple, worshiping day and night in fasting and prayer. Coming on the scene at this precise time, she gave thanks to God and talked about the Child to all who were awaiting the redemption of Jerusalem. When they had fulfilled all the prescriptions of the Law of the Lord they returned to Galilee to their own town of Nazareth. The Child grew in size and strength, filled with wisdom, and the favor of God was upon Him.

> Creed, p. 18.

OFFERTORY Ps. 92, 1. 2   [God, Eternal Ruler]

God has made the world firm, *
  not to be moved. *
Your throne, O God, stands firm from of old; *
  from everlasting You are.

> Offertory Prayers, p. 21.

SECRET   [Grace of Devotion]

Grant, we beseech You, almighty God, that the gift offered in the sight of Your Majesty may obtain for us the grace of reverent devotion and secure us eternal happiness. Through our Lord, etc. People: **Amen.**

> Preface for Christmas, p. 65.

COMMUNION Matt. 2, 20   [Back from Exile]

Take the Child and His Mother, *
  and go into the land of Israel, *
  for those who sought the Child's life are dead.

POSTCOMMUNION   [Fulfillment Assured]

By the working of this sacrament, O Lord, may our sins be erased and our just desires fulfilled. Through our Lord, etc. People: **Amen.**

> Dismissal, p. 42.

"The Name Jesus was given to Him."

OCTAVE DAY OF CHRISTMAS

THOUGHT FOR TODAY: At the beginning of the new civil year we firmly resolve "to live a life of self-control, holiness and piety" in the New Year, looking for the "glorious appearance of our great God."

BIBLE AND LITURGY: A Jewish boy was initiated into God's Chosen People by circumcision. Christian initiation into God's Chosen People now is effected by Faith and Baptism. READ: Gen. 17, 9-14; Acts 15, 1-12; Rom. 2, 25-29; Col. 2, 8-15; John 3, 1-8; Acts 9, 10-19.

INTROIT Isa. 9, 6; Ps. 97, 1   [*The Glorious Child*]

A Child is born to us, a Son is given to us; *
   upon His shoulder dominion rests; *
And His name shall be called *
   the Angel of great counsel. *
(Ps.) Sing to the Lord a new song, *
   for He has done wondrous deeds. *
Glory be to the Father, etc.
A Child is born to us, a Son is given to us; *
   upon His shoulder dominion rests; *
And His name shall be called *
   the Angel of great counsel.

➢ *Kyrie and Gloria, pp. 13-14.*

- 72 -

PRAYER [Mary's Son: Author of Life]

O God, Who by the fruitful virginity of blessed Mary, have bestowed upon mankind the reward of eternal salvation, grant, we beseech You, that we may enjoy the intercession of her through whom we have been found worthy to receive among us the Author of life, our Lord Jesus Christ, Your Son. Who with You, etc. People: **Amen.** ↓

EPISTLE Tit. 2, 11-15 [Hope in Christ]

Beloved: God's favor has appeared, bringing salvation to all men. It trains us, once we have rejected godlessness and worldly lusts, to live a life of self-control, holiness, and piety in the present age while waiting for the blessed object of our hope, the glorious appearance of our great God and Savior Christ Jesus. He gave Himself up for us to redeem us from all iniquity and to cleanse for Himself a people of His very own, enthusiastic for noble deeds. Speak with insistence about these things, in Christ Jesus, our Lord. ↓

GRADUAL Ps. 97, 3. 4. 2 [The World's Salvation]

All the ends of the earth have seen *
   the salvation by our God; *
   sing joyfully to God, all you lands. *
The Lord has made His salvation known: *
   in the sight of the nations He has revealed His
      justice.
Heb. 1, 1. 2
Alleluia, alleluia. * [Fulfillment of Prophecies]
God, Who in diverse ways *
   spoke in times past to the fathers *
   by the prophets; *

last of all, in these days, has spoken to us *
by His Son. Alleluia.

➤ *Prayer before the Gospel, p. 16.*

GOSPEL   Luke 2, 21   [*The Name of Jesus*]

At that time, when the eighth day arrived for the circumcision of the Child, the Name Jesus was given to Him, the Name which the angel had given Him before His conception.

➤ *Creed, p. 18.*

OFFERTORY   Ps. 88, 12. 15   [*The Lord's World*]

Yours are the heavens, and Yours is the earth; *
the world and its fullness You have founded. *
Justice and judgment are the foundation of Your
throne.

➤ *Offertory Prayers, p. 21.*

SECRET   [*Cleansing Sacrifice*]

Accept, we beseech You, O Lord, our offerings and prayers; cleanse us by this heavenly rite, and in Your mercy, hear us. Through our Lord, etc. People: **Amen.** ➤ *Pref. for Christmas, p. 65.*

COMMUNION   Ps. 97, 3   [*Salvation for All*]

All the ends of the earth have seen *
the salvation by our God.

POSTCOMMUNION   [*Our Lady's Help*]

May this Communion, O Lord, cleanse us from guilt and, by the intercession of the Blessed Virgin Mary, Mother of God, impart to us heavenly healing. Through the same, etc. People: **Amen.**

➤ *Dismissal, p. 42.*

"At the Name of Jesus every knee should bend."

HOLY NAME OF JESUS

THOUGHT FOR TODAY: The Son of God made Man, was called Jesus, that is, Savior. This Name recalls God's ineffable mercy "for there is no other name in the whole wide world given to men by which we are to be saved." Let us always use it with gratitude and respect.

BIBLE AND LITURGY: The Redeemer of the world, Lord of God's Chosen People, is called Jesus. There is no other name by which we are to be saved. Jesus means "Savior." READ: Phil. 2, 5-11; Acts 3, 1-16; 1 Cor. 1, 10-16; 2 Thess. 1, 11-12; Rom. 10, 5-13.

INTROIT Phil. 2, 10-11; Ps. 8, 2

[*Adoration from All Creation*]

At the Name of Jesus every knee should bend *
   of those in heaven, on earth, and under the
      earth, *
And every tongue should confess *
   that the Lord Jesus Christ *
   is in the glory of God the Father. *

(Ps.) O Lord, our Lord, *
   how glorious is Your Name over all the
      earth! *

Glory be to the Father, etc.

At the Name of Jesus every knee should bend *
   of those in heaven, on earth, and under the
   earth, *

And every tongue should confess *
   that the Lord Jesus Christ *
   is in the glory of God the Father.

➤ *Kyrie and Gloria, pp. 13-14.*

PRAYER   [Veneration of Jesus' Name]

O God, Who appointed Your Only-begotten Son to be the Savior of the human race, and commanded that He be called Jesus, mercifully grant that we may enjoy in heaven the vision of Him Whose holy Name we venerate on earth. Through the same, etc. People: **Amen.** ↓

EPISTLE   Acts 4, 8-12   [Power of the Name of Jesus]

In those days Peter, filled with the Holy Spirit, spoke up: "Leaders of our people and elders! If we must answer today for a good deed done to a cripple and explain how he was restored to health, then you and all the people of Israel must realize that it was done in the Name of Jesus Christ the Nazorean, Whom you crucified and Whom God raised from the dead. In virtue of that Name this man stands here before you perfectly well. This Jesus is the stone which was rejected by you builders, but has become the corner-stone. There is no salvation in any-one else, for there is no other name in the whole wide world given to men by which we are to be saved." ↓

GRADUAL   Ps. 105, 47; Isa. 63, 16

[*Thanks to the Name of God*]

Save us, O Lord, our God, *
and gather us from among the nations, *
That we may give thanks to Your holy Name *
and glory in praising You. *
You, O Lord, are our Father and our Redeemer; *
from everlasting is Your Name.

Alleluia, alleluia. *   Ps. 144, 21 [*Praise God's Name*]
May my mouth speak the praise of the Lord, *
and may all flesh bless His holy Name.
Alleluia.

➤ *Prayer before the Gospel, p. 16.*

GOSPEL   Luke 2, 21   [*Jesus the Savior*]

A t that time, when the eighth day arrived for
the circumcision of the Child, the Name
Jesus was given to Him, the Name which the
angel had given Him before His conception.

➤ *Creed, p. 18.*

OFFERTORY   Ps. 85, 12. 5

[*Glory to the Name of Our God*]

I will give thanks to You, O Lord my God, *
with all my heart, *
and I will glorify Your Name forever; *
For You, O Lord, are good and forgiving, *
abounding in kindness to all who call upon
You. Alleluia.

➤ *Offertory Prayers, p. 21.*

SECRET   [Glory from the Sacrifice]

May Your blessing, O most merciful God, which makes all creation flourish, sanctify this our sacrifice, which we offer You to the glory of the Name of Your Son, our Lord Jesus Christ, and may it be pleasing to Your Majesty as an act of praise and be profitable to us for our salvation. Through the same, etc. People: **Amen.**

➤ *Preface, p. 65.*

COMMUNION   Ps. 85, 9-10
                    [All Shall Praise the Holy Name]

All the nations You have made shall come *
   and worship You, O Lord, *
   and glorify Your Name. *
For You are great and do wondrous deeds; *
   You alone are God. Alleluia.

POSTCOMMUNION   [Our Names with Christ]

Almighty, eternal God, Who have created and redeemed us, graciously look upon our needs, and deign to receive with kind and favorable countenance the sacrifice of the Saving Victim, which we have offered to Your Majesty, in honor of the Name of Your Son, our Lord Jesus Christ, that, Your grace being poured out upon us, we may have the joy of seeing our names written in heaven, under the glorious Name of Jesus, the sign of eternal predestination. Through the same, etc. People: **Amen.**

➤ *Dismissal, p. 42.*

"They prostrated themselves and did homage to Him."

THE EPIPHANY OF OUR LORD

THOUGHT FOR TODAY: Like the Wise Men we adore the newborn King, and offer Him the gold of a loving heart, the frankincense of persevering prayers, and the myrrh of our readiness to labor and suffer for Him.

BIBLE AND LITURGY: Christ's Epiphany, or Manifestation, to the Gentiles teaches us about His kingdom, power and dominion, which will not be confined to the carnal offspring of Abraham. His kingdom is a spiritualized Israel. It is equally destined for all regardless of race or color. READ: Acts 10, 34-48; 13, 16-52 (esp. 46-49); 28, 17-31 (esp. 28).

INTROIT   Mal. 3, 1; 1 Par. 29, 12; Ps. 71, 1

[The Great Ruler is Here]

Behold the Lord the Ruler is come; *
   and the kingdom is in His hand, *
   and power, and dominion. *
(Ps.) O God, with Your judgment endow the
      king, *
   and with Your justice, the king's son. *
Glory be to the Father, etc.
Behold the Lord the Ruler is come; *
   and the kingdom is in His hand, *
   and power, and dominion.

→ *Kyrie and Gloria, pp. 13-14.*

PRAYER [Revealed to the Gentiles]

O God, Who by the guidance of a star this day revealed Your Only-begotten Son to the Gentiles, mercifully grant that we who know You now by faith, may come to behold You in glory. Through the same, etc. People: **Amen.** ↓

EPISTLE Isa. 60, 1-6 [The New Jerusalem]

Rise up in splendor, Jerusalem! Your light has come,
the glory of the Lord shines upon you.
See, darkness covers the earth, and thick clouds
    cover the peoples;
But upon you the Lord shines, and over you
    appears His glory.

Nations shall walk by your light, and kings by
    your shining radiance.
Raise your eyes and look about; they all gather
    and come to you:
Your sons come from afar, and your daughters
    in the arms of their nurses.

Then you shall be radiant at what you see,
    your heart shall throb and overflow,
For the riches of the sea shall be emptied out
    before you,
the wealth of nations shall be brought to you.
Caravans of camels shall fill you, dromedaries
    from Madian and Epha;
All from Saba shall come bearing gold and
    frankincense,
and proclaiming the praises of the Lord. ↓

GRADUAL   Isa. 60, 6. 1   [Gifts from Afar]

All from Saba shall come, *
   bringing gold and frankincense, *
   and proclaiming the praises of the Lord. *
Rise up in splendor, *
   O Jerusalem, *
   for the glory of the Lord shines upon you.

Alleluia, alleluia. *   Matt. 2, 2[The Star of Salvation]
We have seen His star in the East: *
   and have come with gifts to worship the
      Lord. Alleluia.

➤ *Prayer before the Gospel, p. 16.*

GOSPEL   Matt. 2, 1-12   [Seeking the King]

After Jesus' birth in Bethlehem of Judea during the reign of King Herod, Magi from the
east arrived one day in Jerusalem, inquiring,
"Where is the one born to be King of the Jews?
We observed His star at its rising, and have
come to pay Him homage." At this news, King
Herod became greatly disturbed, and with him,
all Jerusalem. Summoning all the chief priests
and scribes of the people, he inquired of them
where the Messiah was to be born. "In Bethlehem of Judea," they informed him. "Here is
what the prophet has written: 'And you, Bethlehem, land of Juda, are by no means least among
the princes of Juda, since from you will come
a ruler Who is to shepherd My people Israel.'"
So Herod called the Magi aside and found out
from them the exact time of the star's appearance. Then he sent them to Bethlehem with

the order, "Go and get detailed information about the Child. When you have found out, bring word that I may go and offer Him homage too." After their audience with the king, they set out. And now the star, whose rising they had observed, went ahead of them until it came to a stop over the place where the Child was. Seeing the star, they were overjoyed; and on entering the house, they found the Child with Mary His mother. They prostrated themselves and did homage to Him. Then opening their coffers, they presented Him with gifts of gold, frankincense and myrrh. And then, as they had received a message in a dream not to return to Herod, they took another route back home.

➤ *Creed, p.* 18.

OFFERTORY Ps. 71, 10-11

[*Tribute from the whole world*]

The kings of Tharsis and the Isles shall offer gifts; *

the kings of Arabia and Saba shall bring tribute. *

All kings shall pay Him homage, *

all nations shall serve Him.

➤ *Offertory Prayers, p.* 21.

SECRET [*The Church's Gifts*]

O Lord, look favorably upon the gifts of Your Church, which are no longer gifts of gold, frankincense and myrrh, but, as these gifts signify, our offering is Jesus Christ Your Son, our Lord, Who is now sacrifice and food. Who with You, etc. People: **Amen.** ⍐

PREFACE OF THE EPIPHANY

[*Our Prayer of Thanksgiving*]

Right and worthy it is, fitting and for our good that in every time and place our thanks should rise to You, O Lord, holy Father, almighty and eternal God: for, when Your only Son apppeared to us in the reality of our mortal nature, by this new vision of His immortal nature, He healed us. And therefore, with the Angels and Archangels, with the Thrones and Dominations, and all the forces of heaven, we chant the endless hymn of Your glory:

➤ *Sanctus*, p. 27.

COMMUNION   Matt. 2, 2   [*Led by Faith*]

We have seen His star in the East *
   and have come with gifts to worship the Lord.

POSTCOMMUNION

[*Understanding through Purification*]

Grant, we beseech You, almighty God, that, by the understanding of our minds made pure, we may grasp what we celebrate by these solemn rites. Through our Lord, etc. People: **Amen.**

➤ *Dismissal*, p. 42.

*"He went back with them to Nazareth,
and remained obedient to them."*

FEAST OF THE HOLY FAMILY

THOUGHT FOR TODAY: The family is the smaller unit from which society develops. As long as the love of God binds the members of the family together, and the Christian virtues rule in our homes, society will be prosperous and at peace. Ask in your Mass and Holy Communion that your conduct in family life may be guided by the example of the Holy Family at Nazareth.

BIBLE AND LITURGY: The Church wants all Christian families to take the Holy Family as their example. The basic attitudes toward God, one another and fellow men, fostered in that Family, will guide all families to true happiness. READ: Matt. 19, 3-12; Eph. 5, 22-33; 1 Cor. 7, 1-7; 1 John 4, 7-21; 2 Pet. 1, 3-11; Sir. 7, 18-36.

INTROIT Prov. 23, 24, 25; Ps. 83, 2. 3

[*Joy of Joseph and Mary*]

The Father of the Just will exult with glee; *
let Your father and mother have joy; *
let her who bore You exult. *

(Ps.) **How lovely is Your dwelling place,** *
  O Lord of hosts! *
My soul yearns and pines *
  for the courts of the Lord. *

Glory be to the Father, etc.

The Father of the Just will exult with glee; *
  let your father and mother have joy; *
  let her who bore You exult.

➤ *Kyrie and Gloria, pp.* 13-14.

PRAYER   [Example]

O Lord Jesus Christ, Who while subject
to Mary and Joseph, hallowed family life with
virtues beyond description, grant us by their
combined intercession, that, having been taught
by the example of the Holy Family, we may
attain unto their everlasting companionship.
Who live, etc. People: **Amen.** ↓

EPISTLE   Col. 3, 12-17   [Family Virtues]

Brethren: As God's chosen ones, holy and
beloved, you must put on heartfelt mercy,
kindness, humility, meekness, patience. Bear
with one another and forgive whatever griev-
ances you may have against each other; forgive
just as the Lord has forgiven you. And over
all these put on love, which binds them together and makes them perfect. Let the peace
of Christ rule over your hearts; for, as members
of the one body, you have been called to that
peace. Be thankful. Let the word of Christ

dwell in you with all its richness; instruct and admonish one another with perfect wisdom. With heartfelt gratitude sing to God psalms, hymns, and inspired songs. And whatever you do in word or in work, do everything in the name of the Lord Jesus, giving thanks to God the Father through Him. ↓

GRADUAL Ps. 26, 4; 83, 5   [*Happy Household*]

One thing I ask of the Lord; *
  this I seek: *
To dwell in the house of the Lord *
  all the days of my life. *
Happy they who dwell in Your house, O Lord; *
  continually they praise You.

Alleluia, alleluia. * Isa. 45, 15   [*Hidden God*]
  Truly, You are a hidden God, *
  the God of Israel, the Savior. Alleluia.

➤ *Prayer before the Gospel, p. 16.*

GOSPEL Luke 2, 42-52   [*Jesus Ever Obedient*]

When Jesus was twelve they made their customary trip to Jerusalem for the feast. When they were returning at the end of the feast the Child Jesus remained behind in Jerusalem, unknown to His parents. Thinking that He was in the company they continued their journey for a day, looking for Him among their relatives and acquaintances. Not finding Him, they returned to Jerusalem searching for Him;

and after three days they found Him in the temple sitting in the midst of the teachers, listening to them and asking them questions; and all who heard Him were amazed at His intelligence and answers. When they saw Him they were astonished, and His mother said to Him: "Son, why have You done this to us? You see that Your father and I have been searching for You in sorrow." He said to them: "What prompted you to search for Me? Did you not know that I had to be in My Father's house?" And they did not understand what He said to them. Then He went back with them to Nazareth, and remained obedient to them. His mother kept all these things in her heart. And Jesus progressed in wisdom and age and favor before God and men. → *Creed, p. 18.*

OFFERTORY   Luke 2, 22   [Family Worship]

The parents of Jesus took Him up to Jerusalem, * to present Him to the Lord.

→ *Offertory Prayers, p. 21.*

SECRET   [Blessings on the Family]

In appeasement, O Lord, we offer You this sacrifice, humbly praying that through the intercession of the Virgin Mother of God, and that of St. Joseph, You will establish our households in Your peace and grace. Through the same, etc. People: **Amen.**

→ *Preface, p. 83.*

COMMUNION   Luke 2, 51   [*Obedience and Love*]

Jesus went down with them *
  and came to Nazareth, *
  and was subject to them.

POSTCOMMUNION

[*Heavenly Life through the Holy Family*]

Grant, Lord Jesus, that those whom You refresh with the heavenly sacrament may ever imitate the example of Your Holy Family, so that at the hour of our death, with the glorious Virgin Mary and St. Joseph welcoming us, we may be found worthy to be received into Your everlasting home. Who live, etc. People: **Amen.**

➤ *Dismissal, p. 42.*

"Fill the jars with water," Jesus ordered.

SECOND SUNDAY AFTER EPIPHANY

THOUGHT FOR TODAY: Imitating Mary's life of charity and relying on her powerful intercession, we may find a sure way out of our daily troubles, as the bridegroom did at the wedding at Cana.

BIBLE AND LITURGY: Faith is a grace of God, but Jesus' signs can help those "of little Faith" to come to that complete surrender of mind and heart which means "Faith" in the true Biblical meaning of the word. READ: Matt. 9, 1-8 (esp. 8); John 11, 1-53 (esp. 42); 1 Cor. 15, 12-19; John 3, 1-2; Matt. 8, 23-27 (esp. 27).

INTROIT Ps. 65, 4. 1. 2 [*Proclaim His Glory*]

Let all on earth worship You, O God, and sing
    praise to You, *
  sing praise to Your Name, Most High. *

(Ps.) Shout joyfully to God, all you on earth, *
    sing praise to the glory of His Name; *
    proclaim His glorious praise. *

Glory be to the Father, etc.

Let all on earth worship You, O God, and sing
  praise to You, *
sing praise to Your Name, Most High.

→ *Kyrie and Gloria, p. 27.*

PRAYER [Peace]

*Almighty, everlasting God, Who govern
both the heavens and the earth, graciously hear
the humble prayers of Your people and grant
us Your peace all the days of our life. Through
our Lord, etc.* People: **Amen.** ↓

EPISTLE Rom. 12, 6-16 [Christian Renewal]

Brethren: We have gifts which differ according to the favor we received. One's gift may
be prophecy; its use should be in proportion to
his faith. It may be the gift of ministry; it
should be used for ministering. One who is a
teacher should use his gift for teaching; one with
power of exhortation should exhort. He who
gives alms should do so generously; one who
rules should exercise his authority with care;
he who performs works of mercy should do
so with cheerfulness. Your love must be sincere.
Detest what is evil, cling to what is good. Love
one another with the affection of brothers. Anticipate each other in showing honor. Do not
grow slack in diligence, but be fervent in spirit;
it is the Lord whom you serve. Rejoice in hope;
be patient under trial; persevere in prayer. Look
on the needs of the saints as your own; be
prompt in offering hospitality. Bless your persecutors; bless them and do not curse. Rejoice

with those who rejoice; weep with those who weep. Have the same attitude toward all. Put away ambitious thoughts, and associate with those who are lowly. ☥

GRADUAL   Ps. 106, 20-21   [Thanks]

The Lord sent forth His Word to heal them *
   and to snatch them from destruction. *
Let them give thanks to the Lord for His kindness, *
   and His wondrous deeds to the children of men.

Alleluia, alleluia. *   Ps. 148, 2   [Praise]
Praise the Lord, all you His angels, *
   praise Him, all You His hosts. Alleluia.

➔ *Prayer before the Gospel, p. 16.*

GOSPEL   John 2, 1-11   [The First Miracle]

At that time there was a wedding at Cana in Galilee. The Mother of Jesus was there, and Jesus Himself and His disciples had also been invited to the celebration. When the wine ran short, Jesus' Mother told Him, "They have no wine." But Jesus answered her, "Woman, how does this concern of yours involve Me? My hour has not yet come." His Mother instructed the waiters, "Do whatever He tells you." As prescribed for Jewish ceremonial washings, there were at hand six stone water jars, each one holding fifteen to twenty-five gallons. "Fill the jars with water," Jesus ordered, and they filled them to the brim. "Now," He said to them, "draw some out and take it to the headwaiter."

And they did so. But as soon as the headwaiter tasted the water made wine (now he had no idea where it came from; only the waiters knew since they had drawn the water), he called the bridegroom, and pointed out to him, "Everyone serves choice wine first; then when the guests have been drinking a while, the inferior wine. But you have kept the choice wine till now." What Jesus did at Cana in Galilee marked the beginning of His signs; thus He revealed His glory, and His disciples believed in Him.

➤ *Creed, p.* **18.**

OFFERTORY   Ps. 65, 1-2. 16

[The Lord's Goodness to Me]

Shout joyfully to God, all you on earth, *
sing praise to the glory of His Name. *
Hear now, all you who fear God, *
while I declare what the Lord has done for me.

➤ *Offertory Prayers, p.* **21.**

SECRET   [Sanctify and Purify]

Hallow our offerings, O Lord, and cleanse us from the stains of our sins. Through our Lord, etc. People: **Amen.**

➤ *Preface, p.* **26.**

COMMUNION   John 2, 7. 8. 9. 10-11   [The Sign]

The Lord said, *
"Fill the jars with water and take to the chief steward." *

When the chief steward had tasted the water *
    after it had become wine, *
    he said to the bridegroom, *
    "You have kept the good wine until now." *
This first miracle Jesus worked *
    in the presence of His disciples.

POSTCOMMUNION [Sacramental Nourishment]

O Lord, we beseech You that the effects of Your power may ever increase within us; and, strengthened by the divine sacrament, we may be prepared by Your grace to lay hold of what it promises. Through our Lord, etc. People: **Amen.**

➤ *Dismissal, p. 42.*

"Lord, . . . I am not worthy to have You enter my house. Just give an order, and my boy will get better."

THIRD SUNDAY AFTER EPIPHANY

THOUGHT FOR TODAY: Receiving Christ in frequent Communion with humble faith in His Divinity is the best assurance that we shall enter heaven.

BIBLE AND LITURGY: Faith, humility and confidence should mark our approach to God. Like the centurion, many persons in the Bible gave an example of Faith, i.e., total self-surrender to God, who reveals Himself to us. The most outstanding was Abraham, who is considered by the Church as the father of all the faithful. READ: Gen. 15: 1-8 (esp. 6); Gal. 3, 3-9; Rom. 4, 18-25; Matt. 17, 14-20; Luke 17, 5-6.

INTROIT   Ps. 96, 7. 8   [*Adore Him*]

Adore God, all you His angels: *
   Sion hears and is glad, *
   and the cities of Juda rejoice. *

(Ps.) The Lord is King; let the earth rejoice; *
   let the many isles be glad. *

Glory be to the Father, etc.

Adore God, all you His angels: *
Sion hears and is glad, *
and the cities of Juda rejoice.

➤ *Kyrie and Gloria, pp. 13-14.*

PRAYER   [Strengthen Us]

Almighty and everlasting God, look with favor upon our weakness, and stretch forth the right hand of Your Majesty to help and defend us. Through our Lord, etc. People: **Amen.** ℣

EPISTLE   Rom. 12, 16-21   [Love of Enemies]

Brethren: Do not be wise in your own estimation. Never repay injury with injury. See that your conduct is honorable in the eyes of all. If possible, so far as it lies with you, live peaceably with everyone. Do not avenge yourselves, beloved, but leave that to God's wrath, for it is written: "Vengeance belongs to Me; I will repay," says the Lord. But, "If your enemy be hungry, give him food to eat; if he be thirsty, give him to drink; for by doing this you will heap live coals on his head." Do not be conquered by evil, but conquer evil with good. ℣

GRADUAL   Ps. 101, 16. 17   [Revering God's Glory]
The nations shall revere Your Name, O Lord, *
and all the kings of the earth Your glory. *
For the Lord has rebuilt Sion, *
and He shall appear in His Glory.

Alleluia, alleluia. *   Ps. 96, 1 [Rejoice in the King]
The Lord is King; let the earth rejoice; *
let the many isles be glad. Alleluia.

➤ *Prayer before the Gospel, p. 16.*

GOSPEL Matt. 8, 1-13 [*Jesus the Healer*]

At that time, when Jesus came down from the mountain, great crowds followed Him. And suddenly a leper advanced, did Him homage, and said to Him, "Lord, if you will to do so, you can make me clean." He stretched out His hand, touched him and said, "I will to do so. Be clean." Immediately he was clean of leprosy. Then He said to him, "See that you tell no one. Simply go and show yourself to the priest, and offer the gift Moses prescribed. That will be a proof for them." After He had entered Capharnaum, a centurion approached Him with this urgent request, "Lord, my boy is at home in bed paralyzed, suffering terribly." He said to him, "I will come and cure him." "Lord," replied the centurion, "I am not worthy to have You enter my house. Just give an order, and my boy will get better. I myself know how authority works. I have soldiers under me, and if I give one man the order, 'On your way,' off he goes; or another the order, 'Come here,' he comes. If I tell my slave, 'Do this,' he does it." Jesus was surprised to hear this and He remarked to His followers, "I assure you, I have never found an Israelite with faith as great as this. Mark My words! Many from east and west will come and find a place at the banquet in the kingdom of heaven with Abraham, Isaac, and Jacob, while the natural heirs of the kingdom will be driven outside into the darkness, where they will wail and gnash their teeth." To the centurion Jesus said, "Go home.

It shall be done in answer to your faith." The boy got better that very moment.

➤ *Creed, p.* 18.

OFFERTORY   Ps. 117, 16. 17   [*Might of the Lord*]

The right hand of the Lord has struck with power: *
  the right hand of the Lord has exalted me; *
I shall not die, but live, *
  and declare the works of the Lord.

➤ *Offertory Prayers, p.* 21.

SECRET   [*Sanctify Body and Mind*]

May this offering, O Lord, we beseech You, wipe away our transgressions, and make holy the minds and bodies of Your servants for celebrating this sacrifice. Through our Lord, etc.
People: **Amen.**

➤ *Preface, p.* 26.

COMMUNION   Luke 4, 22   [*Marvels of the Word*]

All marveled at the words *
  that came from the mouth of God.

POSTCOMMUNION   [*Fit to benefit*]

O Lord, as You grant us to use this great sacrament, deign, we beseech You, to make us truly worthy of its fruits. Through our Lord, etc.
People: **Amen.**

➤ *Dismissal, p.* 42.

"He stood up, . . . and everything became very calm.

FOURTH SUNDAY AFTER EPIPHANY

THOUGHT FOR TODAY: Our life with its temptations and struggles is often similar to a voyage on a stormy sea. If we do what is in our power and persevere in prayer, the Master of Nature will do the rest, and there will come a great calm and peace.

BIBLE AND LITURGY: Our Lord showed His power by rebuking the wind and the sea. He has that power because He is Lord of all. We must see Christ as Lord of His Church even when His power is temporarily hidden. READ: Matt. 9, 1-8; Luke 4, 33-37; Mark 13, 21-27; Apoc. 5, 9-14; 12, 10-12.

INTROIT Ps. 96, 7. 8. 1 [*Adore Him*]

Adore God, all you His angels: *
  Sion hears and is glad. *
  and the cities of Juda rejoice. *

(Ps.) The Lord is King; let the earth rejoice; *
  let the many isles be glad. *

Glory be to the Father, etc.

Adore God, all you His angels: *
  Sion hears and is glad, *
  and the cities of Juda rejoice.

➤ *Kyrie and Gloria, pp.* 13-14.

PRAYER [*Help Our Frailty*]

O God, Who know that our human frailty cannot stand fast against the great dangers that beset us, grant us health of mind and body, that with Your help we may overcome what we suffer on account of our sins. Through our Lord. etc. People: **Amen.** ↓

EPISTLE Rom. 13, 8-10 [*Love of Neighbor*]

Brethren: Owe no debt to anyone except the debt that binds us to love one another; for whoever loves his neighbor has fulfilled the law. For the commandments, "You shall not commit adultery; you shall not kill; you shall not steal; you shall not covet," and any other commandment there is, are all summed up in this one sentence: "You shall love your neighbor as yourself." Love never does any wrong to one's neighbor; and so love is the fulfillment of the Law. ↓

GRADUAL Ps. 101, 16. 17 [*Revering God's Glory*]

The nations shall revere Your name, O Lord, *
and all the kings of the earth Your glory. *
For the Lord has rebuilt Sion, *
and He shall appear in His glory.

Alleluia, alleluia. * Ps. 96, 1 [*Rejoice in the King*]
The Lord is King; let the earth rejoice; *
let the many isles be glad. Alleluia.

➤ *Prayer before the Gospel, p.* 16.

GOSPEL   Matt. 8, 23-27   [*Calming the Waves*]

At that time Jesus got into the boat, and His disciples followed Him. Without warning, a violent storm came up on the sea, so that the boat was being swamped by the waves. But He was sleeping soundly, so they came and woke Him, with the plea, "Lord, save us! We are going to drown!" But He said to them, "Why such cowardice? What weak faith you have!" Then He stood up, reprimanded the winds and the sea, and everything became very calm. The men expressed their surprise, "What sort of Man is this, that the winds and the sea obey Him?"   ➔ *Creed, p. 18.*

OFFERTORY   Ps. 117, 16. 17   [*Might of the Lord*]

The right hand of the Lord has struck with
     power: *
   the right hand of the Lord has exalted me; *
I shall not die, but live, *
   and declare the works of the Lord.

➔ *Offertory Prayers, p. 21.*

SECRET   [*Protect Us from Evil*]

Grant, we beseech You, almighty God, that the offering of this sacrifice may always cleanse and strengthen the weakness of our nature. Through our Lord, etc. People: **Amen.**

➔ *Preface, p. 26.*

COMMUNION   Luke 4, 22   [*Marvels of the Word*]

All marveled at the words *
   that came from the mouth of God.

POSTCOMMUNION [Detachment]

May Your gifts, O God, free us from the attraction of earthly pleasures and give us new strength through Your heavenly nourishment. Through our Lord, etc. People: **Amen.**

"His enemy came along and sowed weeds all through his wheat."

FIFTH SUNDAY AFTER EPIPHANY

THOUGHT FOR TODAY: God is the Creator of the world, and what He has made is good. How then do we account for the evil in the world? Because man has free will, he can misuse God's gifts and transgress His Commandments and do evil. He can become an enemy of his greatest Benefactor. It would be foolish to delay our conversion until God separates the weeds from the wheat.

BIBLE AND LITURGY: The problem of good and evil is often discussed in the Bible. Man has a free will and can misuse God's favors. God, Who is a loving Father, may also permit good people to undergo suffering and frustration to cleanse them from all attachment to evil. Often evil is a mystery. READ: Gen. 4, 1-16; Job 1—3; Ps. 50.

INTROIT Ps. 96, 7. 8. 1 [Adore Him]

Adore God, all you His angels: *
> **Sion hears and is glad, ***
> **and the cities of Juda rejoice. ***

(Ps.) The Lord is King; let the earth rejoice; *
> **let the many isles be glad. ***

Glory be to the Father, etc.

Adore God, all you His angels: *
  Sion hears and is glad, *
  and the cities of Juda rejoice.

➜ *Kyrie and Gloria, pp. 13-14.*

PRAYER   [*Guard Your Family*]

O Lord, we beseech You to keep Your house-hold continually under Your mercy: that, as it leans only upon the hope of Your heavenly grace, so it may always be protected by Your mighty power. Through our Lord, etc. People: **Amen.** ↓

EPISTLE   Col. 3, 12-17   [*Do All in His Name*]

Brethren: As God's chosen ones, holy and be-loved, you must put on heartfelt mercy, kindness, humility, meekness, patience. Bear with one another and forgive whatever griev-ances you may have against each other; forgive just as the Lord has forgiven you. And over all these put on love, which binds them together and makes them perfect. Let the peace of Christ rule over your hearts; for, as members of the one body, you have been called to that peace. Be thankful. Let the word of Christ dwell in you with all its richness; instruct and admonish one another with perfect wisdom. With heart-felt gratitude sing to God psalms, hymns, and inspired songs. And whatever you do in word or in work, do everything in the Name of the

Lord Jesus, giving thanks to God the Father through Jesus Christ, our Lord. ↓

GRADUAL   Ps. 101, 16-17   [*Revering God's Glory*]

The nations shall revere Your Name, O Lord, *
   and all the kings of the earth Your glory. *
For the Lord has rebuilt Sion, *
   and He shall appear in His glory.

Alleluia, alleluia. *   Ps. 96, 1   [*Rejoice in the King*]
The Lord is King; let the earth rejoice, *
   let the many isles be glad. Alleluia.

➤ *Prayer before the Gospel, p. 16.*

GOSPEL   Matt. 13, 24-30   [*Wheat and Weeds*]

At that time Jesus proposed another parable to the crowds: "The kingdom of heaven may be compared to the situation of a farmer who sowed good seed in his field. But when everyone was asleep, his enemy came along and sowed weeds all through his wheat, and got away. Then when the crop came up and began to ripen, the weeds also made their appearance. So the owner's slaves came and said to him, 'Sir, didn't you sow good seed in your field? Then where do the weeds come from?' 'This is the work of an enemy,' he answered. His slaves said to him, 'Do you want us to go out and pull them up?' 'No,' he replied, 'pull up the weeds, and you might pull up the wheat along with them. Let them both grow together until the harvest; then at harvest time, I will order the harvesters: "Collect the weeds first, and bundle them up to burn. But gather the wheat into my barn."' "

➜ *Creed, p. 18.*

OFFERTORY   Ps. 117, 16. 17   [*Might of the Lord*]

The right hand of the Lord has struck with power: *
  the right hand of the Lord has exalted me; *
I shall not die, but live, *
  and declare the works of the Lord.

➜ *Offertory Prayers, p. 21.*

SECRET   [*Absolve Us*]

We offer You, O Lord, this sacrifice of atonement, that You would mercifully absolve our sins and direct our faltering hearts. Through our Lord, etc. People: **Amen.**

➜ *Preface, p. 26.*

COMMUNION   Luke 4, 22   [*Marvels of the Word*]

All marveled at the words *
  that came from the mouth of God.

POSTCOMMUNION   [*Pledge of Salvation*]

We beseech You, almighty God, that we may obtain that salvation whose pledge we have received in this divine sacrament. Through our Lord, etc. People: **Amen.**

➜ *Dismissal, p. 42.*

"Jesus taught the crowds in the form of parables."

SIXTH SUNDAY AFTER EPIPHANY

THOUGHT FOR TODAY: We thank God for the shelter given us under the tree of Christ's Church. But it would not profit us if the teaching of Christ did not "leaven" our thoughts, words and deeds, and stimulate us to true Catholic Action.

BIBLE AND LITURGY: Jesus instructs us about the very nature of the Church by using parables and comparisons. The parable of the mustard seed and the leaven teach us the influence of the Church all over the world. READ also other parables and comparisons concerning the Church: John 10, 11-18; 18, 33-37; 15, 1-7; 1 Cor. 12, 13-31; Matt. 13, 47-50; Apoc. 21, 1-4.

INTROIT Ps. 96, 7. 8. 1   [Adore Him]

Adore God, all you His angels: *
    Sion hears and is glad, *
    and the cities of Juda rejoice. *

(Ps.) The Lord is King; let the earth rejoice; *
    let the many isles be glad. *

Glory be to the Father, etc.

Adore God, all you His angels: *
Sion hears and is glad, *
and the cities of Juda rejoice.

➜ *Kyrie and Gloria, pp. 13-14.*

PRAYER [Reasonable Thinking]

Grant us, we beseech You, almighty God, ever to think of spiritual things and in every word and work always to do what is well pleasing in Your sight. Through our Lord, etc. People: **Amen.** ↓

EPISTLE 1 Thess. 1, 2-10 [Fervent Christians]

Brethren: We keep thanking God always for all of you, constantly remembering you in our prayers, mindful as we are before our God and Father of the work of your faith, the labor of your love, and the constancy of your hope fixed on our Lord Jesus Christ. We know, too, brothers beloved of God, how you have been chosen: our preaching of the gospel proved to be for you not a matter of words only but also of power and the Holy Spirit and complete conviction. You know as well as we do what manner of men we proved to be for your sakes while we were in your midst. For your own part, you became imitators of us and, indeed, of the Lord, receiving the word in the face of great trial with the joy that comes from the Holy Spirit. Thus you became a model for all the believers of both Macedonia and Achaia. For the word of the Lord has resounded from your midst; not only in Macedonia and Achaia but throughout every region has come report of your faith toward God. Hence it is needless for us to say a thing. Rather, it is they who tell all about us: what kind of admittance we gained with you, and how you turned to God from idols, to serve the living and true God and to await the coming down from heaven of His Son Whom He raised from the dead, Jesus, Who delivers us from the wrath to come. ↓

GRADUAL Ps. 101, 16. 17 [*Revering God's Glory*]

The nations shall revere Your Name, O Lord, *
 and all the kings of the earth Your glory. *
For the Lord has rebuilt Sion, *
 and He shall appear in His glory.

Alleluia, alleluia. * Ps. 96, 1 [*Rejoicing in the King*]
The Lord is King; let the earth rejoice, *
 let the many isles be glad. Alleluia.

→ *Prayer before the Gospel, p. 16.*

GOSPEL Matt. 13, 31-35 [*Kingdom of Heaven*]

At that time Jesus proposed another parable to the crowds: "The kingdom of heaven is like a mustard seed which someone took and sowed in his field. It is the smallest of all seeds, yet, when fully grown, it is the largest of plants. It grows into a tree so that the birds of the sky come, and build their nests in its branches." He told them another parable: "The kingdom of heaven is like yeast which a woman took and kneaded into three measures of flour. Eventually the whole mass of dough began to rise." All these lessons Jesus taught the crowds in the form of parables. It was only by way of the parable that He spoke to them, to fulfill what had been said through the prophet, "I will open My mouth in parables, I will announce what has lain hidden since creation."

➤ *Creed, p.* 18.

OFFERTORY Ps. 117, 16. 17 [*Might of the Lord*]

The right hand of the Lord has struck with power: *

  the right hand of the Lord has exalted me; *
I shall not die, but live, *
  and declare the works of the Lord.

➤ *Offertory Prayers, p.* 21.

SECRET [*Our Renovation*]

May this offering, O God, we beseech You, cleanse and renew us, govern and protect us. Through our Lord, etc. People: **Amen.**

➤ *Preface, p.* 26.

COMMUNION Luke 4, 22 [*Awe for God's Word*]

All marveled at the words *
  that came from the mouth of God.

POSTCOMMUNION [*Seek for True Life*]

Nourished by Your heavenly food, O Lord, we beseech You that we may always have a taste for that same food which gives us true life. Through our Lord, etc. People: **Amen.**

➤ *Dismissal, p.* 42.

THE EASTER CYCLE (I)

PRE-LENT AND LENTEN SEASON—

The Preparation

Man, enslaved by evil, owes our Lord gratitude for two extremely great favors. The first one is His Incarnation, which is celebrated during the Christmas Cycle. The second is our Redemption, which sets the theme for the Cycle of Easter.

We start as repentant sinners, who need redemption (Pre-Lent and Lenten Season). "Mindful, therefore, O Lord, not only of the blessed Passion of the same Christ Your Son, our Lord, but also of His Resurrection from the dead, and finally His glorious Ascension into heaven" (*Canon of the Mass*). This is the setting: Self-restraint, heart-searching, charity, prayer, penance as a participation in Christ's penance-passion, but always with the Christian outlook on our final participation in the Lord's Resurrection and Ascension into heaven.

The basic structure of the Christian approach to life is thoroughly treated during this season. Great themes as: evil-good, light-darkness, life-death appear on the scene in manifold variations. We should assimilate them by meditation and frequent celebration of the liturgical services, composed for Lent. "Was it not necessary for the Messiah first to endure these sufferings and then enter into His glory?" (*Gospel of Monday in Easter week.*) Our life means re-living the life of Christ.

From Easter to Easter we will share more intimately in Christ's glorious Resurrection, but only if a serious partaking in the Lenten exercises came first! "Remember, man, that you are dust and unto dust you shall return" (*Ash Wednesday*) will result in a triumphant challenge "O death, where is your victory?" (1 Cor. 15, 50-55), but only after a valiant preparation!

Holy Mother Church guides us through her Lenten Liturgy.

"The last shall come first, and the first, last."

SEPTUAGESIMA SUNDAY

THOUGHT FOR TODAY: God holds out a great reward to us, but we must work to receive it. Unfortunately, we are by nature more inclined to endure hardships for the perishable goods of this life than we are for our eternal happiness in the Kingdom of God.

BIBLE AND LITURGY: The Church sees human nature as wounded by sin. Man is naturally inclined to evil. That is the reason why life often becomes a battle, labor and hardship. Lent and also the Pre-Lenten season, which begins with this Sunday, remind us of this fact. READ: Gen. 3; Heb. 10, 32-39; 12, 1-13; 1 Cor. 9, 24-27; 2 Tim. 4, 6-8; Ps. 34.

INTROIT   Ps. 17, 5. 6. 7. 2. 3   [*My Help in Terror*]

The terrors of death surged round about me, *
   the cords of the nether world enmeshed me. *
In my distress I called upon the Lord; *
   from His holy temple He heard my voice. *
(Ps.) I love You, O Lord, my strength, *
   O Lord, my rock, my fortress, my deliverer. *
Glory be to the Father, etc.

The terrors of death surged round about me, *
 the cords of the nether world enmeshed me. *
In my distress I called upon the Lord; *
 from His holy temple He heard my voice.

➤ *Kyrie, p. 13. Omit Gloria.*

PRAYER   [*Delivery through Penance*]

O Lord, we beseech You, graciously hear the prayers of Your people, that we who are justly punished for our sins may be mercifully delivered for the glory of Your Name. Through our Lord, etc. People: **Amen.** ⬇

EPISTLE   1 Cor. 9, 24-27; 10, 1-5

[*The Struggle for Eternal Life*]

Brethren: Don't you know that while all the runners in the stadium take part in the race, only one wins the prize? Run to win! Every athlete denies himself many things. And they do this to win a perishable crown, but we an imperishable one. So I do not run like a man who doesn't see the goal. I do not fight like a boxer who punches the air. No, I beat my body and make it my slave, so that after having preached to others, I myself may not be disqualified. Brothers, I want you to remember this: Our fathers were all under the cloud and all passed through the sea; and by the cloud and the sea all were baptized into Moses. And all ate the same spiritual food; and all drank the same spiritual drink (for they drank from the spiritual rock that was following them, and the rock was Christ)—and yet with most of them God was not pleased. ⬇

GRADUAL Ps. 9, 10. 11. 19. 20 [*Trust in God's Help*]

A stronghold in times of distress; *
   they trust in You who cherish You; *
   for You forsake not those who seek You, O
     Lord. *
For the needy shall not always be forgotten; *
   nor shall the hope of the afflicted forever
     perish; *
Rise, O Lord, let not man prevail. ⍖

TRACT Ps. 129, 1-4   [*Mercy for Sinners*]

Out of the depths I cry to You, O Lord; *
   Lord, hear my voice! *
Let Your ears be attentive *
   to the prayer of Your servant. *
If You, O Lord, mark iniquities: *
Lord, who can stand?" *
But with You is forgiveness, *
   and by reason of Your law *
   I have waited for You, O Lord.

➜ *Prayer before the Gospel, p.* 16.

GOSPEL Matt. 20, 1-16

[*Conversion to God Welcome at Any Time*]

At that time Jesus told His disciples this
parable: "The kingdom of heaven is like
the owner of an estate who went out at dawn
to hire workmen for his vineyard. After reaching an agreement with the workmen for the
usual daily wage, he sent them out to his vineyard. He came out about mid-morning, and he
saw other men standing about the market

place without work; so he said to them, 'You go along to my vineyard also; and I'll pay you whatever is fair.' So they went. He again came out around noon, and in the mid-afternoon; and did the same. Finally going out in the late afternoon, he found still others standing around, and he said to them, 'Why have you been standing here idle all day?' 'Nobody has hired us,' they explained. So he said to them, 'You go along to the vineyard too.' When evening came the owner of the vineyard said to his foreman, 'Call the workmen, and give them their pay. But begin with the last group and end with the first.' Now when those hired late in the afternoon came, they received a full day's pay. So when the first group came along, they expected to receive more. Yet they received the same daily wage. On receiving it, they complained against the owner. 'This last group did only an hour's work, but you have made them equal to us, who have carried the heavy part of the day's work and put up with the heat.' 'My friend,' he said to one of them in reply, 'I am doing you no injustice. You agreed on the usual daily wage, didn't you? Take your pay and go home. I choose to give this man who was hired last the same pay as you. Am I not free to do as I choose with what is mine? Or could it be that you are showing envy because I am generous?' Thus, the last shall come first, and the first, last."

➤ *Creed,* p. **18**.

OFFERTORY Ps. 91, 2 [*Thanks and Praise*]

It is good to give thanks to the Lord, *
 and to sing praise to Your Name, Most High.

➔ *Offertory Prayers, p.* 21.

SECRET [*Plea for God's Favors*]

*Since You have accepted our gifts and our
prayers, we beseech You, O Lord, to cleanse us
by this heavenly sacrament and mercifully to
hear us. Through our Lord, etc.* People: **Amen.**

➔ *Preface, p.* 26.

COMMUNION Ps. 30, 17. 18 [*God's Kindness*]

Let Your face shine upon Your servant; *
 save me in Your kindness. *
O Lord, let me not be put to shame, *
 for I call upon You.

POSTCOMMUNION [*Longing for God's Gifts*]

*May Your faithful people, O God, be strength-
ened by Your gifts; that by receiving them, they
may still desire them, and by desiring them, may
evermore receive them. Through our Lord, etc.*
People: **Amen.**

➔ *Dismissal, p.* 42.

"A farmer went out to sow seed."

SEXAGESIMA SUNDAY

THOUGHT FOR TODAY: Jesus is the Divine Sower. His word and example would yield fruit a hundredfold in our hearts as it did in the life of St. Paul, if we would not busy ourselves with thousands of unnecessary things which divert us from the one necessary thing, namely, the salvation of our souls.

BIBLE AND LITURGY: Man, weak in his fallen nature, can be strengthened by the strength of Christ. His Word can dwell in us. But we must receive God's Word with an open mind and cooperate in order that it may grow and bear fruit in us. Hence, regular Bible reading is extremely important. READ: Prov. 30, 5; John 5, 24; Rom. 15, 1-6; 2 Tim. 3, 10-17; 2 Pet. 1, 16-21.

INTROIT Ps. 43, 23-26. 2   [Come to Our Aid]

Awake! Why are You asleep, O Lord?*
　Arise! Cast us not off forever! *
Why do You hide Your face, *
　forgetting our oppression? *
Our bodies are pressed to the earth. *
　Arise, O Lord, help us, and deliver us. *
(Ps.) O God, our ears have heard, *
　our fathers have declared to us. *

Glory be to the Father, etc.

Awake! Why are You asleep, O Lord? *

 Arise! Cast us not off forever! *

Why do You hide Your face, *

 forgetting our oppression? *

Our bodies are pressed to the earth. *

 Arise, O Lord, help us, and deliver us.

➔ *Kyrie, p.* 13. *Omit Gloria.*

PRAYER [Help of St. Paul]

O God, Who see that we put no trust in anything we do, mercifully grant that by the protection of the Doctor of the Gentiles, we may be defended against all adversity. Through our Lord, etc. People: **Amen.** ↓

EPISTLE 2 Cor. 11, 19-33; 12, 1-9 [Paul, the Apostle]

Brethren: You gladly put up with fools, being wise yourselves. Why you even put up with those who try to enslave you, with those who exploit you, with those who impose upon you, with those who put on airs, with those who slap you in the face. To my shame I must confess that we have been too weak to do such things. But what anyone else dares to claim—I am talking foolishly now—I, too, will dare. Are they Hebrews? So am I! Are they Israelites? So am I! Are they offspring of Abraham? So am I! Are they ministers of Christ? Now I am really talking like a fool—I am more! with many more labors, with many more imprisonments, with far worse beatings, frequently in danger of death. Five times at the hands of the Jews I received forty lashes less one; three times I was beaten with rods; once I was stoned; three times I was shipwrecked; I passed a day and a night in the sea. I was continually on journeys with danger from floods, with danger from robbers; in danger from my own people and from the Gentiles; with danger in the city, in the desert and on the sea; in danger from false brothers; with labor and hardship, with many sleepless nights; in hunger and thirst and frequent fastings, in cold and nakedness; and, leaving other sufferings unmentioned, there is that daily tension pressing down on me, my anxiety for all the churches. Who is weak, and I am not affected by it? Who is scandalized, and I am not inflamed with indignation? If I must boast, I will boast about my weaknesses. The God and Father of the Lord Jesus knows —may He be blessed forever!—that I am not lying. In Damascus the ethnarch of King Aretas was keeping a close watch on the city in order to arrest me, but I was lowered in a basket through a window in the wall and I escaped his hands. I must go on boasting, useless though it is. I shall speak of visions and revelations of the Lord. I know a man in Christ, who, fourteen years ago—whether he was in his body, or outside his body, I don't know, but God does—was snatched up even to the third heaven; and I know that this man—whether he was in his body or outside it I don't know, God knows—was snatched up even into Paradise and heard words which can't be uttered, which no man is permitted to speak. About this man I will boast, but I will not boast about

myself, unless it be about my weaknesses. If
I should boast, I would not really be foolish,
because I would be telling the truth. But I
refrain, lest anyone should think more of me
than what he sees in me or hears from me.
Now with respect to the extraordinary revelations, in order that I might not become conceited
I was given a thorn for the flesh, an angel of
Satan to beat me, to keep me from becoming
proud. Three times I begged the Lord about
this, that it might leave me. And He said to
me: "My favor is enough for you, for in weakness power reaches perfection." Gladly, therefore, will I boast rather about my weaknesses,
in order that the power of Christ may rest
upon me.

GRADUAL   Ps. 82, 19. 14   [*You Are the One God*]

Let the nations know that God is Your name; *
You alone are the Most High over all the
earth. *
O my God, make them like leaves in a whirl-
wind, *
like chaff before the wind. ↓

TRACT   Ps. 59, 4. 6   [*The God of Power*]

You have rocked the country, O Lord; *
and split it open. *
Repair the cracks in it, *
for it is tottering. *
That they may flee out of bowshot; *
that Your loved ones may escape.

➤ *Prayer before the Gospel, p. 16.*

GOSPEL　　Luke 8, 4-15　　　　[Sowing of the Word]

At that time a large crowd was gathering, and men were resorting to Jesus city by city. He spoke to them in a parable: "A farmer went out to sow seed. And in the sowing, some seed fell on the footpath, where it was walked on and the birds of the air ate it up. Some fell on rocky ground, sprouted up, and withered through lack of moisture. Some fell among thorns, and the thorns grew up with it, and stifled it. And some fell on good soil, grew up, and yielded grain a hundred for one." As He said this He exclaimed: "Let everyone heed what he has heard." His disciples began asking Him what was the meaning of this parable, and He said: "To you have been confided the mysteries of the kingdom of God, but the rest have only parables that 'seeing they may not perceive and hearing may not understand.' This is the meaning of the parable. 'The seed' is the word of God. 'Those on the footpath' are those who hear, but the devil comes and takes the word out of their hearts lest they should believe and be saved. 'Those on the rocky ground' are they who, when they hear it, receive the word with joy. These have no root; they believe for awhile, but they fall away in time of temptation. 'The seed fallen among thorns' are those who hear, but their progress is stifled by the cares and riches and pleasures of life, and they do not mature. 'The seed in good ground' are they who hear the word with nobility and goodness of

heart, and retain it, and bear fruit in perseverance.''

➤ *Creed, p.* 18.

OFFERTORY Ps. 16, 5. 6. 7 [*God's Care of the Trustful*]

Make my steps steadfast in Your paths, *
that my feet may not falter. *
Incline Your ear to me; *
hear my word. *
Show Your wondrous kindness, O Lord, *
Savior of those who trust in You.

➤ *Offertory Prayers, p.* 21.

SECRET [*Life from the Sacrifice*]

May this sacrifice which we offer You, O Lord,
ever give us new life and protection. Through
our Lord, etc. People: **Amen.**

➤ *Preface, p.* 26.

COMMUNION Ps. 42, 4 [*Joy of God's Altar*]

I will go in to the altar of God, *
the God of my gladness and joy.

POSTCOMMUNION [*Newness of Spirit*]

O almighty God, grant, we humbly beseech You,
that those whom You refresh with Your sacra-
ment may also worthily serve You in a way
that is well pleasing to You. Through our Lord,
etc. People: **Amen.**

➤ *Dismissal, p.* 42.

"Jesus, Son of David, have pity on me!"

QUINQUAGESIMA SUNDAY

THOUGHT FOR TODAY: As the blind man asked sight of Jesus, so we ought to implore Christ to cure our spiritual blindness. We are spiritually blind if we do not see that our busy life on earth is worthless unless it be rooted in the love of God and of our neighbor.

BIBLE AND LITURGY: Charity is the first and most important law of the Christian Religion. It is a sign by which Christians should be recognized. We should pray often: "Lord, that I may see." READ: Luke 10, 25-37; 1 John 2, 3-11; 3, 16-18; 4, 7-21; Matt. 5, 21-26; Eph. 4, 25-32; Matt. 5, 43-48; Gal. 6, 10; John 13, 34-35.

INTROIT Ps. 30, 3. 4. 2   [God, Our Strength]

Be my rock of refuge, O God, *
     a stronghold to give me safety. *
You are my rock and my fortress; *
     for Your Name's sake You will lead and guide me. *

(Ps.) In You, O Lord, I take refuge; *
     let me never be put to shame. *

In Your justice rescue me, *
   and deliver me. *
Glory be to the Father, etc.
Be my rock of refuge, O God, *
   a stronghold to give me safety. *
You are my rock and my fortress; *
   **for Your Name's sake You will lead and guide
      me.**

➤ *Kyrie, p. 13. Omit Gloria.*

PRAYER   [*Make Us Safe*]

*O Lord, we beseech You, mercifully hear our
prayers; loose us from the chains of our sins and
keep us from all adversity. Through our Lord,
etc.* People: **Amen.** ↓

EPISTLE 1 Cor. 13, 1-13   [*Christian Love*]

Brethren: If I should speak with the tongues
of men and of angels, but not have love, I
am a noisy gong and a clanging cymbal. And
if I were a prophet and knew all mysteries and
had all knowledge, and if I should have faith
so great that I could move mountains, but not
have love, I am nothing. And if I were to give
away everything I have to feed the poor, and
if I were to hand over my body to be burned,
but not have love, I would gain nothing. Love is
patient; love is kind. Love is not jealous; it
does not put on airs; it is not snobbish. Love
does nothing rude; it is not self-seeking; it is
not prone to anger; it does not brood over
injuries. Love is not happy over iniquity, but
rejoices along with the truth. Love covers over

everything, believes everything, hopes for everything, puts up with everything. Love never fails. Prophecies will pass away, tongues will be silent and knowledge will pass away. We have only incomplete knowledge and our prophesying is incomplete. When that which is complete comes, then the incomplete will pass away. When I was a child, I used to talk like a child, think like a child, reason like a child. But when I became a man, I put aside childish ways. We see now in a mirror, in a confused sort of way; but then we shall see face to face. Now I have only partial knowledge; then I shall know even as I am known. Here and now there are three gifts that endure: faith, hope, and love. But the greatest of these is love. ↓

GRADUAL Ps. 76, 15. 16 [*God Delivers Us*]

You are the God Who alone works wonders; *
   among the peoples You have made known
      Your power. *
With Your strong arm You delivered Your
      people, *
   the sons of Israel and Joseph. ↓

TRACT Ps. 99, 2-3 [*Sing to God*]

Sing joyfully to God, all you lands; *
   serve the Lord with gladness. *
Come before Him with joyful song; *
Know that the Lord is God. *
   He made us, His we are; *
   His people, the flock He tends.

→ *Prayer before the Gospel, p. 16.*

GOSPEL   Luke 18, 31-43

[*Prophecy of the Cross: Lord, That I May See*]

At that time, taking aside the Twelve, Jesus said to them, "Now we are going up to Jerusalem, and all that was written by the prophets will be accomplished for the Son of Man. He will be delivered up to the pagans. He will be mocked, outraged, and spat upon. They will scourge Him and put Him to death and on the third day He will rise again." But they understood nothing of this; this word remained in the dark for them, and they did not understand what He said. As He drew near Jericho a blind man sat at the side of the road begging. Hearing a crowd go by he asked, "What is that?" They replied that Jesus of Nazareth was passing by. Then he shouted out, "Jesus, Son of David, have pity on me." Those in the lead sternly ordered him to be silent, but he cried out all the more, "Son of David, have pity on me."

Jesus halted and ordered him to be brought to Him. When he drew near, Jesus asked him: "What do you want Me to do for you?" "Lord," he answered, "that I may see." Jesus said to him: "Receive back your sight, your faith has saved you." At that very instant he got back his sight and he followed Him glorifying God. And all the people witnessed it and gave praise to God.

➤ *Creed, p. 18.*

OFFERTORY   Ps. 118, 12-13   [Learning God's Law]

Blessed are You, O Lord; *
   teach me Your statutes. *
With my lips I declare *
   all the ordinances of Your mouth.

➤ *Offertory Prayers, p. 21.*

SECRET   [Sanctify Us]

May this offering, O Lord, we beseech You, wash away our sins; may it sanctify the bodies and souls of Your servants for the celebration of this sacrifice. Through our Lord, etc. People: **Amen.**

➤ *Preface, p. 26.*

COMMUNION   Ps. 77, 29-30   [All Were Filled]

They ate and were wholly surfeited; *
   the Lord had brought them what they craved; *
   they were not defrauded of that which they craved.

POSTCOMMUNION   [Celestial Food]

We beseech You, almighty God, that we who have received the Bread of heaven, may by it be protected from all adversity. Through our Lord, etc. People: **Amen.**

➤ *Dismissal, p. 42.*

"Away with you, Satan! Scripture has it, 'You shall do homage to the Lord your God.'"

FIRST SUNDAY IN LENT

THOUGHT FOR TODAY: Christ permitted Himself to be tempted by Satan. Why, then, should we be surprised if we have to struggle against the malice and snares of the devil! Our strength to resist lies in fasting, in guarding and controlling our senses, in almsgiving, in prayers, and in uniting ourselves with Christ in Holy Mass and Communion.

BIBLE AND LITURGY: Temptation to go freely and deliberately against God's will may come at times from our nature, which is disrupted through sin. At other times, the devil and bad company may bring on temptations. READ: Apoc. 12, 1 Pet. 5, 5-11; 2 Cor. 11, 1-15 (esp. 3 and 14); 2 Tim. 2, 19-26; James 1, 12-18; 1 Cor. 10, 12-13; Matt. 6, 13.

INTROIT   Ps. 90, 15. 16. 1   [*Glorified by Prayer*]

He shall call upon Me, and I will answer him; *
    I will deliver him and glorify him; *
    with length of days I will gratify him. *

(Ps.) **You who dwell in the shelter of the Most High,** *

shall abide in the shadow of the Almighty. *

Glory be to the Father, etc.

He shall call upon Me, and I will answer him; *
I will deliver him and glorify him; *
with length of days I will gratify him.

➤ *Kyrie, p. 13. Omit Gloria.*

PRAYER   [*Power of Good Works*]

O God, Who purify Your Church by the yearly Lenten observance, grant to Your household that what they strive to obtain from You by abstinence, they may achieve by good works. Through our Lord, etc. People: **Amen.** ↓

EPISTLE   2 Cor. 6, 1-10   [*Virtue from Suffering*]

Brethren: We beg you, as your fellow workers, not to receive the favor of God in vain. For He says: "In a favorable time I heard you, and on a day of salvation I helped you." Now is the favorable time; now is the day of salvation. We avoid giving anyone occasion for taking offense in anything, in order that the ministry may not be blamed. On the contrary, in everything we strive to show ourselves as ministers of God, with great fortitude in trials, distress, difficulties, in beatings, imprisonments, riots; with hard work, sleepless nights and fastings; with innocence, knowledge, patience and kindness; with a holy spirit, with sincere love; with

the message of truth and the power of God;
wielding the weapons of justice with right hand
and left; whether honored or dishonored;
whether spoken of well or ill. We are called
impostors, and yet we are truthful; nobodies,
and we are well known; dead, and here we are
alive; punished, and we have not yet been put
to death; sorrowful, and we are always rejoicing; poor, and we are enriching many; we are
said to have nothing, and yet we possess everything. ▼

GRADUAL   Ps. 90, 11-12   [*Our Angel's Care*]

**To His angels God has given command about
you, ***

   that they guard you in all your ways. *
Upon their hands they shall bear you up, *
   lest you dash your foot against a stone. ▼

TRACT   Ps. 90, 1-7. 11-16

          [*The Most High Watches over Us*]

You who dwell in the shelter of the Most High, *
   shall abide in the shadow of the Almighty. *
Say to the Lord, "My refuge and my fortress, *
   my God, in Whom I trust." *
**For He will rescue you from the snare of the
fowler, ***
   from the destroying pestilence. *
With His pinions He will cover you, *
   and under His wings you shall take refuge. *
His faithfulness is a buckler and a shield; *
   you shall not fear the terror of the night. *

Nor the arrow that flies by day; *
  nor the pestilence that roams in darkness; *
  nor the devastating plague at noon. *
Though a thousand fall at your side, *
  ten thousand at your right side, *
  near you it shall not come. *
For to His angels He has given command about
    you, *
  that they may guard you in all your ways. *
Upon their hands they shall bear you up, *
  lest you dash your foot against a stone. *
You shall tread upon the asp and the viper; *
  you shall trample down the lion and the
    dragon. *
Because he clings to Me, I will deliver him; *
  I will set him on high because he acknowl-
    edges My Name. *
He shall call upon Me, and I will answer him; *
  I will be with him in distress. *
I will deliver him and glorify him; *
  with length of days I will gratify him *
  and will show him My salvation.

➤ *Prayer before the Gospel, p.* 16.

GOSPEL Matt. 4, 1-11   [*Christ Conquers*]

At that time, Jesus was led into the desert by
  the Spirit to be tempted by the devil. He
fasted forty days and forty nights, and after-
wards He was hungry. Then the tempter approached and said to Him, "If You are God's
Son, command these stones to turn into bread."
But He replied, "Scripture has it, 'Not on bread

alone is man to live, but on every command that issues from the mouth of God.'" Next the devil took Him to the holy city. He set Him upon the highest point in the Temple area, saying, "If You are God's Son, throw Yourself down. Scripture has it, 'He will bid His angels look after You; with their hands they will support You, that You may never even stumble over a stone.'" Jesus answered him, "Scripture also has it, 'You shall not make trial of the Lord your God.'" Again, the devil took Him along to a lofty mountain peak, and displayed before Him all the kingdoms of the world in their magnificence, promising, "All this will I bestow upon You, if You will prostrate Yourself in homage before me." Then Jesus said to him, "Away with you, Satan! Scripture has it, 'You shall do homage to the Lord your God: Him alone shall you adore.'" At that the devil left Him, and all at once angels came and waited on Him.

➤ *Creed, p.* 18.

OFFERTORY   Ps. 90, 4. 5   [Protection of God]

With His pinions the Lord will cover you. *
and under His wings you shall take refuge; *
His faithfulness is a buckler and a shield.

➤ *Offertory Prayers, p.* 21.

SECRET   [Curbing Sin]

We offer these sacrificial gifts at the beginning of Lent, praying You, O Lord, that while we practice restraint in the use of bodily food, we may also refrain from harmful pleasures. Through our Lord, etc. People: **Amen.** ↓

PREFACE FOR LENT

[*Our Prayer of Thanksgiving*]

Right and worthy it is, fitting and for our good that in every time and place our thanks should rise to You, O Lord, holy Father, almighty and eternal God. When in our bodies we keep the fast, You grant us mastery over vice, You raise our hearts, You strengthen and reward us; through Christ our Lord. Through Him the Angels praise Your Majesty, while Dominations adore and all the powers stand in awe. In one great voice, the heavens, all the hosts of heaven, and the Blessed Seraphim, cry our their praise. In our turn we pray that our voices now may be joined with theirs as, in humble witness, we sing: ➤ *Sanctus, p. 27.*

COMMUNION   Ps. 90, 4. 5   [*Protection of God*]

With His pinions the Lord will cover you, *
  and under His wings you shall take refuge; *
His faithfulness is a buckler and a shield.

POSTCOMMUNION   [*Union with God*]

May the holy offering of Your sacrament renew us, O Lord, and cause us to be purified from our old ways and come to the fellowship of this saving mystery. Through our Lord, etc. People: **Amen.**

➤ *Dismissal, p. 42.*

"And suddenly Moses and Elia appeared to them, conversing with Him."

SECOND SUNDAY IN LENT

THOUGHT FOR TODAY: The Transfiguration of Our Lord gives us an idea of the beauty of a soul in the state of sanctifying grace. "This is the will of God: that you become holy."

BIBLE AND LITURGY: In the midst of trials and tribulations, it is well to keep our eyes on the Transfiguration and preserve the divine life in our souls. Temptations, sufferings, battles and penance, if accepted in Faith, may finally transfigure us completely and make us partakers of Christ's glory. READ: 1 Cor. 6, 12-20; Matt. 10, 16-33; Rom. 7, 24-25; 8, 18-23; 2 Cor. 3, 12-18; 5, 1-10.

INTROIT   Ps. 24, 6. 3. 22. 1. 2   [*The Lord Ever Kind*]

Remember that Your compassion, O Lord, *
   and Your kindness are from of old; *
Let not our enemies exult over us; *
   deliver us, O God of Israel, from all our tribulations. *
(Ps.) To You I lift up my soul, O Lord; *
   in You, O my God, I trust; *
   let me not be put to shame. *
Glory be to the Father, etc.

Remember that Your compassion, O Lord, *
and Your kindness are from of old; *
Let not our enemies exult over us; *
deliver us, O God of Israel, from all our
tribulations.

➔ *Kyrie, p. 13. Omit Gloria.*

PRAYER   [*Our Helplessness*]

*O God, Who see how we are deprived of
all strength, guard us inwardly and outwardly,
that in body we may be protected against all
misfortunes, and in mind cleansed of evil
thoughts. Through our Lord, etc.* People:
Amen. ↓

EPISTLE   1 Thess. 4, 1-7   [*Christian Holiness*]

Brethren: We beg and exhort you by the Lord
Jesus that, as you have learned from us
how to conduct yourselves and please God, as
indeed you are doing, so you make even greater
progress. For you know what instructions we
gave you by the Lord Jesus. This is the will of
God: that you become holy, that you keep away
from immorality, that every one of you preserve
in holiness and honor what is his to use, not in
the passion of desire as do the Gentiles who
do not know God, that he refrain from over-
reaching or deceiving his brother in the matter
at hand; for the Lord is an avenger of all such
things, even as we once told you and testified.
Obviously, God has not called us to remain unclean, but to be made holy in Christ Jesus, our
Lord. ↓

GRADUAL   Ps. 24, 17. 18   [Bring Calm to My Soul]

Relieve the troubles of my heart *
   and bring me out of my distress, O Lord. *
Put an end to my affliction and my suffering, *
   and take away all my sins. ↯

TRACT   Ps. 105, 1-4   [Joy of the Good]

Give thanks to the Lord, for He is good, *
   for His kindness endures forever. *
Who can tell the mighty deeds of the Lord, *
   or proclaim all His praises? *
Happy are they who observe what is right, *
   who do always what is just. *
Remember us, O Lord, as You favor Your people; *
visit us with Your saving help.

➤ *Prayer before the Gospel, p. 16.*

GOSPEL   Matt. 17, 1-9   [Glory of Christ]

At that time Jesus took Peter, James, and his
brother John and led them up a high
mountain by themselves. Then He was trans-
figured before their eyes: His face became as
dazzling as the sun, His clothes as radiant as
light. And suddenly Moses and Elia appeared
to them, conversing with Him. Then Peter spoke
up and said to Jesus, "Lord, it is good that we
are here. With Your permission, I will set up
three tents here: one for You, one for Moses,
and one for Elia." He was still speaking when
suddenly a bright cloud overshadowed them.
And now a voice came out of the cloud, "This
is My beloved Son, in Whom I take delight.
Listen to Him." When they heard this, the

disciples fell face to the ground and were filled with fear. But Jesus came to them, and laying His hand upon them said, "Get up and don't be afraid." When they looked up, they saw only Jesus, no one else. As they were coming down the mountain, Jesus gave them this command, "Don't tell anyone of the vision until the Son of Man is raised from the dead." ↓

OFFERTORY   Ps. 118, 47. 48   [Love of God's Law]

I will delight in Your commands, *
    which I love exceedingly; *
And I will lift up my hands to Your commands, *
    which I love.

➜ *Offertory Prayers, p. 21.*

SECRET   [Gifts of Devotion]

Look with favor, we beseech You, O Lord, upon the offerings here before You, that they may be beneficial for our devotion and for our salvation. Through our Lord, etc. People: **Amen.**

➜ *Preface, p. 132.*

COMMUNION   Ps. 5, 2-4   [Cry to the King]

Attend to my sighing; *
    heed my call for help, my King and my God! *
To You I pray, *
    O Lord.

POSTCOMMUNION [Refreshed by the Sacraments]

O almighty God, we humbly beseech You that those whom You refresh with Your sacrament may also worthily serve You in a way pleasing to You. Through our Lord, etc. People: **Amen.**

➜ *Dismissal, p. 42.*

"If it is by Beelzebul that I cast out devils, by whom do your people cast them out?"

THIRD SUNDAY IN LENT

THOUGHT FOR TODAY: We cannot be neutral in our relationship with God. If we do not serve Him, pride and selfishness will enslave us. "Happy are they who hear the word of God and keep it."

BIBLE AND LITURGY: Being Christians means that we made a decision. The Church teaches today that a compromise with evil is impossible. Faithful penance, abstinence and fasting will keep us from attachment to evil. Hence, they are necessary to be faithful to the decision of our Baptism. READ: 2 Esd. 1, 1-11; Dan. 9, 1-16; Jona 3; Mark 9, 24-28; 2 Cor. 6, 1-10; 1 Cor. 9, 24-27.

INTROIT   Ps. 24, 15-16   [*Looking to the Lord*]

My eyes are ever toward the Lord, *
    for He will free my feet from the snare. *
Look toward me, and have pity on me, *
    for I am alone and afflicted. *
(Ps.) To You I lift up my soul, *
    O Lord. *
In You, O my God, I trust; *
    let me not be put to shame. *

Glory be to the Father, etc.

My eyes are ever toward the Lord, *
  for He will free my feet from the snare. *
Look toward me, and have pity on me, *
  for I am alone and afflicted.

➤ *Kyrie, p. 13. Omit Gloria.*

PRAYER   [*Heed Our Desires*]

*We beseech You, almighty God, hear the prayers
of the humble and stretch forth the right hand of
Your Majesty to protect us. Through our Lord,
etc.* People: **Amen.** ↓

EPISTLE   Eph. 5, 1-9   [*Walk in the Light*]

Brethren: Be imitators of God as very dear
children, and follow the way of love, as
Christ also loved you and gave Himself for us,
an offering to God, a sacrifice of pleasing fragrance. As for fornication or any kind of uncleanness or lust, let it not be mentioned among
you; such is the rule for the saints. Nor should
there be any obscenity, or silly and suggestive
talk; all that is out of place. Instead, give thanks.
And make no mistake about this: no fornicator,
no unclean or lustful person, who is really an
idolator, has any inheritance in the kingdom of
Christ and of God. Do not let anyone deceive
you by worthless arguments; these are the sins
that bring down God's wrath upon the disobedi-
ent; so have nothing to do with them. It is
true that you were once darkness; but now you
are light in the Lord. Live, then, as children of
light; for light produces every kind of goodness
and justice and truth. ↓

GRADUAL Ps. 9, 20. 4   [Defend Us]

Rise, O Lord, let not man prevail; *
  let the nations be judged in Your presence. *
Because my enemies are turned back, *
  overthrown and destroyed before You. ↓

TRACT Ps. 122, 1-3   [Look With Pity]

To You I lift up my eyes, *
  Who are enthroned in heaven. *
Behold, as the eyes of servants *
  are on the hands of their masters. *
As the eyes of a maid *
  are on the hands of her mistress, *
So are our eyes on the Lord our God, *
  till He have pity on us. *
Have pity on us, O Lord, *
  have pity on us.

➤ *Prayer before the Gospel, p.* 16.

GOSPEL Luke 11, 14-28   [Jesus, Conqueror of Evil]

At that time Jesus was casting out a devil which was dumb; and when the devil was cast out the dumb man spoke. And the crowds were amazed. But some of them said: "It is by Beelzebul, the prince of devils, that He casts out devils." Others, to test Him, were demanding of Him a sign from heaven. But He, knowing their thoughts, said to them: "Every kingdom divided against itself is laid waste, and a house divided against itself falls. And if Satan is divided against himself how will his kingdom stand? Seeing that you say that it is by Beelzebul that I cast out devils. If it is by Beelzebul that I cast out devils, by whom do your people cast them out? Therefore they themselves will be your judges. But if it is by the finger of God that I cast out devils, then the kingdom of God has come upon you. When the strong man, fully armed, guards his courtyard, his things are undisturbed. But when someone stronger than himself comes and overpowers him, he carries off all his armor, on which he was relying, and divides the spoils. He who is not with Me is against Me, and he who does not gather with Me scatters. When an unclean spirit has gone out of a man it wanders through parched regions seeking a resting-place; and, failing to find one, it says: "I will return to my former habitation." So it returns and finds the house swept and decorated. Then it goes off and takes with it seven other spirits worse than itself, and they enter in and dwell there. And the man's last state is worse than the first."

While He was saying this a woman from the crowd raised her voice and said: "Happy the womb that bore You and the breasts that fed You." "Rather," He replied, "happy are they who hear the word of God and keep it."

→ *Creed, p.* 18.

OFFERTORY   Ps. 18, 9-12   [*Sweet Are God's Laws*]

The precepts of the Lord are right, *
rejoicing the heart, *
And His ordinances are sweeter than syrup *
or honey from the comb; *
therefore Your servant is careful of them.

→ *Offertory Prayers, p.* 21.

SECRET   [Cleanse Us]

*May this offering, we beseech You, O Lord,
cleanse us of our sins, and make holy the bodies
and minds of Your servants for the celebration
of the sacrificial rite. Through our Lord, etc.*
People: **Amen.**

➤ *Preface, p. 132.*

COMMUNION   Ps. 83, 4. 5   [Family of God]

The sparrow finds a home, *
   and the swallow a nest *
   in which she puts her young: *
Your altars, O Lord of hosts, *
   my King and my God! *
Happy they who dwell in Your house! *
   continually they praise You.

POSTCOMMUNION   [From Guilt and Danger]

*Be merciful, O Lord, we beseech You, and free
from guilt and danger those whom You grant
to share in this great sacrament. Through our
Lord, etc.* People: **Amen.**

➤ *Dismissal, p. 42.*

Jesus then took the loaves, gave thanks, and passed them around to those reclining there.

FOURTH SUNDAY IN LENT

THOUGHT FOR TODAY: A true Christian life requires self-denial and penance. Nevertheless, there is enough joy in it, because self-control leads to the freedom of the children of God. The wonderful Bread which we receive in Holy Communion is another reason for joy because it unites us with God Almighty, the source of all happiness.

BIBLE AND LITURGY: Lenten observance, carried out in Faith, will make us share ever more in the freedom wherewith Christ has made us free. Christ's Word and Sacraments, especially, the Sacrament of His Precious Body and Blood, make it possible to keep ourselves free from the bondage of evil. READ: John 8, 31-38; Rom. 6, 1-23; 1 Cor. 7, 17-24 (esp. 23); Ps. 125.

INTROIT   Isa. 66, 10. 11; Ps. 121, 1   [*Rejoice*]

Rejoice, O Jerusalem, *
    and come together all you who love her: *
Rejoice with joy, *
    you who have been in sorrow: *
That you may exult, *
    **and be filled from the breasts of your consola-
        tion.** *

- 142 -

(Ps.) **I rejoiced because they said to me:** *
   "We will go up to the house of the Lord." *
Glory be to the Father, etc.

Rejoice, O Jerusalem, *
   and come together all you who love her: *
Rejoice with joy, *
   you who have been in sorrow: *
That you may exult, *
   **and be filled from the breasts of your con-
   solation.**

→ *Kyrie, p. 13. Omit Gloria.*

PRAYER   [*Comfort of Grace*]

*Grant, we beseech You, almighty God, that we
who justly suffer for our sins may find relief
in the help of Your grace. Through our Lord,
etc.* People: **Amen.** ↓

EPISTLE   Gal. 4, 22-31   [*Slave and Free*]

Brethren: It is written that Abraham had two
sons, one from the slave-girl, the other from
his free-born wife. The son of the slave-girl had
been born according to the flesh, but the son
of the free woman was the fruit of the promise.
All this is an allegory. The two women stand
for the two covenants, one of which was from
Mt. Sinai (a mountain in Arabia), bringing forth
children into slavery; this is Agar, and corre-
sponds to the Jerusalem of our time, which
also is in slavery along with her children. But
the Jerusalem on high is free-born, and it is
she who is our mother! That is why the Scripture says, "Raise a glad cry, you barren one

who did not bear; break forth in jubilant song, you who were not in labor. For more numerous are the children of the deserted wife than the children of her who has a husband." Now you, my brothers, are children of the promise, in the manner of Isaac. But just as in those days the son born according to the flesh persecuted the one born according to the spirit, it is the very same now. But what does Scripture say? "Cast out the slave-girl with her son; for the son of the slave-girl shall not be heir with the son" of the free-born woman. Therefore, my brothers, we are children not of a slave-girl but of a mother who is free; by the freedom wherewith Christ has made us free. ↓

GRADUAL   Ps. 121, 1. 7   [*The House of God*]

I rejoiced because they said to me: *
    "We will go up to the house of the Lord." *
May peace be within your walls, *
    prosperity in your buildings. ↓

TRACT   Ps. 124, 1-2   [*The Lord Is Close to Us*]

They who trust in the Lord are like Mount Sion, *
    which is immovable; which forever stands. *
Mountains are round about Jerusalem; *
    so the Lord is round about His people, *
    both now and forever.

→ *Prayer before the Gospel, p.* 16.

GOSPEL   John 6, 1-15   [*Christ Feeds His People*]

At that time Jesus crossed the Sea of Galilee to the shore of Tiberias, but a vast crowd kept following Him because they saw the signs

He was performing on the sick. So Jesus went up the mountain and sat down there with His disciples. The Jewish feast of Passover was near. When Jesus looked up and caught sight of a vast crowd coming toward Him, He said to Philip, "Where shall we ever buy bread for them to eat?" (Of course, He was aware of what He was going to do, but He asked this to test him.) Philip replied, "With two hundred days' wages we could not buy loaves enough to let each of them have a morsel." One of His disciples, Andrew, Simon Peter's brother, remarked to Him, "There is a lad here who has five barley loaves and a couple of dried fish, but what good is that for so many?" Jesus said, "Get these people to take their places on the ground." Now the men numbered about five thousand, but there was plenty of grass there for them to find a place. Jesus then took the loaves of bread, gave thanks, and passed them around to those reclining there; and He did the same with the dried fish—just as much as they wanted. When they had enough, He told His disciples, "Collect the fragments that are left over so that nothing will perish." And so they collected twelve baskets full of fragments left over by those who had fed upon the five barley loaves. Now when the people saw the sign He had performed, they began to say, "This is undoubtedly the Prophet Who is to come into the world." At that Jesus realized that they would come and carry Him off to make Him king, so He fled back to the mountain alone.

➤ *Creed, p. 18.*

OFFERTORY Ps. 134, 3. 6 [Praise the Lord]

Praise the Lord, for He is good; *
  sing praise to His Name, for He is sweet; *
All that He wills He does *
  in heaven and on earth.

➤ Offertory Prayers, p. 21.

SECRET [Devotion and Salvation]

Look with favor, we beseech You, O Lord, upon the offerings here before You, that they may be beneficial for our devotion and salvation. Through our Lord, etc. People: **Amen.**

➤ Preface, p. 132.

COMMUNION Ps. 121, 3. 4 [The Heavenly Jerusalem]

Jerusalem, built as a city *
  with compact unity: *
To it the tribes go up, *
  the tribes of the Lord, *
  to give thanks to Your Name, O Lord.

POSTCOMMUNION [The Spiritual Feeding]

Grant, we beseech You, merciful God, that we may treat with sincere reverence, and consume with heartfelt faith Your sacrament, which ever fills us to overflowing. Through our Lord, etc. People: **Amen.**

➤ Dismissal, p. 42.

"Before Abraham even existed, I am."

FIRST PASSION SUNDAY

THOUGHT FOR TODAY: The misled Jewish people tried to stone Christ after He had proclaimed His Divinity. But this was not yet the hour in which Jesus was going to die for us. He proved Himself to be the Master of time and of His life when He "hid Himself and slipped out of the Temple precincts."

BIBLE AND LITURGY: The Church wants to focus our attention and appreciation upon the tremendous fact that Christ became the eternal High Priest of mankind, and at the same time the Victim Who took away the sin of the world. READ: Ex. 24, 4-8; 29, 1-9; Lev. 16, 1-19; Heb. 9, 11-15 (*Ep.*): Heb. 10, 1-18; 1 Cor. 11, 23-26; John 18, 4-11.

INTROIT Ps. 42, 1. 2. 3 [*God, My Strength*]

Do me justice, O God, and fight my fight *
   against a faithless people; *
   from the deceitful and impious man rescue
      me; *
For You are my God *
   and my strength. *

(Ps.) Send forth Your light and Your fidelity; *
they shall lead me on *

And bring me to Your holy mountain, *
to Your dwelling-place. *

Do me justice, O God, and fight my fight *
against a faithless people; *
from the deceitful and impious man rescue
me; *

For You are my God *
and my strength.

➤ *Kyrie, p. 13. Omit Gloria.*

PRAYER   [*Your Family, O God*]

Look graciously upon Your household, almighty
God, we beseech You, that by Your grace we
may be governed in body, and by Your protec-
tion safeguarded in mind. Through our Lord,
etc. People: **Amen.** ↓

EPISTLE   Heb. 9, 11-15   [*Christ, the Great Priest*]

Brethren: When Christ came as High Priest
of the good things which have come to be,
He entered once for all into the sanctuary,
passing through the greater and more perfect
tent not made by hands, that is, not belonging
to this creation. He entered not with the blood
of goats and calves but with His own blood,
and achieved eternal redemption. For if the
blood of goats and bulls and the sprinkling of
a heifer's ashes can make holy those who are
defiled so that their flesh is made clean, how
much more will the blood of Christ, Who
through the eternal Spirit offered Himself up

unblemished to God, cleanse our consciences from dead works to worship the living God? This is why He is mediator of a new covenant: that since His death has taken place for deliverance from transgressions committed under the first covenant, those who have been called may receive the eternal inheritance, in Christ Jesus, our Lord. ↓

GRADUAL   Ps. 142, 9. 10; 17, 48. 49

[Come to My Rescue]

Rescue me from my enemies, O Lord; *
   teach me to do Your will. *
O Lord, my deliverer from the angry nations: *
   truly above my adversaries You exalt me *
   **and from the violent man You have rescued
   me.** ↓

TRACT   Ps. 128, 1-4   [My Afflictions]

Much have they oppressed me from my youth, *
   let Israel say: *
Much have they oppressed me from my youth, *
   yet they have not prevailed against me; *
Upon my back the plowers plowed. *
   Long did they make their furrows. *
But the just Lord has severed *
   the cords of the wicked.

➤ *Prayer before the Gospel, p. 16.*

GOSPEL   John 8, 46-59   [Jesus Rejected]

At that time Jesus said to the crowds of the Jews: "Can any one of you convict Me of sin? If I am telling the truth, why do you not believe Me? The man who belongs to God hears the words of God. The reason why you do not hear is that you do not belong to God." The Jews answered, "Aren't we right, after all, in saying that You are a Samaritan, and are mad?" Jesus replied, "I am not mad, but I do honor My Father, while you fail to honor Me. I do not seek glory for Myself; there is One Who does seek it and He passes judgment. I solemnly assure you, if a man keeps My word, he will never see death." "Now we are sure You are mad," the Jews retorted. "Abraham died; so did the prophets. Yet, You claim, 'A man will never experience death if he keeps My word.' Surely, You don't pretend to be greater than our father Abraham who is dead?—Or the prophets who are dead? Just Who do You pretend to be?" Jesus answered, "If I glorify Myself, My glory amounts to nothing. The One Who glorifies Me is the Father Whom you claim as your God, even though you do not know Him. But I do know Him; and if I say I do not know Him, I shall be just like you—a liar! Yes, I do know Him and I keep His word. Your father Abraham rejoiced at the prospect of seeing My day. When he saw it, he was glad." This caused the Jews to object, "You're not even fifty years old. How can Abraham have seen You?" Jesus answered them, "I solemnly assure you, before Abraham even existed, I am." Then they picked up rocks to throw at Jesus, but He hid Himself and slipped out of the Temple precincts.

→ *Creed, p.* 18.

OFFERTORY   Ps. 110, 1; 118, 17. 107   [*Give Me Life*]

I praise You, O Lord, *
  with all my heart; *
Be good to Your servant, that I may live *
  and keep Your words. *
O Lord, give me life *
  according to Your word.

➤ *Offertory Prayers, p. 21.*

SECRET   [*Loosen Our Bonds*]

*May these offerings, we beseech You, O Lord,
loose the bonds of our wickedness, and obtain
for us the gifts of Your mercy. Through our
Lord, etc.* People: **Amen.** ↓

PREFACE OF THE HOLY CROSS

[*Our Prayer of Thanksgiving*]

Right and worthy it is, fitting and for our good
that in every time and place our thanks should
rise to You, O Lord, holy Father, almighty and
eternal God. By Your decree the race of man
was rescued by the wood of the Cross, so that,
from the ancient source of death, life might
spring anew; while he who triumphed through
a tree be vanquished: through Christ our Lord.
Through Him the Angels praise Your Majesty,
while Dominations adore and all the Powers
stand in awe. In one great voice, the heavens,
all the hosts of heaven, and the Blessed Seraphim, cry out their praise. In our turn we pray
that our voices now may be joined with theirs
as, in humble witness, we sing:

➤ *Sanctus, p. 27.*

COMMUNION   1 Cor. 11, 24. 25   [*This Is Life*]

**This is My Body which shall be given up for
     you:** *
   **this is the cup of the new covenant in My
      Blood,** *
   says the Lord; *
Do this as often as you receive it, *
   in remembrance of Me.

POSTCOMMUNION   [*Refreshed*]

*Stand by us, O Lord our God, and protect by
Your everlasting help those to whom You have
given new strength through Your sacrament.
Through our Lord, etc.* People: **Amen.**

➤ *Dismissal, p. 42.*

"Blessed be He Who comes in the Name of the Lord!"

SECOND PASSION SUNDAY
or PALM SUNDAY

THOUGHT FOR TODAY: The triumphal entry of Jesus into Jerusalem and the sorrowful recollection of His Passion are both expressed in today's Liturgy. It is safer for us to follow Christ along the hard way of fulfilled duties than along the easy road of the world.

BIBLE AND LITURGY: Just as the grain of wheat must die in order to bring forth fruit (John 12, 24-25), so Jesus, in order to be inaugurated as King of His universal Kingdom, had to undergo a bitter Passion and cruel Death. READ (the Bible portions of today's Liturgy): Matt. 21, 1-9; Ps. 147; Phil. 2, 5-11 (*Ep.*); Ps. 21 (*Tract*); Matt. 26, 36-75; 27, 1-60 (*Passion*).

INTROIT Ps. 21, 20. 22. 2 [*Rescue Me*]

O Lord, be not far from me; *
　O my help, hasten to aid me. *
Save me from the lion's mouth; *
　from the horns of the wild bulls, my wretched
　　life. *
(Ps.) My God, my God, look upon me, why have
　　you forsaken me? *
Far from my salvation are the words of my sins. *

O Lord, be not far from me; *
  O my help, hasten to aid me. *
Save me from the lion's mouth; *
  from the horns of the wild bulls, my wretched
    life.

➤ *Kyrie, p. 13. Omit Gloria.*

PRAYER [Our Humble Victim]

Almighty, eternal God, Who, to provide man-kind an example of humility for it to imitate, willed that the Savior should assume our flesh and suffer death upon the Cross, mercifully grant that we may be found worthy of the lesson of His endurance and the fellowship of His resurrection. Through the same, etc. People: **Amen.** ↓

EPISTLE   Phil. 2, 5-11 [He Emptied Himself]

Brethren: Your attitude must be Christ's attitude: He was of divine condition, yet He did not greedily cling to equality of status with God, but emptied Himself, taking the condition of a slave through being born in the likeness of men. He was known as a man, human in form, and in that state He humbled Himself, obediently accepting even death—yes, death on a cross! Because of this, God in turn exalted Him above all else, and bestowed on Him that Name which is above every other name, whose dignity requires that at the mention of Jesus' Name every knee must bend throughout the heavens and on earth and under the earth and every tongue proclaim to the glory of God the Father: "Jesus Christ is Lord!" ↓

GRADUAL Ps. 72, 24. 1-3

[*God's Goodness to His Own*]

You have hold of my right hand; *
   with Your counsel You guide me; *
   and in the end You will receive me in glory. *

How good God is to Israel; *
   to those who are clean of heart! *

But, as for me, I almost lost my balance; *
   my feet all but slipped, *

Because I was envious of sinners *
   when I saw them prosper though they were
      wicked. ↓

TRACT Ps. 21, 2-9. 18. 19. 22. 24. 32

[*The Powers of Evil*]

My God, my God, look upon me, why have You
   forsaken me? *

Far from my salvation are the words of my
   sins. *

O my God, I cry out by day, and You answer
   not; *
   by night, and there is no relief. *

But You are enthroned in the holy place, *
   O glory of Israel! *

In You our fathers trusted; *
   they trusted, and You delivered them. *

To You they cried, and they escaped; *
   in You they trusted, and they were not put
      to shame. *

But I am a worm, not a man; *
   the scorn of men, despised by the people. *

All who see me, scoff at me; *
   they mock me with parted lips, they wag their
      heads. *

"He relied on the Lord; let Him deliver him, *
　　let Him rescue him, if He loves him." *

But they look on and gloat over me; *
　　they divide my garments among them, *
　　and for my vesture they cast lots. *

Save me from the lion's mouth; *
　　from the horns of the wild bulls, my wretched
　　　life. *

You who fear the Lord, praise Him; *
　　all you descendants of Jacob, give glory to
　　　Him. *

There shall be declared to the Lord a generation
　　to come: *
　　and the heavens shall show forth His justice. *

To a people that shall be born, *
　　which the Lord has made.

➤ *Prayer before the Gospel, p. 16.*

PASSION OF OUR LORD JESUS CHRIST

Matt. 26, 36-75; 27, 1-60　　　[*The Story of Our Redemption*]

At that time Jesus went with His disciples to a place called Gethsemani. "Sit down here," He said to His disciples, "while I go over there and pray." But He took along Peter and Zebedee's two sons, and He began to experience sorrow and distress. Then He said to them, "My heart is near breaking with sorrow. Remain here, and stay awake with Me." He advanced a little and fell prostrate in prayer: "O my Father, if it is possible, let this cup pass Me by. Still, let it be as You will, not as I will." When He returned to His disciples, He found them asleep. He said to Peter, "So you could not stay awake with Me for even an hour? Stay awake, and pray that you may not be subject to the trial. The spirit may be eager, but human nature is weak." Going back yet a second time, He began to pray, "O My Father, if this cannot pass Me by without My drinking it, may Your will be done!" Once again, He found them asleep on His return, for they could not keep their eyes open. Again He left them and withdrew, and began to pray a third time, saying the same words once more. Finally He returned to His disciples and said to them, "Still asleep? Still enjoying your rest? See, the hour is upon us, in which the Son of Man is handed over into the power of evil men. Get up! Let us be on our way. Look, My betrayer is here."

While He was still speaking, suddenly Judas, one of the Twelve, arrived, accompanied by a great crowd with swords and clubs, sent by the chief priests and elders of the people. Now His betrayer had arranged to give them a signal, saying, "The Man I shall kiss is the One; arrest Him." And immediately he went over to Jesus, and said, "Good evening, Rabbi," and kissed Him. But Jesus said to him, "Do what you are here for, My friend!" At that moment, they stepped forward, laid hands on Jesus and arrested Him. But suddenly, one of those accompanying Jesus put his hand to his sword, drew it, and slashed at the high priest's slave, cutting off his ear. Then Jesus said to him, "Put your sword back where it belongs! Those who use the sword are all destroyed by the sword. Or do you think that I cannot appeal to My Father to put more than twelve legions of angels at My immediate service? But then how could the Scriptures be fulfilled which state that it must happen this way?" In that same hour, Jesus said to the crowds, "You have come out to seize Me, armed with swords and clubs, as if against a bandit. Daily I sat teaching in the Temple precincts, yet you never arrested Me. Still, this has all happened in order that the writings of the prophets might be fulfilled." Then all the disciples deserted Him, and fled.

Those who had arrested Jesus led Him off to Caiaphas the high priest, where the scribes and elders were convened. Peter was following Him at a distance as far as the high priest's palace. Going inside, he sat down with the Temple police to see the outcome. The chief priests with the whole Sanhedrin were busy trying to obtain false testimony against Jesus, so that they might put Him to death. However, they discovered none, although many false witnesses took the stand, until two men finally came forward. They stated, "This Man has declared, 'I can destroy God's sanctuary and rebuild it in three days.'" The high priest rose to his feet, and addressed Him, "Have You no answer to what these men testify against You?" But Jesus remained silent. So the high priest said to Him, "I order You to tell us under oath before the living God whether You are the Messiah, the Son of God." Jesus answered, "As you say. Still I tell you that very soon you will see the Son of Man seated at the right hand of the Power and coming on the clouds of heaven." At this the high priest tore His robes; "He has blasphemed!" he declared, "What further need do we have of witnesses? Remember, you have now heard the blasphemy. What is your opinion?" They replied, "He deserves death!" Then they began to spit in His face and to hit Him, and others slapped Him, saying, "Play the prophet for us, O Messiah! Who is it that struck you?"

Now Peter was sitting in the courtyard, when one of the servant girls came over to him and said, "You too were with Jesus the Galilean." But he denied it in front of everybody, "I don't know what you are talking about!" When he went out to the gate, another girl saw him, and said to those nearby, "This man was with Jesus the Nazorean." Again he denied it with an oath, "I don't know the fellow!" A little later, the bystanders came over to Peter and said, "Obviously you are also one of them! Why, even your accent gives you away!" Then he began to curse and swear, "I don't even know the fellow!" Just then a cock crowed and Peter remembered the prediction Jesus had made, "Before the cock crows, you will three times disown Me." He went outside and wept bitterly. At daybreak all the chief priests and the elders of the people hatched a plot against Jesus to put Him to death. So they bound Him and led Him away, and handed Him over to the governor Pilate.

Then Judas, who had handed Him over, saw that He had been condemned and began to regret his action. He took the thirty pieces of silver back to the chief priests and elders, saying, "I did wrong to hand over an innocent man!" But they retorted, "What's that to us? That's your responsibility!" So he flung the money into the sanctuary, and left. He went off and hanged himself. But the chief priests picked up the silver with the remark, "It is not right to deposit this in the Temple treasury since it is blood money." So after consultation they used it to buy the Potter's Field as a cemetery for foreigners. That is why that field, even today is called Blood Field. Then what was said through Jeremia the prophet was fulfilled, "They took the thirty pieces of silver, the value of a man with a price on his head, a price set by the Israelites, and they paid it out for the Potter's Field, just as the Lord had commanded me."

Now Jesus was arraigned before the governor, who questioned Him, "Are You the King of the Jews?" "As you say," Jesus answered. Yet when He was accused by the chief priests and elders, He made no reply. Then Pilate said to Him, "Surely You hear how many charges they are bringing against You?" Still, He did not answer him on a single count, much to the governor's surprise. Now on the occasion of a festival, the governor was accustomed to release one prisoner whom the crowd would designate. At that time, they had a notorious prisoner whose name was Barabbas. So, since they were already assembled, Pilate said to them, "Which one do you wish me to release for you, Barabbas or Jesus, the so-called Messiah?" He knew, of course, that it was out of jealousy that they had handed Him over. While he was still presiding on the bench, his wife sent him a message, "Do not interfere with that holy man. I had a dream about Him today which has greatly upset me." Meanwhile, the chief priests and elders convinced the crowds that they should ask for Barabbas, and have Jesus put to death. So when the governor asked them, "Which one do you wish me to release for you?" they said, "Barabbas." Pilate said to them, "Then what am I to do with Jesus, the so-called Messiah?" "Have Him crucified!" they all cried. But he said, "Why, what crime has He committed?" They only shouted the louder, "Have Him crucified!" Pilate finally realized that he was making no impression but that instead a riot was starting. Calling for water, he washed his hands in front of the crowd and declared, "I am innocent of this holy man's blood. It is your responsibility." Then the whole people said in reply, "Let His blood be on us and on our children!" At that, he released Barabbas to them. But after scourging Jesus, he handed Him over to be crucified.

Then the governor's soldiers took Jesus in charge to the Pretorium and collected the whole cohort around Him. They stripped off His clothes and wrapped a scarlet military cloak about Him. Weaving a crown out of thorns, they fixed it on His head and stuck a reed in His right hand. They began to mock Him by genuflecting before Him and saying, "All hail, King of the Jews!" and they spat at Him. They snatched the reed and kept striking Him on the head. Then, when they had finished mocking Him, they stripped Him of the cloak, dressed Him in His own clothes, and led Him off to crucifixion.

Now as they were marching out, they met a Cyrenian called Simon. This man they pressed into service to carry the cross. Upon arriving at a place called Golgotha (a name which means Skull-Place), they gave Him a drink of wine flavored with gall. But on tasting it, He refused to drink it. When they had crucified Him, they divided up His garments by rolling dice; then they sat down there and kept watch over Him. Above His head they had put a written notice of His offense, "This is Jesus, the King of the Jews." Next, two bandits were crucified with Him, one at the right and one at the left. People going by kept insulting Him, wagging their heads and saying, "So You were going to destroy the sanctuary and rebuild it in three days! Now save Yourself! Come down off that cross, if You are God's Son!" The chief priests, the scribes and the elders also joined in: "Other men He saved," they jeered, "Himself He cannot save! And He is 'King of Israel'! Let Him come down off that cross, and we'll put our faith in Him. He relied on God; let Him deliver Him now, if He wants Him. After all, He claimed, 'I am God's Son.'" In the same way, the bandits, who had been crucified with Him, also kept taunting Him.

From noon on, darkness fell upon the whole land, lasting until mid-afternoon. Then toward mid-afternoon, Jesus cried in a loud voice, "Eli, Eli, lema sabachthani?" that is, "My God, My God, why have You forsaken Me?" So some of the bystanders who heard it remarked, "The fellow is invoking Elia!" And immediately, one of their number ran off and got a sponge. He soaked it in sour wine; and, sticking it on a reed, he tried to make Him drink. But the rest said, "Leave Him alone. Let's see whether Elia comes to save Him." Again Jesus cried out in a loud voice, and gave up His spirit. (*Here all kneel and pause a few moments*) And suddenly the curtain in the sanctuary was torn in two from top to bottom. The earth quaked, boulders split, tombs opened; and many bodies of saints who had fallen asleep were raised. After His resurrection, they came forth from their tombs, and entered the holy city, and appeared to many people. Now the centurion and his men, who were keeping watch over Jesus, were terror-stricken at the sight of the earthquake and these happenings, and they declared, "It is clear this was God's Son!" There were present many women looking on from a distance. They had followed Jesus from Galilee to attend to His needs. Among them were Mary Magdalene, and Mary, the mother of James and Joseph, and the mother of Zebedee's sons.

When it grew dark, a wealthy man from Arimathea arrived, whose name was Joseph. He too was one of Jesus' disciples and had gone to Pilate to request the body of Jesus. Pilate then issued an order for its release. So taking the body, Joseph wrapped it in fresh linen, and laid it in his own new tomb which had been cut out of rock. Then he rolled a huge stone across the entrance of the tomb and went away.

A Priest who celebrates a second or third Mass today is not bound to repeat the reading of the Lord's Passion; in place of it the following Gospel is read in the usual manner:

GOSPEL Matt. 27, 45-52 [*He Gave Up His Spirit*]

After they crucified Jesus, darkness fell upon the whole land from noon until mid-afternoon. Then toward mid-afternoon, Jesus cried out in a loud voice, "Eli, Eli, lema sabachthani?" that is, "My God, My God, why have You forsaken Me?" So some of the bystanders who heard it remarked, "The fellow is invoking Elia!" And immediately, one of their number ran off and got a sponge. He soaked it in sour wine; and, sticking it on a reed, he tried to make Him drink. But the rest said, "Leave Him alone. Let's see whether Elia comes to save Him." Again Jesus cried out in a loud voice, and gave up His spirit. (*Here all kneel and pause a few moments.*) And suddenly the curtain in the sanctuary was torn in two from top to bottom. The earth quaked, boulders split, tombs opened; and many bodies of saints who had fallen asleep were raised.

➤ *Creed, p. 18.*

OFFERTORY Ps. 68, 21-22 [*I Found None to Help*]

Insult has broken my heart, and I am weak; *
I looked for sympathy, but there was none; *
for comforters, and I found none; *
Rather they put gall in my food, *
and in my thirst they gave me vinegar to drink.

➤ *Offertory Prayers, p. 21.*

SECRET [*The Grace of Devotion*]

Grant, we beseech You, almighty God, that the gift offered in the sight of Your Majesty may obtain for us the grace of reverent devotion and assure us eternal happiness. Through our Lord, etc. People: **Amen.** ⍦

PREFACE OF THE HOLY CROSS
[*Our Prayer of Thanksgiving*]

Right and worthy it is, fitting and for our good that in every time and place our thanks should rise to You, O Lord, holy Father, almighty and eternal God. By Your decree the race of man was rescued by the wood of the Cross, so that, from the ancient source of death, life might spring anew; while he who triumphed through a tree be vanquished: through Christ our Lord. Through Him the Angels praise Your Majesty, while Dominations adore and all the Powers stand in awe. In one great voice, the heavens, all the hosts of heaven, and the Blessed Seraphim, cry out their praise. In our turn we pray that our voices now may be joined with theirs as, in humble witness, we sing:

➤ *Sanctus, p. 27.*

COMMUNION   Matt. 26, 42   [*Christ Accepts*]

Father, if this cup cannot pass away, *
   unless I drink it, *
   Your will be done.

POSTCOMMUNION   [*Fulfill Our Desires*]

By the working of this sacred rite, O Lord, may our sins be erased and our just desires fulfilled. Through our Lord, etc. People: **Amen.**

➤ *Dismissal, p. 42.*

———————

THE EASTER CYCLE (II)

EASTER — ASCENSION — PENTECOST —

The Festive Celebrations

In our analysis of Advent, we mentioned that creation and ourselves in it, as unfinished beings, are in a process of evolution. The Creator evolves His plan and the first creature in Whom this master-plan was fully realized is our risen Lord Jesus Christ. Creation, where it became self-conscious man , did not cooperate. Man sinned; hence God re-established all things in Christ Jesus (Eph. 1, 10).

According to the purpose of God's will, we are predestined to grow into the full realization of that Divine plan (Eph. 1, 5), presupposing the cooperation we have given during Lent. In Christ all will be made to live. But each in his own turn, Christ as first fruits, then they who are Christ's, who have believed, at His coming (1 Cor. 15, 22-23).

It is through Faith and Baptism that we share in Christ's glorious Resurrection now already, till we will fully share in it partaking in His Ascension into heaven. Therefore both mysteries: Christ's Resurrection and our partaking in it through Baptism, are celebrated in the Easter Liturgy.

And after we had heard the good news of our salvation and believed in it, we were sealed with the Holy Spirit (Eph. 1, 13). Our full initiation into God's people by Confirmation! The feast of Pentecost celebrates the outpouring of this Pledge of our inheritance (Eph. 1, 14).

Again, both Easter, Ascension and Pentecost are not past but present to us. (Note "this day" in the Propers of these feasts!) See the Christmas Cycle (II).

We should read about God's plan of Salvation in Eph. 1, 3-14 and consider prayerfully how it is celebrated at Easter, the Ascension and Pentecost.

The Sundays after Pentecost are an after-glow, repeating and elaborating themes of this cycle in various ways and modifications.

"He has been raised: He is not here."

EASTER SUNDAY

THOUGHT FOR TODAY: The Resurrection of Christ is a historical fact. When His enemies believed that they had destroyed Him, His real triumph began. To die to sin and to live with Christ is our way to victory and glorious resurrection.

BIBLE AND LITURGY: The Jews celebrated the Feast of "Passover" because the Lord "passed over" the houses of the Israelites, whose doorposts were sprinkled with the blood of the "passover" (paschal) lamb. Our Passover Lamb is Christ. His Blood, shed on Calvary, keeps the devil from harming us and makes us partakers of His glorious Resurrection. READ: Ex. 12, 21-28; 1 Cor. 5, 7-8 (*Ep.*); Rom. 6, 1-11; Cor. 15, 12-58; 1 Thess. 4, 13-18.

INTROIT   Ps. 138, 18. 5. 6. 1. 2   [*Christ Has Risen*]

I arose, and am still with You, alleluia; *
    You rest Your hand upon Me, alleluia; *
    Your knowledge is too wonderful, alleluia, alleluia. *

(Ps.) Lord, You have probed Me and You know Me; *
    You know when I sit and when I stand. *

Glory be to the Father, etc.

I arose, and am still with You, alleluia; *
    You rest Your hand upon Me, alleluia; *
    Your knowledge is too wonderful, alleluia, alleluia.

➤ *Kyrie and Gloria, pp.* 13-14.

PRAYER   [Desire for Life]

O God, Who this day, through Your Only-begotten Son, have conquered death and opened the gate of eternity, help us to fulfill the desires You have Yourself awakened in us. Through the same, etc. People: **Amen.** ↓

EPISTLE   1 Cor. 5, 7-8   [Renewal in Christ]

Brethren: Clean out the old yeast, that you may be fresh dough, as you really are unleavened. For indeed, our passover, Christ, has been sacrificed. Let us celebrate the feast, then, not with the old yeast, the yeast of malice and wickedness, but with the unleavened bread of sincerity and truth. ↓

GRADUAL   Ps. 117, 24. 1   [This Is the Day]

This is the day the Lord has made; *
    let us be glad and rejoice in it. *
Give thanks to the Lord, for He is good, *
    for His mercy endures forever.

Alleluia, alleluia. * 1 Cor. 5, 7 [Christ Our Passover]
Christ, our Passover, *
    has been sacrificed. ↓

SEQUENCE   [The Miracle]

Christians, to the Paschal Victim *
   Offer your thankful praises! *
A lamb the sheep redeemeth: Christ, *
      Who only is sinless, *
   Reconcileth sinners to the Father. *
Death and life have contended in that combat
      stupendous: *
   The Prince of life, Who died, reigns im-
      mortal. *

Speak, Mary, declaring *
   What thou sawest, wayfaring. *
"The tomb of Christ Who is living, *
   The glory of Jesus' resurrection; *
Bright angels attesting, *
   The shroud and napkin resting. *
Yea, Christ my hope is arisen: *
   To Galilee He goes before you." *

Christ indeed from death is risen, our new life
      obtaining. *
   Have mercy, victor King, ever reigning!
      Amen. Alleluia.

➤ *Prayer before the Gospel, p. 16.*

GOSPEL   Mark 16, 1-7   [He Is Risen]

At that time Mary Magdalene, and Mary the
mother of James, and Salome, bought per-
fumed oils, intending to come and anoint Jesus.
Then, very early in the morning, on the first
day of the week, they came to the tomb, after
sunrise. They were saying to one another, "Who
will roll back the stone for us from the entrance

to the tomb?" But when they looked up, they
observed that the stone had been rolled back
(and it was indeed huge). On entering the
tomb, they saw a young man sitting at the
right, dressed in a white robe. This thoroughly
amazed them. But he reassured them, "No need
to be amazed! You are looking for Jesus of
Nazareth, the crucified. He has been raised: He
is not here. See the spot where they laid Him.
Now go, tell His disciples and Peter, 'He is
going to Galilee ahead of you, where you will
see Him, just as He told you.' "

➤ *Creed, p.* 18.

OFFERTORY   Ps. 75, 9. 10   [*Triumph*]

The earth feared and was silent, *
  when God arose for judgment. Alleluia.

➤ *Offertory Prayers, p.* 21.

SECRET   [Easter the Foretaste]

*Accept, O Lord, we beseech You, the prayers
and sacrificial offerings of Your people, so that
what has begun with the Easter rites may, with
Your help, become for us a remedy unto life
everlasting. Through our Lord, etc.* People:
Amen. ↓

PREFACE FOR EASTER
[Our Prayer of Thanksgiving]

**Right and worthy it is, fitting and for our good
that in every time and place our praise should
rise to You, O Lord. But above all** *on this great
day,* ***** **when Christ, our Paschal Lamb, was of-**

* *On Sundays after Easter substitute "at this great time."*

fered, greater still must be our praise. For He is the true Lamb Who has taken away the sins of the world. By dying He destroyed our death and by rising He gave us life remade. And therefore, with the Angels and Archangels, with the Thrones and Dominations, and all the forces of heaven, we chant the endless hymn of Your glory: ➤ *Sanctus, p.* 27.

COMMUNION 1 Cor. 5, 7. 8 [*The Paschal Victim*]

Christ our passover, has been sacrificed, alle-luia: *
 therefore let us keep festival with the un-leavened bread of sincerity and truth, *
 alleluia, alleluia, alleluia.

POSTCOMMUNION [*One Mind in Love*]

Pour upon us, O Lord, the Spirit of Your love, so that we whom You have filled with the Easter Sacrament may, by Your gentle mercy, be made of one mind. Through . . . in the unity of the same, etc. People: **Amen.**

➤ *Dismissal, p.* 42.

Thomas said to Him, "My Lord and my God!"

FIRST SUNDAY AFTER EASTER

THOUGHT FOR TODAY: Despite all convincing proofs, many doubting Thomases are still saying, "I'll never believe." We should repeat the words of the believing Thomas, "My Lord and my God," as often as we lift our eyes up to the Blessed Sacrament.

BIBLE AND LITURGY: It is through Baptism, sealing and perfecting a beginning Faith, that man is initiated into God's Holy People. Through Faith and Baptism man undergoes a mysterious rebirth and shares in God's life. READ: Acts 8, 26-39; John 3, 1-6; Acts 2, 37-41; 8, 4-13; 16, 11-15; 18. 1-11; 19, 1-7.

INTROIT   1 Pet. 2, 2; Ps. 80, 2   [*New Life*]

Crave as newborn babes, alleluia: *
   pure spiritual milk: *
   alleluia, alleluia, alleluia. *

(Ps.) Sing joyfully to God our strength; *
   acclaim the God of Jacob. *

Glory be to the Father, etc.

Crave as newborn babes, alleluia: *
   pure spiritual milk: *
   alleluia, alleluia, alleluia.

➤ *Kyrie and Gloria, pp. 13-14.*

PRAYER   [Easter in Daily Life]

Grant, we beseech You, almighty God, that we, who have well performed the Easter rites, by Your bounty, may cling to them in our conduct and life. Through our Lord, etc. People: **Amen.**
↓

EPISTLE   1 John 5, 4-10   [Christ the Victor]

Beloved: Whatever is begotten by God conquers the world; and the conquest that has conquered the world is this faith of ours. Who is the conqueror of the world?—none other than he who believes that Jesus is the Son of God. Jesus Christ is the One Who came through water and blood, not in water only, but in water and in blood. And it is the Spirit that testifies to this because the Spirit is truth. Thus there are three who testify to this: the Spirit and water and blood, and these three are of one accord. If we accept human testimony, the testimony of God is far better; for God's testimony consists of what He Himself has testified about His Son. Whoever believes in the Son of God possesses that testimony in his own heart. ↓

Alleluia, alleluia. *   Matt. 28, 7: John 20, 26   [Peace]
"On the day of My Resurrection," says the
 Lord, *
 "I will go before you into Galilee." *
Alleluia. After eight days, the doors being
 closed, *
 Jesus stood in the midst of His disciples, and
 said, *
 "Peace be to you!" Alleluia.

➤ *Prayer before the Gospel, p. 16.*

GOSPEL   John 20, 19-31

[Forgive Sins: First Fruit of Redemption]

At that time, on the evening of that first day of the week, even though, for fear of the Jews, the disciples had locked the doors of the place where they were, Jesus came and stood in front of them. "Peace be with you," He said. And when He had said this, He showed them His hands and side. At the sight of the Lord the disciples rejoiced. "Peace be with you," He said to them again. "As the Father has sent Me, so do I send you." After these words He breathed on them, saying, "Receive the Holy Spirit. If you forgive men's sins, their sins are forgiven; if you hold them, they are held fast." It happened that one of the Twelve, Thomas (this name means "Twin"), was absent when Jesus came. So the other disciples kept telling him: "We have seen the Lord!" But he answered them, "I'll never believe without first examining the marks of the nails on His hands, and putting my finger right into the mark of the nails and my hand into His side." Now, a week later, His disciples were once more in the room; this time Thomas was with them. Even though the doors were locked, Jesus came and stood in front of them. "Peace be with you," He said. Then He told Thomas, "Take your finger and examine My hands; take your hand and put it into My side; and don't persist in your disbelief. Become a believer!" Thomas answered with the words, "My Lord and my God!" Jesus told him, "You have believed because you have seen Me. Happy those who have not seen but have believed." Of course, Jesus also performed many other signs in the presence of His disciples, signs not written down in this book. But these have been written so that you may have faith that Jesus is the Messiah, the Son of God, and that, through this faith, you may have life in His name.

➤ *Creed, p. 18.*

OFFERTORY   Matt. 28, 2. 5. 6   [*Risen As He Said*]

An angel of the Lord came down from heaven, *
and said to the women, *
"He Whom you seek has risen, *
even as He said," alleluia.

➤ *Offertory Prayers, p. 21.*

SECRET   [*Church Exultant*]

Accept, we pray You, O Lord, the gifts of Your jubilant Church, and, as You have given her reason for such great joy, grant her the fruit of unending gladness. Through our Lord, etc. People: **Amen.**

➤ *Preface, p. 170.*

COMMUNION   John 20, 27   [*Believe*]

Put in your hand, *
and know the place of the nails, alleluia; *
And be not unbelieving, *
but believing, alleluia, alleluia.

POSTCOMMUNION   [*Eternal Remedy*]

We beseech You, O Lord our God, that the sacrament You have given as the bulwark of our atonement may be made a saving remedy for us in this life and in the life to come. Through our Lord, etc. People: **Amen.**

➤ *Dismissal, p. 42.*

"There will be one flock, one Shepherd."

SECOND SUNDAY AFTER EASTER

THOUGHT FOR TODAY: Our good example and prayers will help to bring back to Christ the sheep going astray, that there may be "one flock, one Shepherd."

BIBLE AND LITURGY: Christ used examples, taken from the rural life of His audience, to explain heavenly truth. The writers of both the Old and the New Testaments did the same. READ: John 10, 1-19; Jer. 31, 1-13; Ezech. 34; John 21, 15-17.

INTROIT   Ps. 32, 5. 6. 1   [*God's Kindness Everywhere*]

Of the kindness of the Lord the earth is full, alleluia; *

   by the word of the Lord the heavens were made, alleluia, alleluia. *

(Ps.) Exult, you just, in the Lord; *
praise from the upright is fitting. *

Glory be to the Father, etc.

Of the kindness of the Lord the earth is full, alleluia; *

   by the word of the Lord the heavens were made, alleluia, alleluia.

➤ *Kyrie and Gloria, pp. 13-14.*

PRAYER   [*Everlasting Joy*]

O God, Who by the self-abasement of Your Son raised a fallen world, grant lasting gladness to Your faithful and assure unfailing happiness to those whom You have saved from falling into eternal death. Through the same, etc. People: **Amen.** ↓

EPISTLE   1 Pet. 2, 21-25   [*Reclaimed Sheep*]

Beloved: Christ suffered for you, leaving you an example, so that you may follow in His steps. He committed no sin, and no falsehood was found in His speech. When He was insulted, He returned no insults; when He suffered, He did not threaten, but surrendered Himself to the One Who judges justly. He bore our sins Himself, in His own body, onto the tree, that we might die to the sins and live to justice. By His stripes you were healed. For you were astray like sheep, but now you have been brought back to the Shepherd and Guardian of your souls. ↓

Luke 24, 35; John 10, 14
[*It Is the Lord*]

Alleluia, alleluia. *
The disciples recognized the Lord Jesus *
  in the breaking of the bread. *
Alleluia. I am the Good Shepherd, *
  and I know My sheep, *
  and Mine know Me. Alleluia.

➤ *Prayer before the Gospel, p.* 16.

GOSPEL   John 10, 11-16   [*Good Shepherd*]

At that time Jesus said to the Pharisees: "I am the Good Shepherd: the good shepherd lays down his life for the sheep. The hired hand, who is not the shepherd and does not own the sheep, catches sight of the wolf coming and runs away, leaving the sheep to be snatched and scattered by the wolf. And this is because he works for pay and has no concern for the sheep. I am the Good Shepherd: I know My sheep and Mine know Me, just as the Father knows Me and I know the Father. And for these sheep I lay down My life. I have other sheep, too, that do not belong to this fold. These also must I lead, and they will listen to My voice. Then there will be one flock, one Shepherd."

➤ *Creed, p. 18.*

OFFERTORY   Ps. 62, 2, 5   [Longing for God]

O God, my God, to You do I watch at break of day, *
   and in Your Name I will lift up my hands, alleluia.

➤ *Offertory Prayers, p. 21.*

SECRET   [Saving Blessing]

May the sacred offering, O Lord, ever be a blessing to us, so that what is performed as a sacramental rite may yield its full effect. Through our Lord, etc. People: **Amen.**

➤ *Preface, p. 170.*

COMMUNION   John 10, 14   [I Know Mine]

I am the Good Shepherd, alleluia: *
   and I know My sheep, *
   and Mine know Me: alleluia, alleluia.

POSTCOMMUNION   [Glory in God's Gift]

Grant us, we beseech You, almighty God, that, having received the grace of life, we may ever glory in Your gift. Through our Lord, etc. People: **Amen.**

➤ *Dismissal, p. 42.*

"There is just a little while before you lose sight of Me."

THIRD SUNDAY AFTER EASTER

THOUGHT FOR TODAY: All those who resolve to live up to their Christian principles will meet with opposition and persecution. But our life on earth is only "a little while," and our "grief will be changed to joy."

BIBLE AND LITURGY: We must regard suffering, pain, frustration, opposition and disillusionment in the same perspective as Christian abstinence and penance. God permits the former and Christians freely embrace the latter for the same end—an ever more perfect detachment from evil and a greater freedom to unite themselves to God in a bond of love. READ: Matt. 5, 10; Luke 6, 20-26; Rom. 8, 35-39; 2 Cor. 4, 7-18; 2 Thess. 1, 3-10; 2 Tim. 3, 10-17.

INTROIT   Ps. 65, 1. 2. 3   [Sing Joyfully]

Shout joyfully to God, all you on earth, alleluia; *
   sing praise to the glory of His Name, alleluia; *
   proclaim His glorious praise, alleluia, alleluia,
   alleluia. *

(Ps.) Say to God, "How tremendous are Your
      deeds, O Lord! *
   For Your great strength Your enemies fawn
      upon You."*

Glory be to the Father, etc.

Shout joyfully to God, all you on earth, alleluia; *
sing praise to the glory of His Name, alleluia; *
proclaim His glorious praise, alleluia, alleluia,
alleluia.

➜ *Kyrie and Gloria, pp.* 13-14.

PRAYER   *[True Christians]*

*O God, Who give the light of Your truth to
those who go astray, that it may help them to
return to the way of righteousness, grant unto
all who are numbered as Christians, that they
may reject whatever is opposed to their faith,
and strive for whatever befits it. Through our
Lord, etc.* People: **Amen.** ↓

EPISTLE   1 Pet. 2, 11-19   *[Freedom without License]*

Beloved: I urge you as strangers and way-
farers to avoid fleshly desires which war
against the soul. Keep your behavior good
among the Gentiles, so that from accusing you
as wrongdoers, they may, when faced with your
good works, glorify God on the day of retribution. Submit to every human institution for the
Lord's sake; whether it be the king in his
supremacy, or rulers sent by him for the chas-
tisement of wrongdoers and the praise of those
who excel. It is the will of God for you to muzzle
the ignorance of impious people in this way,
by excelling. Submit as free men, who do not
make this freedom a veil for wickedness, but
who live as God's slaves. Honor all men; love
the brotherhood; fear God; honor the king. You
who are servants, be subject to your masters in

all reverence—not only to the good and considerate, but even to the perverse; for this is a gift from God: in Christ Jesus, our Lord. ↯

Ps. 110, 9; Luke 24, 46

Alleluia, alleluia. * [*Salvation through Suffering*]
The Lord has sent deliverance *
   to His people. *
Alleluia. It behooved Christ to suffer *
   and to rise again from the dead, *
   and so to enter into His glory. Alleluia.

➤ *Prayer before the Gospel, p.* 16.

GOSPEL   John 16, 16-22   [*A Little While*]

At that time Jesus said to His disciples: "There is just a little while before you lose sight of Me, and again a little while before you see Me." At this some of His disciples remarked to one another, "What does He mean by this: 'There is just a little while before you lose sight of Me, and again a little while before you see Me' and 'Because I am going to the Father'?" So they kept saying, "What does He mean by this 'little while'? We don't understand what He is talking about." Since Jesus knew that they wanted to question Him, He said, "You are asking yourselves about My saying, 'There is just a little while before you lose sight of Me, and again a little while before you see Me.' Truly I assure you, you will weep and go into mourning while the world will rejoice; you will grieve but your grief will be changed to joy. When a woman is in labor, she is in pain since her hour has come. But once the child is born, her joy makes her forget her trial because a man has been born into the world! So you too are in pain now; but I shall see you again, and your hearts will rejoice with a joy that no one can take from you."

➤ *Creed, p.* 18.

OFFERTORY   Ps. 145, 2   [Lifelong Praise]

Praise the Lord, O my soul; *
  I will praise the Lord all my life; *
  I will sing praise to my God while I live. Alleluia.

➤ *Offertory Prayers, p.* 21.

SECRET   [Longing for Heaven]

O Lord, may grace be given us, through these sacramental actions, so that, curbing our earthly desires, we may learn to love heavenly things. Through our Lord, etc. People: **Amen.**

➤ *Preface, p.* 170.

COMMUNION   John 16, 16   [I Go to the Father]

A little while, and you shall not see Me, alleluia: *
  and again a little while, and you shall see Me: *
  because I go to the Father, alleluia, alleluia.

POSTCOMMUNION   [Strength of Body and Soul]

May the sacrament we have received, renew us with spiritual food, we beseech You, O Lord, and may it sustain us with bodily help. Through our Lord, etc. People: **Amen.**

➤ *Dismissal, p.* 42.

"When He comes ... the Spirit of Truth ..."

FOURTH SUNDAY AFTER EASTER

THOUGHT FOR TODAY: The Holy Spirit, promised by Christ to His Church, continues to "prove the world wrong about sin, about justice, about condemnation." Only among those guided by the Spirit of Truth can there be lasting peace on earth.

BIBLE AND LITURGY: The typical attitude of an unbeliever is skepticism. All knowledge is uncertain to him. Pilate asked: "What is truth?" (John 18, 38). We know the truth through God's Spirit, Who has been poured into our souls by Faith, Baptism and Confirmation. READ: John 18, 37-38; 1, 1-18 (esp. 14); 8, 12-33 (esp. 32); 8, 42-47; 15, 26-27.

INTROIT Ps. 97, 1. 2. 1   [*Deeds of the Lord*]

Sing to the Lord a new song, alleluia; *

    for the Lord has done wondrous deeds, alleluia; *

    in the sight of the nations, He has revealed His justice, alleluia, alleluia, alleluia. *

(Ps.) His right hand has won victory for Him, * His holy arm. *

Glory be to the Father, etc.

Sing to the Lord a new song, alleluia; *
for the Lord has done wondrous deeds, alleluia; *
in the sight of the nations, He has revealed His justice, alleluia, alleluia, alleluia.

➤ *Kyrie and Gloria, pp. 13-14.*

PRAYER   [*Unity of Mind*]

O God, Who make the minds of the faithful of one accord, grant that Your people may love what You command and desire, what You promise, so that amid the passing things of this world, our hearts may rest where true joys abide. Through our Lord, etc. People: **Amen.** ↓

EPISTLE   James 1, 17-21   [*The Saving Word*]

Beloved: Each good gift and every best favor comes from above, comes down from the Father of the lights of the sky, Who has never known change, Who is never shadowed over. He has willed to bring us to birth with a revelation of truth, so that we might be a kind of first-fruits of His creatures. Remember this, my beloved brothers. Then let every man be quick to hear, slow to speak, slow to anger; for a man's anger does not accomplish God's just purpose. So strip away everything filthy, every vicious excess. Humbly welcome the revelation that has struck its roots into you, that has the power to save your souls. ↓   Ps. 117, 16; Rom. 6, 9
                                        [*Power of God*]
Alleluia, alleluia. *
The right hand of the Lord has struck with power; *
the right hand of the Lord has exalted me. *

Alleluia. Christ, having risen from the dead, dies now no more; *

death shall no longer have dominion over Him. Alleluia.

➤ *Prayer before the Gospel, p. 16.*

GOSPEL   John 16, 5-14   [*Promising the Paraclete*]

At that time Jesus said to His disciples: "Now I am going away to Him Who sent Me. Yet not one of you asks Me, 'Where are You going?' Just because I have said this to you, your hearts are full of sorrow. Still, I am telling you the truth: it is better for you that I go away. If I do not go, the Paraclete will never come to you; whereas, if I do go, I shall send Him to you. And when He does come, He will prove the world wrong about sin, about justice, about condemnation. First, sin—because they refuse to believe in Me. Then, justice—because I am going to the Father and you can no longer see Me. Finally, condemnation—because the Prince of this world has been condemned. I have much more to tell you, but you cannot bear it now. When He comes, however, being the Spirit of Truth, He will guide you along the way of all truth. For He will not speak on His own, but will speak only what He hears and will announce to you the things to come. He will glorify Me because He will take what is Mine and announce it to you."

➤ *Creed, p. 18.*

OFFERTORY   Ps. 65, 1. 2. 16   [Declaring the Lord]

Shout joyfully to God, all you on earth, *
  sing praise to the glory of His Name; *
Hear now, all you who fear God, while I declare *
  what the Lord has done for me. Alleluia.

➔ *Offertory Prayers, p. 21.*

SECRET   [Faith for Salvation]

O God, Who through the gifts we have exchanged with You in this sacrament, have made us partakers of the supreme Godhead, grant, we beseech You, that, as we have knowledge of Your truth, so we may fully live up to it. Through our Lord, etc. People: **Amen.**

➔ *Preface, p. 170.*

COMMUNION   John 16, 8   [Work of the Holy Spirit]

When the Paraclete has come, the Spirit of
  Truth, *
He will convict the world *
of sin, and of justice, and of judgment, alleluia,
  alleluia.

POSTCOMMUNION

Be near us, O Lord, our God, that through those things which we have received in faith, we may be cleansed of sin and rescued from all dangers. Through our Lord, etc. People: **Amen.**

➔ *Dismissal, p. 42.*

"Now I am leaving the world and I am going to the Father."

FIFTH SUNDAY AFTER EASTER

THOUGHT FOR TODAY: At the opening of the Rogation-Week we are reminded of Christ's promise that our petitions will be granted if we ask anything in His Name. To speak in His Name we must be "doers," not "hearers" only, of the word of God.

BIBLE AND LITURGY: Being God's children through Faith and Baptism, we can preserve our relationship with our heavenly Father by prayer. Praying means to direct our heart to God. This is possible only with God's help. That is the reason why Jesus teaches and helps us. READ: Luke 11, 1-13; Matt. 6, 5-15; 7, 7-11; Gen. 19, 16-33; Acts 12, 1-17 (esp. 5 and 13); Tobias 3; Ps. 140.

INTROIT   Isa. 48, 20; Ps. 65, 1. 2

[*Proclaiming God's Goodness*]

Declare the word of joy, *
    and let it be heard, alleluia: *
Declare it even to the ends of the earth; *
    the Lord has delivered His people: alleluia,
    alleluia. *

(Ps.) Shout joyfully to God, all you on earth, *
    sing praise to the glory of His Name; *
    proclaim His glorious praise. *

Glory be to the Father, etc.

Declare the word of joy, *
  and let it be heard, alleluia: *

Declare it even to the ends of the earth; *
  **the Lord has delivered His people: alleluia,
  alleluia.**

➤ *Kyrie and Gloria, pp. 13-14.*

PRAYER   [*Think and Do Rightly*]

*O God, from Whom all good things come, grant,
we beseech You, that by Your inspiration, we
may think what is right and under Your guidance, accomplish it. Through our Lord, etc.*
People: **Amen.** ↓

EPISTLE James 1, 22-27 [*Doers, Not Just Hearers*]

Beloved: Act on this revelation. If you only
listen to it, you are fooling yourselves. For a
man who listens to divine revelation but does
not put it into practice is like a man who looks
in a mirror at the face he was born with. He
looks at himself, then off he goes and promptly
forgets how he appeared. But then there is the
man who peers into the ideal law that is char-
acterized by freedom, and he does so continually. He is no forgetful listener but he does
things in practice. Happy will this man be in
his accomplishment. Then there is the case of
a man whose tongue is not controlled. He im-
agines that he is devout, but this is self-decep-
tion. That man's worship is pointless. Looking
after orphans and widows in their distress,
keeping oneself unspotted by the world, this is
pure and stainless worship before our God and
Father. ↓

John 16, 28

Alleluia, alleluia. *   [*The Redeeming Christ*]

Christ is risen, and has shone upon us, *
   whom He redeemed with His Blood. *

Alleluia. I came forth from the Father, *
   and have come into the world. *

Again I leave the world, *
   and go to the Father. Alleluia.

➔ *Prayer before the Gospel, p. 16.*

GOSPEL   John 16, 23-30   [*Christ Our Mediator*]

At that time Jesus said to His disciples: "Truly I assure you, whatever you ask the Father, He will give you in My name. Until now you have not asked for anything in My name. Ask and you shall receive that your joy may be complete. I have said all this to you in figures of speech. An hour is coming when I shall no longer speak to you in figures, but tell you plainly about the Father. On that day you will ask in My name; and this does not mean that I shall have to petition the Father for you. For the Father Himself loves you, since you have loved Me and have believed that I came forth from God. I came forth from the Father and I have come into the world. Now I am leaving the world and I am going to the Father." "Why, at last," His disciples exclaimed, "You are talking plainly without any figure of speech! Now we know that You know everything—no need for anybody to ask You questions. Because of this we believe that You came forth from God."

➔ *Creed, p. 18.*

OFFERTORY Ps. 65, 8. 9. 20

[*Giver of Life and Protector*]

Bless the Lord our God, you peoples, *
loudly sound His praise; *
He has given life to my soul, *
and has not let my feet slip. *
Blessed be the Lord, Who refused me not *
my prayer, or His kindness. Alleluia.

➤ *Offertory Prayers, p.* 21.

SECRET [*Heavenly Glory Through These Gifts*]

*Accept, O Lord, the prayers and gifts of Your
faithful people, that, through these rites of love
and devotion we may pass to the glory of
heaven. Through our Lord, etc.* People: **Amen.**

➤ *Preface, p.* 170.

COMMUNION Ps. 95, 2 [*Sing of Salvation*]

Sing to the Lord, alleluia; *
sing to the Lord; *
Bless His Name; *
announce His salvation day after day, alleluia,
alleluia.

POSTCOMMUNION [*Desire What Is Right*]

*Grant, O Lord, that we who have been fed with
the strengthening food of Your heavenly table,
may desire what is right and obtain what we
desire. Through our Lord, etc.* People: **Amen.**

➤ *Dismissal, p.* 42.

"He was lifted up before their very eyes . . ."

ASCENSION DAY

THOUGHT FOR TODAY: Our Lord ascended into heaven to prepare a place for us. His apostles were sent to teach all nations what He had commanded them. We must now cleanse our hearts from sin, which cannot enter heaven, and store up good deeds, performed in the state of grace. These will speak for us when we appear before God.

BIBLE AND LITURGY: The Bible theme of the First Passion Sunday teaches the Christian vision on Christ's eternal priesthood. Christ went up into heaven, sits at the right hand of God the Father (i.e., shares power with Him) and is constantly interceding for us. He is our Mediator and High Priest in heaven. READ: John 14, 1-24; Heb. 7, 11-28 (esp. 25); 8, 1-13; 1 John 2, 1-2; Apoc. 21, 22-27; 22, 3-5.

INTROIT   Acts 1, 11; Ps. 46. 2   *[Why Look Up]*

Men of Galilee, *

  why do you stand looking up to heaven? Alleluia. *

He shall come in the same way *

  as you have seen Him going up to heaven: alleluia, alleluia, alleluia. *

(Ps.) **All you peoples, clap your hands,** *
   shout to God with cries of gladness. *

Glory be to the Father, etc.

Men of Galilee, *
   why do you stand looking up to heaven? Alleluia. *

He shall come in the same way *
   **as you have seen Him going up to heaven:
   alleluia, alleluia, alleluia.**

➤ *Kyrie and Gloria, pp. 13-14.*

PRAYER [Ascending Minds]

*Grant, we beseech You, almighty God, that we
who believe Your Only-begotten Son, our Redeemer, ascended into heaven on this day, may
also dwell in spirit in those heavenly places.
Through our Lord, etc.* People: **Amen.** ↓

EPISTLE Acts. 1, 1-11 [Seeing Christ Ascend]

In my first account, Theophilus, I dealt with
all that Jesus did and taught until the day
He was taken up to heaven, after He had instructed His chosen apostles through the Holy
Spirit. For after His Passion He showed them
in many convincing ways that He was alive,
appearing to them during forty days and speaking to them about the kingdom of God. Once
when He met with them, He told them not to
leave Jerusalem. "Wait, rather, for the fulfillment of My Father's promise about which you
have heard Me speak. John baptized with water,
but within a few days you will be baptized with
the Holy Spirit." When they were with Him,

they used to ask, "Lord, is this the time when You are going to restore the kingdom to Israel?" He answered, "It is not for you to know the exact time; the Father has reserved that to Himself. You will receive power when the Holy Spirit comes upon you, and you are to be My witnesses in Jerusalem, throughout Judea and Samaria—yes, even to the ends of the earth." When He had said this He was lifted up before their very eyes, and a cloud took Him from their sight. They were still staring after Him into the sky when two men dressed in white stood beside them. "Men of Galilee," they said, "why do you stand here looking at the sky? This Jesus Who has been taken away from you up to heaven will come back in the same way that you saw Him go." ↓

Ps. 46, 6; 67, 18. 19

Alleluia, alleluia. *   [*Glory of Christ's Mission*]

God mounts His throne amid shouts of joy; *
  the Lord, amid trumpet blasts. *

Alleluia. The Lord advances from Sinai to the
  sanctuary; *

  ascending on high. *

  He has led captivity captive. Alleluia.

➤ *Prayer before the Gospel, p. 16.*

GOSPEL   Mark 16, 14-20   [*Preach to the World*]

At that time, as they were at table, Jesus appeared to the Eleven. He reproached them for their disbelief and stubbornness, since they had put no faith in those who had seen Him after He had been raised. And He told them, "Go into the whole world, and proclaim the good news to the whole of creation. The man who believes in it and accepts baptism will be saved: the man who refuses to believe in it will be condemned. And signs like these will accompany those who have professed their faith: they will use My name to expel demons; they will speak entirely new languages; they will be able to handle serpents; they will even be able to drink deadly poison without harm; and the sick upon whom they lay their hands will recover." Then, after speaking to them, the Lord Jesus was taken up into heaven and took His seat at God's right hand. But they went forth and preached everywhere, while the Lord worked with them and confirmed the message through the signs which accompanied them.

➤ *Creed, p.* 18.

OFFERTORY   Ps. 46. 6   [*Triumph*]

God mounts His throne amid shouts of joy; *
the Lord, amid trumpet blasts. Alleluia.

➤ *Offertory Prayers, p.* 21.

SECRET   [*Our Leader to Heaven*]

Accept, O Lord, the gifts we offer for Your Son's ascension into the glory of heaven, and mercifully grant that we may be saved from present dangers and gain life everlasting. Through the same, etc. People: **Amen.** ⱱ

PREFACE FOR ASCENSION

[*Our Prayer of Thanksgiving*]

Right and worthy it is, fitting and for our good that in every time and place our thanks should rise to You, O Lord, holy Father, almighty and eternal God: through Christ our Lord. For, after His Resurrection, He showed Himself clearly to all His disciples and, even as they watched, was carried up to heaven, in order to make us share in His Godhead. And therefore, with the Angels and Archangels, with the Thrones and Dominations, and all the forces of heaven, we chant the endless hymn of Your glory:

➤ *Sanctus, p. 27.*

COMMUNION   Ps. 67, 33. 34

[*Praise to Christ in Triumph*]

Chant praise to the Lord, *
Who rises on the heights of the heavens to the East. Alleluia.

POSTCOMMUNION   [*Prayer for Grace*]

Grant, we beseech You, almighty and merciful God, that we may receive the invisible effects of the food we have eaten in this visible rite. Through our Lord, etc. People: **Amen.**

➤ *Dismissal, p. 42.*

"He will give evidence on My behalf."

SUNDAY AFTER THE ASCENSION

THOUGHT FOR TODAY: Fervent prayers are being said during this week in preparation for Pentecost. To make these prayers more acceptable to God, "maintain constant charity toward each other, because charity does away with a multitude of sins."

BIBLE AND LITURGY: Jesus promised to send the Spirit, Who proceeds from the Father. The Spirit is God just as the Father and the Son. He sanctifies us into the image of God. It is the Spirit also Who gives wisdom, understanding, fortitude and godliness to God's Chosen People. READ: Isa. 11, 1-10; Matt. 3, 13-17; Rom. 8, 1-17; 8, 26-27; 1 Cor. 2, 6-16; 3, 10-17.

INTROIT   Ps. 26, 7. 8. 9. 1   [*My Heart Speaks*]

Hear, O Lord, the sound of my call, alleluia; *
   to You my heart speaks, Your glance I seek; *
Your presence, O Lord, I seek. *
   Hide not Your face from me, alleluia, alleluia. *

(Ps.) The Lord is my light and my salvation; *
   whom should I fear? *

Glory be to the Father, etc.

Hear, O Lord, the sound of my call, alleluia; *
   to You my heart speaks, Your glance I seek; *
Your presence, O Lord, I seek. *
   Hide not Your face from me, alleluia, alleluia.

➔ *Kyrie and Gloria, pp.* **13-14.**

PRAYER   [*Serving Sincerely*]

*Almighty and eternal God, give us a will ever
dedicated to You, and a true heart to serve Your
Majesty. Through our Lord, etc.* People: **Amen.** ↓

EPISTLE   1 Pet. 4, 7-11   [*Godlike Charity*]

Beloved: Be responsible, and earnest in prayers. Above all maintain constant charity
toward each other, because charity does away
with a multitude of sins. Be hospitable to one
another without grumbling. Let each of you,
according to the gift he has received, share it
with the rest, as good stewards of the manifold
gift of God. When one of you speaks, let it be
like the things said by God; when one of you
shares, let it be as from the resources which
God provides; so that in all of you God may be
glorified, through Jesus Christ our Lord. ↓

                          Ps. 46, 9; John 14, 18
Alleluia, alleluia. *   [*Children of a King*]
The Lord reigns over all the nations, *
   God sits upon His holy throne. *
Alleluia. I will not leave you orphans; *
   I go away and I come to you, *
   and your heart shall rejoice. Alleluia.

➔ *Prayer before the Gospel, p.* **16.**

GOSPEL   John 15, 26-27; 16, 1-4 [*Bravery in the Spirit*]

A t that time Jesus said to His disciples: "When the Paraclete comes, the Spirit of Truth Who comes forth from the Father and Whom I shall send you from the Father, He will give evidence on My behalf. You too will give evidence because you have been with Me from the beginning. I have said all this to you to prevent your faith from being shaken. They are going to put you out of the synagogue. In fact, a time will come when anyone who puts you to death will think he is paying homage to God! And they will do such things because they never knew the Father nor Me. For My part, I have said all this to you so that, when their hour comes, you may remember what I told you."

➤ *Creed, p.* 18.

OFFERTORY   Ps. 46, 6   [*Triumph*]

God mounts His throne amid shouts of joy; *
the Lord, amid trumpet blasts. Alleluia.

➤ *Offertory Prayers, p.* 21.

SECRET   [*Vigorous Grace*]

May this pure sacrifice cleanse us, O Lord, and impart to our minds the strength of heavenly grace. Through our Lord, etc. People: **Amen.**

➤ *Preface, p.* 195.

COMMUNION   John 17, 12. 13. 15

[*Keep Them from Evil*]

Father, while I was with them, *
I kept them whom You have given Me, alleluia; *

But now I am coming to You: *

    I do not pray that You take them out of the world, *

    but that You keep them from evil, alleluia, alleluia.

POSTCOMMUNION   *[Giving Thanks]*

We who have been filled with heavenly gifts beseech You, O Lord, grant us to continue giving thanks to You. Through our Lord, etc. People: **Amen**.

➤ *Dismissal, p. 42.*

"They were all filled with the Holy Spirit."

PENTECOST SUNDAY

THOUGHT FOR TODAY: Jesus had instructed His disciples on several occasions about the coming of the Holy Spirit. The marvelous events which accompanied His arrival were signs of the far greater effects of grace He produces in the souls of those who receive Him. We pray with the Church: "Come, Holy Spirit, fill the hearts of Your faithful, and kindle in them the fire of Your love."

BIBLE AND LITURGY: The Spirit of God, another Advocate and Consoler, worked marvels in the Apostles and continues to do so in the Church. Faith, Baptism and Confirmation gave us this Spirit of God. Our constant prayer should be the prayer after the Epistle of this Mass: "Come, Holy Spirit, fill the hearts of Your faithful!" READ: Joel 2, 28-32; Acts 2, 14-21; 2, 37-41; 1 Cor. 12, 1-16; Eph. 4, 25-32; Acts 10, 34. 32-48; 8, 14-17.

INTROIT Wis. 1, 7; Ps. 67, 2 [*The Spirit Fills the World*]

The Spirit of the Lord fills the world, alleluia, *
is all-embracing, and knows man's utterance,
alleluia, alleluia, alleluia. *

(Ps.) **God arises; His enemies are scattered,** *
and those who hate Him flee before Him. *
Glory be to the Father, etc.

The Spirit of the Lord fills the world, alleluia, *
is all-embracing, and knows man's utterance,
alleluia, alleluia, alleluia.

➔ *Kyrie and Gloria, pp. 13-14.*

PRAYER   [Comfort of the Spirit]

O God, Who on this day have taught the
hearts of the faithful by the light of the Holy
Spirit, grant us by that Holy Spirit Himself, to
know what is right and ever to rejoice in His
help. Through...in the unity of the same, etc.
People: **Amen.** ↓

EPISTLE   Acts 2, 1-11   [Coming of the Holy Spirit]

When the day of Pentecost had come, the
disciples were all gathered together. Suddenly from the sky there was a noise like a
strong driving wind that filled the whole house
where they sat. There appeared to them tongues
as of fire that parted and came to rest on each
one of them. They were all filled with the Holy
Spirit and began to speak in other tongues and
to proclaim according to the promptings of the
Spirit. Now there were living in Jerusalem devout people, Jews of every nation under heaven,
who on hearing the sound gathered in a crowd.
But they were confused because each one heard
the speakers in his own language. This as-
tounded them and they asked in amazement,
"Aren't these men who are speaking all Galile-
ans? How is it, then, that each of us hears them

in his native language? We are Parthians, Medes and Elamites; inhabitants of Mesopotamia, of Judea and Cappadocia, of Pontus and Asia, of Phrygia and Pamphylia, of Egypt and the regions of Libya around Cyrene; even visitors from Rome—all Jews or Jewish converts (Cretans and Arabs too). And yet we hear them speaking in our own tongues about the great things which God has done." ↓

Alleluia, alleluia. *   Ps. 103, 30   [Fire of New Love]
Send forth Your Spirit, and they shall be created; *
  and You shall renew the face of the earth. *
Alleluia. *
(Here genuflect.)
  Come, Holy Spirit, fill the hearts of Your faithful: *
  and kindle in them the fire of Your love. ↓

SEQUENCE   [Cry of Mankind to the Lifegiver]

Come, Thou Holy Spirit, come! *
  And from Thy celestial home *
  Shed a ray of light divine! *

Come, Thou Father of the poor! *
Come, Thou source of all our store! *
  Come, within our bosoms shine! *

Thou, of comforters the best; *
Thou, the soul's most welcome Guest; *
  Sweet refreshment here below; *

In our labor, rest most sweet; *
Grateful coolness in the heat; *
  Solace in the midst of woe. *

O most blessed Light divine, *
Shine within these hearts of Thine, *
  And our inmost being fill! *

Where Thou art not, man hath naught, *
Nothing good in deed or thought, *
  Nothing free from taint of ill. *

Heal our wounds, our strength renew; *
On our dryness pour Thy dew; *
  Wash the stains of guilt away: *

Bend the stubborn heart and will; *
Melt the frozen, warm the chill; *
  Guide the steps that go astray. *

On the faithful, who adore *
And confess Thee, evermore *
  In Thy sev'nfold gift descend; *

Give them virtue's sure reward; *
Give them Thy salvation, Lord; *
  Give them joys that never end. *
      Amen. Alleluia.

➤ *Prayer before the Gospel, p.* 16.

GOSPEL   John 14, 23-31   [*Indwelling*]

At that time Jesus said to His disciples: "If anyone loves Me, he will keep My word. Then My Father will love him, and We shall come to him and make Our dwelling-place with him. Whoever does not love Me does not keep My words; yet the word that you hear is not My own but comes from the Father Who sent Me. All this have I spoken to you during My stay with you. But the Paraclete, the Holy Spirit, Whom the Father will send in My name, will teach you everything and remind you of all that I told you Myself. 'Peace' is My farewell to you. My 'peace' is My gift to you, and I do not give it to you as the world gives it. Do not let your hearts be troubled or fearful. You have heard Me say to you, 'I am going away,' and 'I am coming back to you.' If you loved Me, you would rejoice to have Me go to the Father, for the Father is greater than I. But I have told you this now even before it happens so that, when it does happen, you may believe. I shall no longer speak at length with you, for the Prince of the world is coming. Actually, He has no hold on Me; but the world must recognize that I love the Father and that I do exactly as the Father has commanded me."

➤ *Creed, p.* 18.

OFFERTORY   Ps. 67, 29. 30

Confirm, O God. * [Continue the Work of the Spirit]
  what You have wrought in us; *
From Your temple, which is in Jerusalem, *
  kings shall offer gifts to You. Alleluia.

➤ *Offertory Prayers, p.* 21.

SECRET   [Purified by the Spirit]

Sanctify these offerings, we beseech You, O Lord, and cleanse our hearts by the light of the Holy Spirit. Through . . . in the unity of the same, etc. People: **Amen.** ↓

PREFACE FOR PENTECOST

[*Our Prayer of Thanksgiving*]

Right and worthy it is, fitting and for our good that in every time and place our thanks should rise to You, O Lord, holy Father, almighty and eternal God: through Christ our Lord. Rising up above all the heavens, and taking His place at Your right hand, as He promised, He sent down on this day the Holy Spirit upon those who by adoption are Your children. This is why the whole world now rejoices with a joy beyond all joy. The Powers high above, and the angelic hosts, chant, as one, the endless hymn of Your glory: ⇢ *Sanctus, p. 27.*

COMMUNION   Acts 2, 2. 4 [*Filled with the Holy Spirit*]

Suddenly there came a sound from heaven, *
   as of a violent wind blowing, *
   where they were sitting, alleluia: *
And they were all filled with the Holy Spirit, *
   speaking of the wonderful works of God,
      alleluia, alleluia.

POSTCOMMUNION   [*Endued with the Spirit*]

May the inpouring of the Holy Spirit cleanse our hearts, O Lord, and make them fertile through the dew He sprinkles upon them. Through . . . in the unity of the same, etc. People: **Amen.**

⇢ *Dismissal, p. 42.*

"Blessed be the Holy Trinity and undivided Unity!"

TRINITY SUNDAY

THOUGHT FOR TODAY: Our intellect is too limited to comprehend the inner life of the infinite God, the Mystery of one God in three Divine Persons. But we know that everything in our Christian Religion is related to the Holy Trinity: Creation, Sanctification and Salvation. The "Glory be to the Father, and to the Son, and to the Holy Spirit" is an expression of our reverence and gratitude.

BIBLE AND LITURGY: Divine Revelation teaches us about the Father (see first part of the Nicene Creed, p. 18), the Son (see second part of the Nicene Creed, p. 18) and the Holy Spirit (see third part of the Nicene Creed, p. 20). These three Persons: Father, Son and Holy Spirit—all of them are God. "One God in three Persons" is also called "The Blessed Trinity." We cannot understand this mystery in God. We should approach it in Faith and profound adoration. READ: Acts 17, 16-34; Matt. 3, 13-17; 2 Cor. 13, 1-13; 1 Pet. 1, 1-12; Jude 20-24.

INTROIT   Tob. 12, 6; Ps. 8, 2   [*Glorious Trinity*]

Blessed be the Holy Trinity and undivided Unity: *

We will give glory to Him, *
  because He has shown His mercy to us. *

(Ps.) **O Lord, our Lord,** *
  how glorious is Your Name over all the earth! *

Glory be to the Father, etc.

Blessed be the Holy Trinity and undivided Unity: *

We will give glory to Him, *
  because He has shown His mercy to us.

➔ *Kyrie and Gloria, pp. 13-14.*

PRAYER   [Steadfast Faith]

Almighty, eternal God, Who have given Your servants, in the confession of the true Faith, to acknowledge the glory of the eternal Trinity, and in the power of that Majesty to adore its Unity, grant, we beseech You, that in the firmness of this Faith we may ever be protected from all harm. Through our Lord, etc.
People: **Amen.** ↓

EPISTLE   Rom. 11, 33-36   [Depth of the Mystery]

Oh, the depth of the riches and the wisdom and the knowledge of God! How inscrutable His judgments are, how unsearchable His ways! For "Who has known the mind of the Lord? Or who was ever His counselor? Who has given Him anything first, so as to earn a due return?" For from Him and through Him and for Him are all things. To Him be glory forever. ↓

GRADUAL   Dan. 3, 55. 56   [*Reigning Supreme*]

Blessed are You, O Lord, *
  Who look into the depths *
  from Your throne upon the Cherubim. *
Blessed are You, O Lord, *
  in the firmament of heaven, *
  and praiseworthy forever.

Alleluia, alleluia. *   Dan. 3, 52   [*Eternal Praise*]
Blessed are You, O Lord, the God of our
    fathers, *
  and praiseworthy forever. Alleluia.

➤ *Prayer before the Gospel, p.* 16.

GOSPEL   Matt. 28, 18-20   [*Baptize All*]

A t that time Jesus addressed His disciples in
  these words, "Complete authority has been
conferred on Me in heaven as on earth; go,
therefore, and make disciples of all the nations
by baptizing them in the Name 'of the Father,
and of the Son, and of the Holy Spirit,' by
teaching them to carry out everything that I
have commanded you. And remember, I am
with you always until the end of the world."

➤ *Creed, p.* 18.

OFFERTORY   Tob. 12, 6   [*Mercy from the Trinity*]
Blessed be God the Father, *
  and the Only-begotten Son of God, *
  and also the Holy Spirit: *
Because He has shown His mercy to us.

➤ *Offertory Prayers, p.* 21.

SECRET [*Everlasting Offering*]

We call upon Your Name, O Lord, and beseech You to hallow this sacrificial offering and through it to make us an eternal offering to You. Through our Lord, etc. People: **Amen**.

➤ *Preface, p. 26.*

COMMUNION   Tob. 12, 6 [*Bless God*]

We bless the God of heaven, *
 and before all living we will praise Him; *
Because He has shown His mercy to us.

POSTCOMMUNION [*Faith for Salvation*]

May the reception of this sacrament, O Lord our God, and the profession of our faith in the eternal holy Trinity and undivided Unity, benefit us for the salvation of body and soul. Through our Lord, etc. People: **Amen.**

➤ *Dismissal, p. 42.*

"Lo the Angels' Food is given. . .

FEAST OF CORPUS CHRISTI

THURSDAY AFTER TRINITY SUNDAY

THOUGHT FOR TODAY: The joy of the institution of the Holy Eucharist is not fully expressed on Holy Thursday because of the nearness of Good Friday. Hence wherever possible, public homage and adoration are paid to Jesus in the Blessed Sacrament on this Feast of Corpus Christi, and the faithful accompany Christ in a colorful procession.

BIBLE AND LITURGY: This feast expresses the joy of God's people, because Christ is with us in the Holy Eucharist. READ: Gen. 14, 18-20 and Heb. 7; Mal. 1, 10-11; John 6; Mark, 14, 17-21.

INTROIT   Ps. 80, 17. 2   [*Food for God's People*]

He fed them with the best of wheat, alleluia; *
 and filled them with honey from the rock,
  alleluia, alleluia, alleluia. *

(Ps.) Sing joyfully to God our strength; *
 acclaim the God of Jacob. *

Glory be to the Father, etc.

He fed them with the best of wheat, alleluia; *
and filled them with honey from the rock,
alleluia, alleluia, alleluia.

➔ *Kyrie and Gloria, pp. 13-14.*

PRAYER   [*Fruit of Redemption*]

*O God, Who in this wondrous Sacrament
have left us a memorial of Your Passion, grant
us, we beseech You, so to venerate the sacred
mysteries of Your Body and Blood that we may
ever experience within us the effect of Your
redemption. Who live, etc. People:* **Amen.** ↓

EPISTLE   1 Cor. 11, 23-29

[*Testimony to Apostolic Belief*]

Brethren: I received from the Lord, what I
also handed on to you, that the Lord Jesus,
on the night in which He was betrayed, took
bread and having given thanks, broke it and
said: "This is My Body which is for you. Do
this as a remembrance of Me." In the same
way, after the supper, He took the cup saying:
"This cup is the new covenant in My Blood. Do
this, whenever you drink it, as a remembrance
of Me." Every time, then, that you eat this
Bread and drink this cup, you proclaim the
death of the Lord, until He comes. So, whoever eats the Bread or drinks the cup of the
Lord unworthily will have to answer for the
Body and the Blood of the Lord. A man should
first examine himself. Only then should he eat
of the Bread and drink of the cup. For he who
eats and drinks without recognizing the Body,
eats and drinks a judgment against himself. ↓

GRADUAL   Ps. 144, 15-16   [*Hope*]

The eyes of all look hopefully to You, O Lord; *
  and You give them their food in due season. *
You open Your hand; *
  and satisfy the desire of every living thing.

Alleluia, alleluia. * John 6, 56-57 [*The Heavenly Food*]
My Flesh is food indeed, *
  and My Blood is drink indeed. *
He who eats My Flesh, and drinks my Blood, *
  abides in Me, and I in him.

SEQUENCE   [*Song of the Eucharist*]

L aud, O Sion thy salvation, *
    Laud with hymns of exultation, *
  Christ, thy King and Shepherd true: *

Bring Him all the praise thou knowest, *
He is more than thou bestowest, *
  Never canst thou reach His due. *

Special theme for glad thanksgiving *
Is the quick'ning and the living *
  Bread today before thee set: *

From His hands of old partaken, *
As we know, by faith unshaken, *
  Where the Twelve at supper met. *

Full and clear ring out thy chanting, *
Joy nor sweetest grace be wanting, *
  From thy heart let praises burst: *

For today the feast is holden, *
When the institution olden *
  Of that supper was rehearsed. *

Here the new law's new oblation, *
By the new King's revelation, *
  Ends the form of ancient rite: *

Now the new the old effaceth, *
Truth away the shadow chaseth, *
  Light dispels the gloom of night. *

What He did at supper seated, *
Christ ordained to be repeated, *
  His memorial ne'er to cease: *

And His rule for guidance taking, *
Bread and wine we hallow, making *
  Thus our sacrifice of peace. *

This the truth each Christian learneth, *
Bread into His Flesh He turneth, *
  To His Precious Blood the wine: *

Sight hath fail'd, nor thought conceiveth, *
But a dauntless faith believeth, *
  Resting on a pow'r divine. *

Here beneath these signs are hidden *
Priceless things to sense forbidden; *
  Signs, not things are all we see: *

Blood is poured and Flesh is broken, *
Yet in either wondrous token *
  Christ entire we know to be. *

Whoso of this Food partaketh, *
Rendeth not the Lord nor breaketh *
  Christ is whole to all that taste: *

Thousands are, as one, receivers, *
One, as thousands of believers, *
  Eats of Him Who cannot waste. *

Bad and good the feast are sharing, *
Of what divers doom preparing, *
  Endless death, or endless life. *

Life to these, to those damnation, *
See how like participation *
  Is with unlike issues rife. *

When the sacrament is broken, *
Doubt not, but believe 'tis spoken, *
  That each sever'd outward token *
    doth the very whole contain. *

Nought the precious gift divideth, *
Breaking but the sign betideth *
  Jesus still the same abideth, *
    still unbroken doth remain. *

Lo the Angels' Food is given *
To the pilgrim who hath striven; *
  See the children's Bread from heaven, *
    which on dogs may not be spent. *

Truth the ancient types fulfilling, *
Isaac bound, a victim willing, *
  Paschal lamb, its life blood spilling, *
    manna to the fathers sent. *

Very Bread, Good Shepherd, tend us, *
Jesu, of Thy love befriend us, *
  Thou refresh us, Thou defend us, *
  Thine eternal goodness send us *
In the land of life to see. *

Thou who all things canst and knowest, *
Who on earth such Food bestowest, *
  Grant us with Thy saints, though lowest, *
  Where the heav'nly feast Thou showest, *
Fellow heirs and guests to be. Amen. Alleluia.

➜ *Prayer before the Gospel, p. 16.*

GOSPEL   John 6, 55-59   [*Our Lord's Promise*]

At that time Jesus said to the crowds of the Jews: "My Flesh is real food and My Blood, real drink. The man who feeds on My Flesh and drinks My Blood abides in Me and I in him. Just as the Father Who has life sent Me and I have life because of the Father, so the man who feeds on Me will have life because of Me. This is the Bread which came down from heaven. Unlike your ancestors who ate and yet died, the man who feeds on this Bread will live forever." ➤ *Creed, p.* **18.**

OFFERTORY   Lev. 21, 6   [*Solemn Liturgy*]

The priests of the Lord *
    offer incense and loaves to God, *
And therefore they shall be sacred to their God *
    and shall not profane His Name. Alleluia.

➤ *Offertory Prayers, p.* **21.**

SECRET   [*Unity and Peace*]

Graciously give Your Church, we beseech You, O Lord, the gifts of unity and peace which are betokened by the gifts we offer. Through our Lord, etc. People: **Amen.** ↓

PREFACE OF THE BLESSED SACRAMENT

Right and worthy it is, fitting and for our good that in every time and place our thanks should rise to You, O Lord, holy Father, almighty and eternal God: through Christ our Lord. The animal victims that foreshadowed Him He set aside, and urged upon us His own Body and

Blood for sacrifice, that in every place there might rise to Your Name the clean offering, the only one pleasing in Your sight. So, in this mystery of Wisdom beyond reach and of Love without limit, the very thing He accomplished once upon the Cross He now accomplishes unceasingly, offering Himself and being offered. One victim with Himself He made us, and now He invites us to the sacred meal of fellowship in which it is He Himself Who is eaten as our food, His Passion is brought to mind, the soul is filled with grace, and we are given the pledge of future glory. And therefore with the Angels and Archangels, with the Thrones and Dominations, and all the forces of heaven, we chant the endless hymn of Your glory: *Sanctus, p. 27.*

COMMUNION   1 Cor. 11, 26-27 [*The Divine Command*]

As often as you shall eat this Bread *
  and drink the cup, *
You proclaim the death of the Lord, *
  until He comes. *
Therefore whoever eats this Bread *
  or drinks the cup of the Lord unworthily, *
Will be guilty *
  of the Body and Blood of the Lord, alleluia.

POSTCOMMUNION   [*Divinity Expressed*]

Grant, we beseech You, O Lord, that we may be filled with that everlasting enjoyment of Your Godhead, as foreshadowed here on earth by the partaking of Your precious Body and Blood. Who live, etc. People: **Amen.** ➤ *Dismissal, p. 42.*

"Bring in here the poor, and the crippled . . ."

SECOND SUNDAY AFTER PENTECOST

THOUGHT FOR TODAY: The Communion-Banquet to which we are invited is not only for the just, but for all who acknowledge that they are poor, feeble, blind, and lame in their religious life and desire to be cured.

BIBLE AND LITURGY: Faith and eternal happiness in the future life are a favor and an invitation of God. We should gratefully accept this invitation. To refuse it by carelessly losing our Faith may result in eternal punishment. READ: Matt. 23, 37-39; John 8, 43-59; 9 (*Note the attitude toward Faith of parents, Pharisees and blind man!*); 12, 37-50.

INTROIT   Ps. 17, 19. 20. 2. 3   [Act for Love]

The Lord came to my support; *
   He set me free in the open, *
   and rescued me, because He loves me. *

(Ps.) I love You, O Lord, my strength, *
   O Lord, my rock, my fortress, my deliverer. *

Glory be to the Father, etc.

The Lord came to my support; *
   He set me free in the open, *
   and rescued me, because He loves me.

➤ *Kyrie and Gloria, pp. 13-14.*

PRAYER   [*Firm in God's Love*]

Grant, O Lord, that we may always fear and love Your holy Name, for You never fail to guide those whom You firmly establish in Your love. Through our Lord, etc. People: **Amen.** ↓

EPISTLE   1 John 3, 13-18   [*Love of One Another*]

Beloved: No need to be surprised if the world hates you. That we have passed from death to life we know, because we love the brothers. The man without love is still in the abode of death. Everyone who hates his brother is a murderer; and, as you know, no murderer has eternal life abiding within him. The way we came to understand love was that He laid down His life for us; so must we too lay down our lives for the brothers. Now, how can divine love abide within a man who has enough of this world's livelihood and yet closes his heart to his brother when he observes him in need? Little children, let us show with deeds that our love is genuine and not merely express it with words. ↓

GRADUAL   Ps. 119, 1-2   [*Deliver Me*]

In my distress I called to the Lord, *
   and He answered me. *
O Lord, deliver me from lying lip, *
   from treacherous tongue.

Alleluia, alleluia. * Ps. 7, 2   [Rescue Me]
O Lord, my God, in You I take refuge; *
   save me from all my pursuers and rescue me.
      Alleluia.

➤ *Prayer before the Gospel, p. 16.*

GOSPEL Luke 14, 16-24   [Bring All to the Banquet]

At that time Jesus spoke this parable to the Pharisees: "A man was giving a great dinner and he invited many. At dinner time he sent his servant to say to those invited: 'Come along, everything is now ready.' But they began to excuse themselves, one and all. The first said to the servant: 'I have bought some land, and I must go out and inspect it. Please excuse me.' Another said: 'I have bought five pair of oxen, and am going to test them. Please excuse me.' A third said: 'I am newly married and therefore cannot come.'

"On his return the servant reported all this to his master. The master of the house was angry and said to his servant: 'Go out quickly into the streets and alleys of the town, and bring in here the poor, and the crippled, and the blind, and the lame!' The servant said: 'Your orders, my lord, have been carried out, and there is still room.' And the master said to the servant: 'Go out into the highways and along the hedges and force them to come in so that my house may be filled! For I tell you that none of those men who were invited shall taste my dinner.'"

➤ *Creed, p. 18.*

OFFERTORY   Ps. 6, 5   [Protecting Love]

Return, O Lord, save my life; *
  rescue me because of Your kindness.

➤ *Offertory Prayers, p. 21.*

SECRET   [Reality of Heaven]

May the sacrifice we are about to offer unto
Your holy Name, O Lord, make us pure, and day
by day help us to live a more heavenly life.
Through our Lord, etc. People: **Amen.**

➤ *Preface, p. 26.*

COMMUNION   Ps. 12, 6   [Sing to God's Goodness]

I will sing of the Lord, *
  "He has been good to me"; *
And I will sing to the Name *
  of the Lord the Most High.

POSTCOMMUNION   [Closer to Salvation]

We beseech You, O Lord, that having received
Your gifts, each partaking of this sacrament
may increase within us its saving effect.
Through our Lord, etc. People: **Amen.**

➤ *Dismissal, p. 42.*

"The thoughts of His Heart are to all generations."

FEAST OF THE SACRED HEART

FRIDAY AFTER THE SECOND SUNDAY
AFTER PENTECOST

The Feast of the Sacred Heart of Jesus is a reminder of all that we owe to the love of our Divine Redeemer. Appearing to St. Margaret Mary Alacoque during the Octave of Corpus Christi in the year 1675, Jesus said to her: "This is the heart which has loved men so much and in turn is so little loved by them." Let us consecrate our good will to the Sacred Heart and offer to Him the sacrifice of a holy life.

THOUGHT FOR TODAY: The Sacred Heart of Jesus is always eager to forgive whenever a sinner sincerely repents, and desires to return to God, the Source of joy and peace. Why then hesitate? "Cast your care upon the Lord, and He will support you."

BIBLE AND LITURGY: God is love. All love in this world merely springs forth from God's abundance of love. His love and goodness became visible in Christ, Whose Sacred Heart is a symbol of that Love. **READ:** Cant. (*Read first the Introduction!*); John 15, 1-11; Rom. 8, 35-39; Ps. 17, 1-4; John 20, 11-18.

INTROIT Ps. 32, 11. 19. 1   [*Love for All*]

The thoughts of His Heart *
  are to all generations: *

To deliver them from death *
   and preserve them in spite of famine. (P.T.
      Alleluia, alleluia.) *

(Ps.) Exult, you just, in the Lord; *
   praise from the upright is fitting. *

Glory be to the Father, etc.

The thoughts of His Heart *
   are to all generations: *

To deliver them from death *
   and preserve them in spite of famine. (P.T.
      Alleluia, alleluia.)

➔ *Kyrie and Gloria, pp.* 13-14.

PRAYER   [Reparation]

*O God, Who in the Heart of Your Son, wounded
by our sins, mercifully lavish upon us the infinite
riches of love, grant, we beseech You, that as
we offer Him the faithful service of our devotion, we may also show forth fitting reparation.
Through the same Lord, etc.* People: **Amen.** ↓

EPISTLE   Eph. 3, 8-12. 14-19   [Immeasurable Love]

Brethren: To me, less than least of all the
saints, this favor was given, to preach to
the Gentiles the unfathomable riches of Christ,
and to enlighten all men on the working out
of the mystery which for ages was hidden in
God, the Creator of all things, so that now
through the Church the manifold wisdom of
God might become known to the Principalities
and Powers of heaven, in fulfillment of the
eternal decree which He carried out in Christ
Jesus our Lord. In Him and through faith in

Him we can speak freely to God and draw
near to Him with confidence. For this reason I
kneel before the Father from Whom every family
in heaven and on earth takes its name; and I
pray that He will bestow on you gifts corresponding to the richness of His glory. May He
strengthen your inner selves with power through
His Spirit. May Christ dwell in your hearts
through faith; and may love be the root and
foundation of your life. Thus you will be able
to grasp fully with all the saints the breadth
and length and height and depth, and to know
that the love of Christ surpasses all knowledge,
so that you will be filled with all the fullness
of God. ℣

GRADUAL   Ps. 24, 8-9   [The Guide]

Good and upright is the Lord, *
  thus He shows sinners the way. *
He guides the humble to justice; *
  He teaches the humble His way.

Alleluia, alleluia. *   Matt. 11, 29   [Learn]
Take My yoke upon you, *
  and learn from Me, *
For I am meek, and humble of heart: *
  and you will find rest for your souls. Alleluia.

*In Votive Masses after Septuagesima, the Alleluia
and versicle are omitted and the following Tract is said:*

TRACT   Ps. 102, 8-10   [Forgiving Lord]

Merciful and gracious is the Lord, *
  slow to anger and abounding in kindness. *
He will not always chide, *
  nor does He keep His wrath forever. *

Not according to our sins does He deal with us, *
nor does He requite us according to our crimes.

During Paschaltime, the Gradual and Tract are omitted and the following Alleluia is said:

Alleluia, alleluia. *   Matt. 11, 29   [Learn of Me]
Take My yoke upon you, *
  and learn from Me, *
For I am meek, and humble of heart; *
  and you will find rest for your souls. *

Alleluia. Come to Me, all you who labor and are burdened, *
  and I will give you rest. Alleluia.

➤ *Prayer before the Gospel, p. 16.*

GOSPEL   John 19, 31-37   [Pierced Heart]

At that time, since it was Preparation Day, the Jews did not want the bodies left on the cross during the Sabbath, for that Sabbath was a solemn feast day. So they asked Pilate to have the legs broken and the bodies taken down. Accordingly, the soldiers came and broke the legs of the men crucified with Jesus, first of the one, then of the other. But when they came to Jesus and saw that He was already dead, they did not break His legs. However, one of the soldiers jabbed His side with a lance, and immediately blood and water flowed out. (This testimony has been given by an eyewitness, and His testimony is true. He is telling what He knows to be true that you too may have faith.) These events took place in order to have the Scripture fulfilled: "None of its bones are to be broken." And still another Scripture passage says: "They shall look on Him whom they have pierced."

→ *Creed, p. 18.*

OFFERTORY   Ps. 68, 21   [No One to Comfort]

My heart expected reproach and misery; *
I looked for sympathy, but there was none; *
for comforters, and I found none.

In Votive Masses during Paschaltime, the Offertory is as follows:

OFFERTORY   Ps. 39, 7-9   [Obedient Love]

Holocausts or sin-offerings You sought not; *
then said I: "Behold I come; *
in the written scroll it is prescribed for Me; *
To do Your will, O My God, is My delight, *
and Your law is within My Heart." Alleluia.

→ *Offertory Prayers, p. 21.*

SECRET   ['Atonement]

Look, we beseech You, O Lord, upon the Heart of Your beloved Son, with its boundless love, so that what we offer, may be an acceptable gift in Your sight and an atonement for our sins. Through the same Lord, etc. People: **Amen.**

PREFACE OF THE SACRED HEART

Right and worthy it is, fitting and for our good that in every time and place our thanks should rise to You, O Lord, holy Father, almighty and eternal God. For it was Your wish that the soldier's lance should pierce the body of Your only Son as He hung upon the Cross. And from His opened Heart, the holy place of Your mercy, there was to flow a mighty tide of grace and pardon. This Heart, which has never failed to burn with love for us, would become for the good a place of rest, and for those who turn from sin a place of refuge. And therefore with the Angels and Archangels, with the Thrones and Dominations, and all the forces of heaven, we chant the endless hymn of Your glory:

➤ *Sanctus, p. 27.*

COMMUNION   John 19, 34   [Blood and Water]

One of the soldiers opened His side with a lance, *
   and immediately there came out blood and water.

In Votive Masses during Paschaltime, the Communion is as follows:

COMMUNION   John 7, 37   [Thirst No More]

If anyone thirst, *
   let him come to Me and drink, alleluia, alleluia.

POSTCOMMUNION   [Divine Fervor]

May Your sacrament, O Lord Jesus, give us holy zeal, so that, seeing the sweetness of Your most loving Heart, we may learn to despise the things of earth and love those of heaven. Who live, etc. People: **Amen.**

➤ *Dismissal, p. 42.*

"Rejoice with me because I have found my lost sheep."

THIRD SUNDAY AFTER PENTECOST

THOUGHT FOR TODAY: The Catholic Church is a hospice for souls that are spiritually ill. Some people are scandalized because She is kind to sinners and forgives them over and over again. They forget that She obeys the merciful Heart of the Physician of souls.

BIBLE AND LITURGY: Since we are inclined to evil and fall into it again and again, we should strive constantly as Christians to be converted (turned back) to God. READ: 2 Kgs. 11; 12, 1-3; Luke 7, 36-50; 22, 54-62 and Matt. 27, 3-5; Ps. 50.

INTROIT Ps. 24, 16. 18. 1. 2 [*I Lift My Soul*]

Look toward me, and have pity on me, O Lord, *
 for I am alone and afflicted. *
Put an end to my affliction and my suffering, *
 and take away all my sins, O my God. *

(Ps.) To You, I lift up my soul, O Lord. *
 In You, O my God, I trust; *
 let me not be put to shame. *

Glory be to the Father, etc.

Look toward me, and have pity on me, O Lord, *
   for I am alone and afflicted. *
Put an end to my affliction and my suffering, *
   and take away all my sins, O my God.

➤ *Kyrie and Gloria, pp.* 13-14.

PRAYER [*Safe for Eternity*]

O God, Protector of all who hope in You, with-
out Whom nothing is strong, nothing is holy,
increase Your mercy toward us, that, with Your
guidance and direction we may so pass through
the things of this temporal life as not to lose
those of life eternal. Through our Lord, etc.
People: **Amen.** ⱱ

EPISTLE 1 Pet. 5, 6-11 [*Strength for Battle*]

Beloved: Humble yourselves beneath the
mighty hand of God, that He may exalt
you when the time comes. Cast upon Him all
your anxiety, because He it is Who takes care
of you. Be earnest, be vigilant! Your opponent,
the devil, is going about like a roaring lion,
seeking someone to devour. Withstand him,
strong in the faith, aware that in the world the
identical sufferings are being inflicted on your
brotherhood. And the God of all grace, Who
called you into His eternal glory in Christ, when
you have suffered briefly, will Himself form,
support, strengthen and establish you. His is
the sovereignty forever and ever. Amen. ⱱ

GRADUAL Ps. 54, 23. 17. 19 [*God, Our Helper*]

Cast your care upon the Lord, *
   and He will support you. *

When I called upon the Lord, *
   He heard my voice, *
   and freed me from those who war against me.

Alleluia, alleluia. * Ps. 7, 12   [A Strong God]

A just judge is God, strong and patient; *
   is He angry every day? Alleluia.

➔ *Prayer before the Gospel, p. 16.*

GOSPEL   Luke 15, 1-10   [*Searching for Sinners*]

At that time the tax gatherers and sinners were drawing near Jesus to hear Him. And the Pharisees and the scribes murmured saying: "This man makes sinners welcome and dines with them."

He addressed this parable to them: "What man of you, owning a hundred sheep and losing one, does not abandon the ninety-nine in the desert and go after the lost one until he finds it? When he finds it, he lays it on his shoulders in jubilation, and comes to his house, and invites his friends and neighbors in, saying, 'Rejoice with me because I have found my lost sheep.' In the same way, I tell you, there will be more rejoicing in heaven over one sinner who repents than over ninety-nine upright people who have no need of repentance.

"Or what woman of you, who has ten dimes and loses one, does not light a lamp, and sweep the house, and search carefully until she finds it? And when she has found it, she calls in the friends and neighbors, and says: 'Rejoice with me because I have found the dime which I lost.' In the same way, I tell you, there will be re-

joicing among the angels of God over one sinner
who repents."

➤ *Creed, p.* 18.

OFFERTORY   Ps. 9, 11. 12. 13   [*He Forgets Not*]

**They trust in You who cherish Your Name, O
    Lord,** *
for You forsake not those who seek You. *
Sing praise to the Lord enthroned in Sion, *
**for He has not forgotten the cry of the
    afflicted.**

➤ *Offertory Prayers, p.* 21.

SECRET   [*Salvation for Partakers*]

*Look favorably, O Lord, upon the offerings of
Your prayerful Church and grant that those
who believe may, in continual holiness, partake
of them for their salvation. Through our Lord,
etc.* People: **Amen.**

➤ *Preface, p.* 26.

COMMUNION   Luke 15, 10   [*Joy over Repentance*]

I say to you: *
there is joy among the angels of God *
over one sinner who repents.

POSTCOMMUNION   [*Cleansed from Sin*]

*May the holy things of which we have partaken
bring us to life and prepare for Your everlasting
mercy those whom You have cleansed from
sin. Through our Lord, etc.* People: **Amen.**

➤ *Dismissal, p.* 42.

"They caught a great number of fish . . ."

FOURTH SUNDAY AFTER PENTECOST

THOUGHT FOR TODAY: Let us always work as Christians laboring in union with, and for, the honor of Christ. We must also be fishers of men, eager to draw them into the boat of Peter, the Catholic Church.

BIBLE AND LITURGY: God's wisdom is not our wisdom. We should learn to adapt our way of thinking to God's way of thinking by frequent contact with His Word in the Bible. Simon Peter achieved success by heeding the Word of Christ, the Son of God. READ: Prov. 2, 1-22; 3, 1-24; Wisd. 6, 1-21; Rom. 8, 5-11; 12, 9-21 (esp. 17); 1 Cor. 1, 17-31.

INTROIT   Ps. 26, 1. 2. 3   [My Light and Strength]

The Lord is my light and my salvation; *
  whom should I fear? *

The Lord is my life's refuge; *
  of whom should I be afraid? *

My enemies that trouble me, *
  themselves stumble and fall. *

(Ps.) Though an army encamp against me, *
  my heart will not fear. *

Glory be to the Father, etc.

The Lord is my light and my salvation; *
whom should I fear? *
The Lord is my life's refuge; *
of whom should I be afraid? *
My enemies that trouble me, *
themselves stumble and fall.

➤ *Kyrie and Gloria, pp. 13-14.*

PRAYER   [*Govern the World*]

Grant us, we beseech You, O Lord, that the course of the world may be directed according to Your rule in peace and that Your Church may have the joy of serving You undisturbed. Through our Lord, etc. People: **Amen.** ↓

EPISTLE Rom. 8, 18-23 [*Creation Longs for the Creator*]

Brethren: I consider the sufferings of the present time unworthy to be compared with the glory that one day will be revealed in us. Even creation itself is waiting with eager longing for that revelation of the sons of God. For creation was condemned to a futile existence, not willingly, but by the will of Him Who doomed it. Yet hope still remained that even creation itself would be delivered from its slavery to corruption and would come to share in the glorious liberty of the children of God. Up to the present, as we know, the whole of creation has been groaning together as it undergoes the pains of childbirth. And not only creation, but we ourselves also groan in our hearts, for, even though we have the Spirit as first fruits of our harvest, we are still waiting for the full adoption that will come to us through the redemption of our bodies: in Christ Jesus, our Lord. ↓

GRADUAL   Ps. 78, 9. 10   [*We Have Pardon*]

Pardon our sins, O Lord; *
   why should the nations say, *
   "Where is their God?" *
Help us, O God our Savior; *
   because of the glory of Your Name, *
   O Lord, deliver us.

Alleluia, alleluia. *   Ps. 9, 5. 10   [*We Have Defense*]

O God, seated on Your throne, judging justly: *
   **be a stronghold for the oppressed in times of
   distress. Alleluia.**

➤ *Prayer before the Gospel, p. 16.*

GOSPEL   Luke 5, 1-11   [*The Great Catch*]

At that time as Jesus stood by the Lake of
Genesareth and the crowd pressed upon
Him to hear the word of God, He saw two
boats moored by the side of the lake; the fish-
ermen had disembarked and were washing their
nets. He got into one of the boats, the one belonging to Simon, and asked Him to pull out a
short distance from the shore. Then He sat down
and went on teaching the crowds from the
boat. When He finished speaking He said to
Simon: "Put out into the deep water and lower
your nets for a catch."

Simon answered: "Master, we worked hard
all night long and caught nothing; but at your
word I will lower the nets." Upon doing so they
caught a great number of fish, and their nets
were at breaking point. They signaled to their
mates in the other boat to come and help them.
These came and they filled both boats to the
point of sinking.

At the sight of this Simon Peter fell at the knees of Jesus, saying: "Depart from me because I am a sinful man, Lord." For amazement at the haul of fish which they had made had seized him and all his companions, and also James and John, sons of Zebedee, who were partners with Simon. Jesus said to Simon: "Do not be afraid. From now on you will be catching men." Then they brought their boats to land, left everything, and followed Him.

→ *Creed, p. 18.*

OFFERTORY   Ps. 12, 4. 5   [Keep Me Alive]

Give light to my eyes that I may never sleep in death, *
   lest my enemy say, "I have overcome him."

→ *Offertory Prayers, p. 21.*

SECRET   [Turn Our Wills]

Be appeased, we beseech You, O Lord, by accepting our offerings, and in Your kindness make even our rebellious wills turn to You. Through our Lord, etc. People: **Amen.**

→ *Preface, p. 26.*

COMMUNION   Ps. 17, 3   [Refuge]

O Lord, my rock, my fortress, my deliverer: *
   my God, my rock of refuge!

POSTCOMMUNION   [Power from the Mass]

May the sacrament we have received cleanse us, we beseech You, O Lord, and by its grace protect us. Through our Lord, etc. People: **Amen.**

→ *Dismissal, p. 42.*

"Go first and seek a reconciliation with your brother . . ."

FIFTH SUNDAY AFTER PENTECOST

THOUGHT FOR TODAY: Purely external practices of devotion like those of the Pharisees have no value in God's eyes. We must first "revere the Lord Christ in (our) hearts." From this inner grace and pure intention will spring patience and readiness to help and forgive even an offending neighbor.

BIBLE AND LITURGY: The Christian ideal is to be honest with oneself, with God and His commandments. "Unless you have more religion than the Scribes and Pharisees . . ." In the life of a Christian there should be no room for hypocrisy and self-satisfaction. READ: Job. 20, 1-29; Matt. 6, 1-34; 23; Luke 11, 29-54; 12, 1-3; James 2, 14-26.

INTROIT   Ps. 26, 7. 9. 1   [*Hear Us*]

Hear, O Lord, the sound of my call, *
  be my helper: *
Forsake me not: *
  despise me not, O God my Savior. *
(Ps.) The Lord is my light and my salvation; *
  whom should I fear? *
Glory be to the Father, etc.

Hear, O Lord, the sound of my call, *
  be my helper: *
Forsake me not: *
  despise me not, O God my Savior.

➤ *Kyrie and Gloria, pp. 13-14.*

PRAYER   [*Marvelous Promises*]

O God, Who have prepared good things as yet unseen for those who love You, pour a burning love into our hearts, so that we, loving You in and above all things, may obtain Your promises which surpass all desire. Through our Lord, etc. People: **Amen.** ↓

EPISTLE   1 Pet. 3, 8-15   [*Good for Evil*]

Beloved: All of you should be of one mind, compassionate, loving one another, merciful, humble. Do not return evil for evil, or insult for insult, but on the contrary, return a blessing; because to this you were called, that you might share in a blessing. For,

He who proposes to love life
  and to see good days
Must keep his tongue from evil
  and his lips from speaking falsehoods;

He must turn from evil and do good,
  seek peace, and follow it.
The Lord has eyes for the just,
  and ears for their cry,
But the Lord confronts the evildoers.

And who can harm you, if you are enthusiastic for what is good? Yes, even if you suffer for the sake of justice, happy are you! But, "Have no fear of them, and do not be disturbed"; instead revere the Lord Christ in your hearts. ↓

GRADUAL   Ps. 83, 10. 9   [Look Upon Us]

Behold, O God, our protector, *
  and look on Your servants. *
O Lord God of hosts, *
  hear the prayers of Your servants.

Alleluia, alleluia. ⁘   Ps. 20, 1   [God's Strength]

O Lord, in Your strength the king is glad; *
  in Your victory how greatly he rejoices!
  Alleluia.

→ *Prayer before the Gospel, p. 16.*

GOSPEL   Matt. 5, 20-24
                    [The New Law]

At that time Jesus said to His disciples: "I assure you, unless you have more religion than the scribes and Pharisees, you shall not enter the kingdom of heaven. You have heard the commandment imposed upon our ancestors, 'You shall not kill.' Every murderer will be liable to judgment. But now I warn you, everyone who becomes angry with his brother will be liable to judgment. Any man who says 'Raka' to his brother will be answerable to the Sanhedrin. Any man who says, 'You impious fool,' will be liable to fiery Gehenna. Therefore, if at the moment you are bringing your gift to the altar, you recall that your brother has a grievance against you, leave your gift there at the altar. Go first and seek a reconciliation with your brother. Then come and offer your gift."

→ *Creed, p. 18.*

OFFERTORY Ps. 15, 7. 8   [*Eyes on God*]

I bless the Lord Who counsels me; *
  I set God ever before me; *
With Him at my right hand *
  I shall not be disturbed.

➤ *Offertory Prayers, p. 21.*

SECRET   [*Offerings for Salvation*]

Be favorable, O Lord, to our humble prayers, and graciously accept these offerings of Your servants, men and women, that what each has offered to the honor of Your Name may profit for the salvation of all. Through our Lord, etc.
People: **Amen.**

➤ *Preface, p. 26.*

COMMUNION Ps. 26, 4   [*God's House*]

One thing I ask of the Lord
  this I seek: *
To dwell in the house of the Lord *
  all the days of my life.

POSTCOMMUNION   [*Cleanse and Deliver*]

Grant us, we beseech You, O Lord, that we whom You have filled with the heavenly gift may be cleansed of our hidden sins and delivered from the snares of our enemies. Through our Lord, etc. People: **Amen.**

➤ *Dismissal, p. 42.*

"Taking the seven loaves, He ... gave them to His disciples to distribute ..."

SIXTH SUNDAY AFTER PENTECOST

THOUGHT FOR TODAY: Easter time has passed but its spirit should never pass. Christ died once and now lives His glorious unending life. Having risen from sin, let us strive to live in union with Christ the new life of holiness, sustaining ourselves by the Holy Eucharist prefigured in the miracle of the multiplication of the loaves.

BIBLE AND LITURGY: Death to sin, symbolized by immersion in the Baptismal water, and a new life with Christ should be our constant concern not only at Easter, but throughout the entire year. This is possible only through a close contact with Christ, His Word and His Holy Signs, especially frequent Communion. READ: Ezech. 18; Mark 2, 13-17; Col. 2, 20-23; Rom. 3, 21-26; 5, 1-19; 8, 1-4; Gal. 3, 23-29.

INTROIT Ps. 27, 8. 9. 1   [Saving Refuge]

The Lord is the strength of His people, *
    the saving refuge of His anointed. *
Save Your people, O Lord, and bless Your
    inheritance; *
    and rule them forever! *
(Ps.) To You, O Lord, I call; *
    O my God, be not deaf to me, *

Lest, if You heed me not, *
  **I become one of those going down into the
    pit.** *

Glory be to the Father, etc.

The Lord is the strength of His people, *
  the saving refuge of His anointed. *

**Save Your people, O Lord, and bless Your
    inheritance;** *
  and rule them forever.

> *Kyrie and Gloria, pp.* 13-14.

PRAYER   [*Love of God's Name*]

*O God of the heavenly powers, Creator of all good
things, implant in our hearts the love of Your
Name, and bestow upon us an increase of godliness, fostering what is good, and, by Your
loving care, guarding what You have fostered.
Through our Lord, etc.* People: **Amen.** ↓

EPISTLE   Rom. 6, 3-11   [*New Life of Baptism*]

Brethren: All of us who were baptized into
Christ Jesus were baptized into His death.
By baptism into His death we were buried together with Him, in order that just as Christ
was raised from the dead by the glory of the
Father, so we too might live a new life. For
if we have been united with Him by likeness
to His death, so shall we be united with Him
by likeness to His resurrection. We know this:
our old self was crucified with Him, so that
the sinful body might be destroyed and we
might no longer be slaves of sin. For a man
who is dead has been freed from sin. If we
have died with Christ, we believe that we shall
live together with Him. We know that Christ,

raised from the dead, will never die again;
death has no more power over Him. His death
was a death to sin, once for all; but His life
is life for God. So you also must regard yourself as dead to sin but living for God in Christ
Jesus, our Lord. ↓

GRADUAL   Ps. 89, 13. 1   [Return to Us]

Return, O Lord! How long? *
Have pity on Your servants! *
O Lord, You have been our refuge *
through all generations.

Alleluia, alleluia. *   Ps. 30, 2. 3   [Save Me]
In You, O Lord, I take refuge; *
let me never be put to shame. *
In Your justice rescue me and release me; *
incline Your ear to me, *
make haste to deliver me! Alleluia.

→ *Prayer before the Gospel, p. 16.*

GOSPEL   Mark 8, 1-9   [Giver of Food]

At that time a large crowd was present with
Jesus, and again they had nothing to eat.
So He summoned the disciples and told them,
"My heart is moved to pity for the crowd. For
three days now they have been in My company,
and have nothing left to eat. And if I send
them home hungry, they will become weak
on the way. Some of them, you know, have
come a long distance." But His disciples replied, "How could anyone satisfy these people
with bread here in this isolated spot?" Still He
asked them, "How many loaves do you have?"
"Seven," they replied. Then He directed the
crowd to take their places on the ground. And
taking the seven loaves, He gave thanks, broke

them, and gave them to His disciples to distribute; and they distributed them to the
crowd. They also had a few tiny fish; and
blessing them, He told them to distribute them
also. They ate until they were full. Then they
gathered up seven hampers of fragments. There
were about four thousand in number, and He
dismissed them. ➙ *Creed, p. 18.*

OFFERTORY · Ps. 16, 5. 6. 7   [Direct Us]

Make my steps steadfast in Your paths, *
   that my feet may not falter. *
Incline Your ear to me; *
   hear my word. *
Show Your wondrous kindness, O Lord, *
   O Savior of those who trust in You.

➙ *Offertory Prayers, p. 21.*

SECRET   [No Prayer in Vain]

*Mercifully hear our humble prayers, O Lord,
and graciously accept these offerings of Your
people, and grant that no prayer may be without effect, no petition in vain, so that what we
ask in faith we may really obtain. Through our
Lord, etc.* People: **Amen.** ➙ *Preface, p. 26.*

COMMUNION   Ps. 26, 6   [Sacrifice and Song]

I will go round and offer in His tent, *
   sacrifices with shouts of gladness; *
I will sing and chant praise to the Lord.

POSTCOMMUNION   [Strength]

*We have been filled with Your gifts, O Lord;
grant, we beseech You, that we may be cleansed
and strengthened by their effect. Through our
Lord, etc.* People: **Amen.** ➙ *Dismissal, p. 42.*

"You will recognize them by their fruit."

7th SUNDAY AFTER PENTECOST

THOUGHT FOR TODAY: As good trees we must bring forth good fruit. We hear enough pious words, but we do not see enough good deeds. Thus, we pray, "O Lord, lead us to do good."

BIBLE AND LITURGY: Christians should be known "by their fruit" in this life and will be known by this fruit in the future life. Heaven is not just a pay check for a good life. Heaven is what we now make of it, just as the exertion of youth is rewarded in later life. READ: Eph. 4, 7-16; Matt. 13, 24-30; Eph. 2, 1-22 (esp. 22); 1 Pet. 2, 1-10 (esp. 2); 2 Pet. 3, 18; Gal. 6, 8-10; Col. 1, 1-14.

INTROIT   Ps. 46, 2. 3   [*Gladness*]

All you peoples, clap your hands, *
  shout to God with cries of gladness. *

(Ps.) For the Lord, the Most High, the awesome, *
  is the great King over all the earth. *

Glory be to the Father, etc.

All you peoples, clap your hands, *
  shout to God with cries of gladness.

➔ *Kyrie and Gloria, pp. 13-14.*

PRAYER [Provide for Us]

O God, Whose providence never fails to set things in order, we humbly beseech You to remove from us whatever is harmful and grant whatever is for our benefit. Through our Lord, etc. People: **Amen.** ↓

EPISTLE Rom. 6, 19-23 [A Free People]

Brethren: Because of your weak human nature, I am using quite human language. Just as formerly you presented your bodily organs to uncleanness and lawlessness as slaves for the doing of lawless deeds, present them now as slaves to justice so that you may become holy. When you were slaves of sin, you were free from justice. But what fruit did you reap? Now you are ashamed of those things. And their goal is death. But now that you have been freed from sin and have become slaves of God, the fruit of this is that you be made holy and your goal is eternal life. For the wages of sin is death, but God's gift is eternal life in Christ Jesus, our Lord. ↓

GRADUAL Ps. 33, 12. 6 [Fear with Hope]

Come, children, hear me; *
 I will teach you the fear of the Lord. *
Look to Him that you may be radiant with joy, *
 and your faces may not blush with shame.

Alleluia, alleluia. * Ps. 46, 2 [Rejoice]
All you peoples, clap your hands, *
 shout to God with cries of gladness. Alleluia.

→ *Prayer before the Gospel, p. 16.*

GOSPEL   Matt. 7, 15-21   [False Prophets]

At that time Jesus said to His disciples: "Be on your guard against false prophets, who come to you in sheep's clothing but actually are prowling wolves. You will recognize them by their fruit. Do you ever pick grapes off thorn-bushes, or figs off thistles? No! The fact is, any healthy tree produces good fruit, but a rotten tree produces bad fruit. A healthy tree cannot bear bad fruit, any more than a rotten tree can bear good fruit. (Every tree that does not bear good fruit is chopped down and thrown into the fire.) That is why you will recognize them by their fruit. It is not the man who says to Me, 'Lord, Lord,' who will enter into the kingdom of heaven, but he who does My heavenly Father's will."

➤ *Creed, p.* 18.

OFFERTORY   Dan. 3, 40   [Pleasing Sacrifice]

As though it were holocausts of rams and
   bullocks, *
   or thousands of fat lambs, *
So let our sacrifice be in Your presence today, *
   that it may please You; *
For those who trust in You *
   cannot be put to shame, O Lord.

➤ *Offertory Prayers, p.* 21.

SECRET   [Sanctified Gifts]

O God, Who have given us in one perfect sacrifice the fulfillment of the various sacrifices made under the Old Law, accept these

*sacrificial gifts offered You by Your devoted
servants, and make them holy as You did the
gifts of Abel, so that what each one of us has
offered in praise of Your Majesty may profit
for the salvation of all. Through our Lord, etc.*
People: **Amen.**

➤ *Preface, p. 26.*

COMMUNION   Ps. 30, 3   [Save Us]

Incline Your ear to me, *
    make haste to deliver me.

POSTCOMMUNION   [Lead Us]

*May Your healing action, O Lord, mercifully
rid us of our evil inclinations and lead us to do
good. Through our Lord, etc.* People: **Amen**

➤ *Dismissal, p. 42.*

"Give an accounting of your stewardship . . ."

8th SUNDAY AFTER PENTECOST

THOUGHT FOR TODAY: The parable of the steward shows how "the children of light" neglected so many opportunities to gain a happy eternity by not participating in the Holy Sacrifice of the Mass and by letting other means of sanctification go by unused.

BIBLE AND LITURGY: The cleverness and devotion of "the children of this age" should shame quite a few Christians. Inertia does not fit into the mentality of Christ, Who said: "I have come to bring a sword, not peace" (Matt. 10, 34). READ: Matt. 10, 16-42; 1 Cor. 9, 24-27; Apoc. 2, 1-11; 2 Mach. 7; Acts 7, 54-60.

INTROIT   Ps. 47, 10. 11. 2

[*Glorify God in His Sanctuary*]

O God, we ponder Your kindness *
  within Your temple. *
As Your Name, O God, so also Your praise *
  reaches to the ends of the earth. *
  Of justice Your right hand is full. *

(Ps.) Great is the Lord and wholly to be
    praised *
  in the city of our God, His holy mountain. *

Glory be to the Father, etc.

O God, we ponder Your kindness *
   within Your temple. *

As Your Name, O God, so also Your praise *
   reaches to the ends of the earth. *
   Of justice Your right hand is full.

➤ *Kyrie and Gloria, pp.* 13-14.

PRAYER   [Entirely Dependent]

Ever graciously bestow upon us, we beseech You, O Lord, the spirit of thinking and doing what is right, so that we, who cannot exist without You, may have the strength to live in accordance with Your law. Through our Lord, etc. People: **Amen.** ↓

EPISTLE   Rom. 8, 12-17   [Sons of God]

Brethren: We are debtors—but not to the flesh so that we must live according to the flesh. If you live according to the flesh, you will die. But if by the spirit you put the evil deeds of the body to death, you will live. Now, all who are led by the Spirit of God are sons of God. You did not receive a spirit of slavery, leading you back into fear, but a spirit of adoption through which we cry out *"Abba!"* (that is, "Father!"). And the Spirit Itself gives witness together with our spirit that we are children of God. But if children, heirs too, heirs of God, heirs together with Christ. ↓

GRADUAL   Ps. 30, 3; 70, 1   [Make Me Safe]

Be my rock of refuge, O God, *
   a stronghold to give me safety. *

In You, O God, I take refuge; *
  O Lord, let me never be put to shame.

Ps. 47, 2

Alleluia, alleluia. *   [*Praise in the Sanctuary*]
Great is the Lord and wholly to be praised *
  in the city of our God, His holy mountain.
    Alleluia.

→ *Prayer before the Gospel, p.* 16.

GOSPEL   Luke 16, 1-9   [*True Wisdom*]

At that time Jesus spoke this parable to His disciples: "There was a rich man who had a steward, who was reported to him for dissipating his property. He called him and said to him: 'What is this I hear about you? Give an accounting of your stewardship, for you can't be steward any longer.' The steward thought to himself, 'What must I do, in view of the fact that my master is taking my job away from me? I am unable to dig and ashamed to beg. I know what I must do to ensure that, when I am dismissed, they will receive me with open doors.' So he called in each one of his master's debtors. He said to the first: 'How much do you owe my master?' He replied: 'A hundred jars of oil.' The steward said: 'Take your invoice, sit down quickly and make it fifty.' Then he said to a second: 'How much do you owe?' He answered: 'A hundred measures of wheat,' and the steward said, 'Take your invoice and make it eighty.'

"The master gave the unjust steward credit for being so enterprising. For the children of this age are more enterprising than the children of light toward their own kind. And I say to you, make friends for yourselves with the help of wicked money so that when it runs out they may receive you into an everlasting abode."

➤ *Creed, p.* 18.

OFFERTORY   Ps. 17, 28. 32   [*Love for the Humble*]

Lowly people You save, O Lord, *
   but haughty eyes You bring low; *
For who is God except You, O Lord?

➤ *Offertory Prayers, p.* 21.

SECRET   [*Sanctification*]

Accept, we beseech You, O Lord, the gifts which we bring to You out of Your own bounty, so that these most holy sacramental rites may, by the power of Your grace, sanctify us in the conduct of our present life, and lead us to everlasting joy. Through our Lord, etc. People: **Amen.**

➤ *Preface, p.* 26.

COMMUNION   Ps. 33, 9   [*Taste and See*]

Taste and see how good the Lord is; *
   happy the man who takes refuge in Him.

POSTCOMMUNION   [*Renew Us*]

May the heavenly sacrament, O Lord, renew our minds and bodies, so that we may feel the benefit of the worship we perform. Through our Lord, etc. People: **Amen.**

➤ *Dismissal, p.* 42.

"My house shall be a house of prayer; but you have made it a bandits' den."

9th SUNDAY AFTER PENTECOST

THOUGHT FOR TODAY: The Holy Scriptures prove that God rewards and punishes even here on earth. Jerusalem rejected the Savior and it was destroyed. No temptation is so strong that we cannot conquer it with the grace of God. "He will not let you be tested beyond your strength."

BIBLE AND LITURGY: What really matters in life is the worship we give to God. We must worship God by doing our daily duties and by saying our private prayers, but its peak should be our weekly community worship in the parish church. What the temple was for the Jews, the parish church is for a Christian community. Every Catholic is responsible for the Church and Public Worship. READ: Ex. 25, 1-40; 27, 1-2; 28, 1; 29, 38-42; Heb. 10, 8-9; Matt. 18, 19-20; 1 Cor. 11, 17-34; Deut. 14, 22-29; 1 Cor. 9, 13-14; Ps. 150.

INTROIT   Ps. 53, 6. 7. 3   [Sustain My Life]

Behold, God is my helper, *
   the Lord sustains my life. *
Turn back the evil upon my foes; *
   in Your faithfulness destroy them, O Lord,
    my protector. *

(Ps.) **O God, by Your Name, save me,** *
   and by Your might deliver me. *
Glory be to the Father, etc.

Behold, God is my helper, *
   the Lord sustains my life. *
Turn back the evil upon my foes; *
   in Your faithfulness destroy them, O Lord,
     my protector.

➔ *Kyrie and Gloria, pp.* 13-14.

PRAYER   [Wise Requests]

*May Your merciful ears be open, O Lord, to
the prayers of those who humbly entreat You;
grant that they may ask for what pleases You
so that You may fulfill their desires. Through
our Lord, etc.* People: **Amen.** ↓

EPISTLE   1 Cor. 10, 6-13   [Pride before a Fall]

Brethren: We should not desire evil things
as our fathers did. Do not become idolators
as some of them did, as it is written: "The
people sat down to eat and drink, and they
got up to play." Let us not give ourselves up
to immorality, as some of them did, so that
in one day twenty-three thousand perished. Let
us not test the Lord as some of them put Him
to the test and were destroyed by the serpents.
And do not grumble as some of them grumbled
and were killed by the destroying angel. Now
these things overtook them to serve as an
example. And they have been written down
as a warning to us, who are living in the end
of the ages. So then, let him who thinks he is

standing firm, watch out that he does not fall.
No test has been sent you that doesn't come
to all men. Moreover, God keeps His promise.
He will not let you be tested beyond your
strength. He will give you with the test a
way of emerging from it successfully, that you
may be able to endure it. ↓

GRADUAL   Ps. 8, 2   [*Glorious Lord*]

O Lord, our Lord, *
   how glorious is Your Name over all the earth! *
   You have elevated Your Majesty above the
      heavens.

Alleluia, alleluia. *   Ps. 58, 2   [*Defend Us*]
Rescue me from my enemies, O my God; *
   from my adversaries defend me. Alleluia.

➔ *Prayer before the Gospel, p.* 16.

GOSPEL   Luke 19, 41-47   [*Rejection*]

At that time when Jesus was near, within
sight of the city, He wept over it, saying,
"If only you too had known this day the way
to peace. But, as it is, it is hidden from your
eyes. For days will come upon you, and your
enemies will encircle you with a rampart; they
will invest you, and press you in on every side;
they will wipe you out, you and your children
within your walls, and they will not leave in
you a stone upon a stone, because you failed
to recognize the moment of your visitation."
Then He entered the Temple precincts and began ejecting the traders, saying to them: "It is
written, 'My house shall be a house of prayer';

but you have made it 'a bandits' den.' " He
was teaching daily in the Temple.

➤ *Creed, p. 18.*

OFFERTORY   Ps. 18, 9. 10. 11. 12   [The Law Is Sweet]

The precepts of the Lord are right, *
  rejoicing the heart, *
And His ordinances sweeter than syrup *
  or honey from the comb; *
    therefore Your servant is careful of them.

➤ *Offertory Prayers, p. 21.*

SECRET   [Redemption Continued]

*Grant us, we beseech You, O Lord, to take part
worthily and frequently in this sacramental
action: for as often as this sacrifice of commemoration is offered, the work of our redemption is performed. Through our Lord, etc.*
People: **Amen.**

➤ *Preface, p. 26.*

COMMUNION   John 6, 57   [Union with Christ]

"He who eats My Flesh, *
  and drinks My Blood, *
Abides in Me, *
  and I in him," says the Lord.

POSTCOMMUNION   [United through the Sacrifice]

*May the partaking of Your sacrament, we be-
seech You, O Lord, cleanse us and unite us.
Through our Lord, etc.* People: **Amen.**

➤ *Dismissal, p. 42.*

"I give You thanks, God, that I am not like the rest of men . . . or even like this tax-gatherer."

10th SUNDAY AFTER PENTECOST

THOUGHT FOR TODAY: Humility is the foundation of all Christian virtues. God reveals Himself to the humble and despises arrogance and pride. We may be aware of our capabilities and accomplishments, but we must remember that "the one and the same Spirit produces all these gifts." Therefore, give glory to God.

BIBLE AND LITURGY: We should be humble. Everything we possess: Faith, our very existence, health, career and happiness in life, is a favor of God. Moreover, being sinners, we have God's mercy as our hope in life. READ: Judith 9; Ps. 33; Matt. 11, 25-30; 18, 1-4; 20, 20-28; Luke 22, 24-30.

INTROIT   Ps. 54, 17. 18. 20. 23. 2-3

[*The Lord Our Support*]

When I called upon the Lord, *
  He heard my voice, *
And freed me from those who war against me; *
  and He humbled them, *
He Who is before all ages, *
  and remains forever; *
Cast your care upon the Lord, *
  and He will support you. *

(Ps.) **Hearken, O God, to my prayer;** *
  turn not away from my pleading; *
  give heed to me, and answer me. *

Glory be to the Father, etc.

When I called upon the Lord, *
  He heard my voice, *
And freed me from those who war against me; *
  and He humbled them, *
He Who is before all ages, *
  and remains forever; *
Cast your care upon the Lord, *
  and He will support you. ➤ *Kyrie p.* **13.**

PRAYER   [*Belief in God's Promises*]

O God, Who manifest Your power, particularly in forbearance and pity, show us Your mercy again and again, so that hastening toward Your promises we may become partakers of the blessings of heaven. Through our Lord, etc.
People: **Amen.** ↓

EPISTLE   1 Cor. 12, 2-11   [*Each Has a Place*]

Brethren: You know that when you were pagans you were led astray to mute idols, whenever the impulse drove you. That is why I am telling you that nobody who speaks under the impulse of God's Spirit ever says: "Cursed be Jesus." And nobody can say: "Jesus is Lord," unless he is inspired by the Holy Spirit.

There are different gifts, but the one same Spirit; and there are different ministries, but the one same Lord; and there are different functions, but the one same God, Who is the cause of all of them in everyone. To each individual the manifestation of the Spirit is given for the common good. To one the Spirit imparts the expression of wisdom; to another the same Spirit imparts the expression of knowledge. By the same Spirit one receives faith; by the same Spirit another is given the gift of healing, while still another gets miraculous powers. Prophecy is given to one, to another ability to distinguish one spirit from another. One gets the gift of tongues, another that of interpreting the tongues. But the one and the same Spirit produces all of these gifts, distributing them to each one just as He wills. ↓

GRADUAL Ps. 16, 8. 2 [Guard Me]

Keep me, O Lord, as the apple of Your eye; *
   hide me in the shadow of Your wings. *
From You let judgment come; *
   Your eyes behold what is right.

Alleluia, alleluia. * Ps. 64, 2 [Debt of Praise]

To You we owe our hymn of praise, *
   O God, in Sion; *
   to You must vows be fulfilled in Jerusalem.
   Alleluia.

→ *Prayer before the Gospel, p. 16.*

GOSPEL Luke 18, 9-14 [Good in the Eyes of God]

At that time Jesus spoke this parable, addressed to those who believed in their own righteousness and held everyone else in contempt. "Two men went up to the Temple to pray; one was a Pharisee, the other a tax-gatherer. The Pharisee stood forward and prayed as follows: 'I give You thanks, God, that I am not like the rest of men, grasping, unjust, adulterous, or even like this tax-gatherer.

I fast twice weekly; I tithe all that I possess.' The tax-gatherer, however, kept his distance and would not dare to raise his eyes to heaven, but beat his breast, saying, "O God, be merciful to me, a sinner.' I tell you, this man went home from the Temple justified, but not the other. For everyone who exalts himself will be humbled, and he who humbles himself will be exalted." ➤ *Creed, p.* 18.

OFFERTORY   Ps. 24, 1-3   [Patient Prayer]

To You I lift up my soul, O Lord. *
In You, O my God, I trust; *
 let me not be put to shame, *
 let not my enemies exult over me. *
No one who waits for You shall be put to shame.

➤ *Offertory Prayers, p.* 21.

SECRET   [A Pleasing Sacrifice]

Let the sacred gifts be offered to You, O Lord, Who have given them to be presented for the honor of Your Name, for in them You have given us a remedy for all our ills. Through our Lord, etc. People: **Amen.** ➤ *Preface, p.* 26.

COMMUNION   Ps. 50, 21   [Appeasing Sacrifice]

You shall be pleased with due sacrifices, *
 burnt offerings and holocausts *
 on Your altar, O Lord.

POSTCOMMUNION   [Aid for Partakers]

We beseech You, O Lord our God, that in Your mercy You will not withhold Your help from those whom You constantly restore with divine sacraments. Through our Lord, etc. People: **Amen.** ➤ *Dismissal, p.* 42.

"Ephphatha!" *(that is, "Be opened")*.

11th SUNDAY AFTER PENTECOST

THOUGHT FOR TODAY: If we did not take so many things as a matter of course, we would marvel at the beauty of our Religion, and we could speak intelligently about our religious belief to others.

BIBLE AND LITURGY: What Christ did to the deaf and dumb man, the priest did to us on the day of our Baptism, also saying: "Ephphatha!" (that is, "Be opened"). We should pray always to have an openminded willingness for God, Who approaches us with His favors. St. Paul did so finally, and became a great saint. READ: Deut. 32, 1-14; Gen. 1 and Acts 17, 22-34; 1 Tim. 6, 11-16; Titus 2, 11-15; Matt. 22, 1-14.

INTROIT   Ps. 67, 6. 7. 36. 2   [*God Brings Unity*]

God is in His holy dwelling, *
  God Who makes men of one mind to dwell in a house; *
  He shall give power and strength to His people. *

(Ps.) God arises; His enemies are scattered, *
  and those who hate Him flee before Him. *

Glory be to the Father, etc.

God is in His holy dwelling, *
   **God Who makes men of one mind to dwell
   in a house;** *
**He shall give power and strength to His
   people.**

→ *Kyrie and Gloria, pp. 13-14.*

PRAYER   [*Grant Our Secret Desires*]

*Almighty, eternal God, Who in the abun-
dance of Your love always grant more than
Your humble petitioners deserve, and even more
than they desire, pour forth Your mercy upon
us that You may forgive whatever our conscience dreads, and give in addition what our
prayer does not venture to ask. Through our
Lord, etc.* People: **Amen.** ↓

EPISTLE   1 Cor. 15, 1-10   [*Events of Salvation*]

Brethren: I want to remind you of the gospel
that I preached to you, which you welcomed and in which you are standing firm. By
it you are even now being saved, if you are
holding on to it just as I preached it to you—
unless you have believed in vain. I handed on
to you first of all what I myself received, namely, that Christ died for our sins in accordance
with the Scriptures; that He was buried and, in
accordance with the Scriptures, rose on the
third day; that He was seen by Cephas, then by
the Twelve. After that He was seen by more
than five hundred brethren at the same time,
most of whom are still alive, although some
have fallen asleep. Then He was seen by James,
then by all the apostles. And last of all He

showed Himself to me, to one strangely born into the apostolic family. Indeed, I am the least of all the apostles. I do not deserve the name "apostle," because I persecuted the Church of God. But by God's favor I am what I am, and His favor to me has not proved fruitless. ✟

GRADUAL   Ps. 27, 7. 1   [Exult in Trust]

In God my heart trusts, and I find help; *
   then my heart exults, and with my song I give
      Him thanks. *
To You, O Lord, I call; *
   O my God, be not deaf to me; *
   depart not from me.

Alleluia, alleluia. *   Ps. 80, 2. 3   [Sing with Joy]
Sing joyfully to God our strength; *
   acclaim the God of Jacob. *
   Take up a pleasant psalm with the harp. Al-
      leluia.

➔ *Prayer before the Gospel, p. 16.*

GOSPEL   Mark 7, 31-37   [Hearing the Truth]

At that time, Jesus left Tyrian territory and returned via Sidon to the sea of Galilee, into the district of the Ten Cities. And some people brought Him a deaf man with a speech impediment, and begged Him to lay His hand upon Him. So He took him off by himself, away from the crowd. He put His fingers into his ears and spitting, touched his tongue; then He looked up to heaven, and groaned, saying to him, "Ephphatha!" (that is, "Be opened"). At once his ears were opened, and the knot in his tongue was untied, and he began to speak plainly. Then He strictly enjoined them not to tell anyone. But the more He ordered them not to, all the more they proclaimed it; and their amazement knew no bounds: "All He has accomplished is wonderful! He even gives hearing to the deaf, speech to the mute." ➤ *Creed, p.* 18.

OFFERTORY   Ps. 29, 2-3   [*Prayer Answered*]

I will extol You, O Lord, for You drew me clear *
   and did not let my enemies rejoice over me; *
O Lord, I cried out to You *
   and You healed me.

➤ *Offertory Prayers, p.* 21.

SECRET   [*Strength from God*]

Look with mercy, we beseech You, O Lord, upon our act of worship that the gift we offer may be acceptable to You and may support us in our frailty. Through our Lord, etc. People: **Amen.** ➤ *Preface, p.* 26.

COMMUNION   Prov. 3, 9-10   [*Offer Sacrifice*]

Honor the Lord with your wealth, *
   with first fruits of all your produce. *
Then will your barns be filled with grain, *
   with new wine your vats will overflow.

POSTCOMMUNION   [*Support of Mind and Body*]

By receiving Your sacrament, O Lord, may we experience Your help in mind and body, that being cured in both, we may glory in the full effect of the heavenly remedy. Through our Lord, etc. People: **Amen.** ➤ *Dismissal, p.* 42.

*The Good Samaritan "bound up his wounds,
applying oil and wine."*

12th SUNDAY AFTER PENTECOST

THOUGHT FOR TODAY: "Happy are the eyes which see what you are seeing." Assisting at Mass, we see the re-presentation and continuation of the Sacrifice on Calvary. We see with the eyes of Faith, Christ present in the Consecrated Host. Personally and actively to participate in the Mass makes us love God, and increases in us a spirit of kindness in dealing with others.

BIBLE AND LITURGY: Christ teaches us through His Church to love our neighbor regardless of race or color. And a Catholic who does not have the courage to translate the words "charity" and "love" into "justice" is a hypocrite, just as so many so-called Christians who try to prove segregation from the Bible. READ: 4 Kgs. 17, 1-6 and 24-28; John 4, 1-45 (esp. 9); Luke 10, 30-37 (*Ep.*); Num. 12, 1-16; Philemon (esp. 15-17); Gal 3, 27-28.

INTROIT   Ps. 69, 2-3. 4   [*Conquer My Foes*]

Deign, O God, to rescue me; *

> **O Lord, make haste to help me. ***

Let them be put to shame and confounded *

> **who seek my life. ***

(Ps.) **Let them be turned back in disgrace** *
   who desire my ruin. *

Glory be to the Father, etc.

Deign, O God, to rescue me; *
   O Lord, make haste to help me. *
Let them be put to shame and confounded *
   who seek my life.

➔ *Kyrie and Gloria, pp. 13-14.*

PRAYER   [God the Magnet]

*Almighty and merciful God, by Whose grace
Your faithful people serve You worthily and
righteously, grant, we beseech You, that we
may hasten without stumbling to those things
You have promised us. Through our Lord, etc.*
People: **Amen.** ↓

EPISTLE   2 Cor. 3, 4-9   [Fulfillment in the New Law]

Brethren: It is through Christ that we have
such great confidence in our relations with
God. Not that we are self-sufficient and can
take personal credit for anything. But our ca-
pability is from God, Who has made us qualified
ministers of the new covenant; not of the letter,
but of the Spirit. For the letter kills, but the
Spirit gives life. Now if the ministry of death,
carved in writing on stone, was inaugurated
with such glory that the Israelites could not
look steadily at Moses' face, because of the
glory that shone on it, even though it was a
fading glory; how much greater glory will not
the ministry of the Spirit have? For if the

ministry of condemnation had glory, much greater will be the glory of the ministry of justification. ⌄

GRADUAL   Ps. 33, 2. 3   [*Bless the Lord Always*]

I will bless the Lord at all times; *
>   His praise shall be ever in my mouth. *
Let my soul glory in the Lord; *
>   the lowly will hear and be glad.

Alleluia, alleluia. *   Ps. 87, 2   [*Call upon God*]
O Lord, the God of my salvation, by day I cry out, *
>   at night I clamor in Your presence. Alleluia.

➤ *Prayer before the Gospel, p.* 16.

GOSPEL   Luke 10, 23-37   [*The Fundamental Law*]

At that time Jesus said to His disciples: "Happy are the eyes which see what you are seeing. I tell you, many prophets and kings wished to see what you see and have not seen it, and to hear what you hear and have not heard it."

Then a certain lawyer stood up to pose this problem to Him: "Master, what must I do to inherit eternal life?" Jesus answered him: "What is written in the Law? How do you interpret it?" He replied:

" 'You shall love the Lord your God
>   with all your heart,
>   with all your soul,
>   with all your strength,

and with all your mind,
and your neighbor as yourself.' "

Jesus said to him: "You have answered rightly. Do this and you will live." But he, wishing to justify himself, said to Jesus: "And who is my neighbor?" Jesus replied: "A man was going down from Jerusalem to Jericho, and he fell into the hands of robbers who stripped him, beat him, and went off leaving him half dead. A priest happened to be going down the same road; he saw him but passed on. Likewise a Levite also came the same way, saw him, and passed on. But a Samaritan who was on his way came upon him, and was moved to pity at the sight. He went to him and bound up his wounds, applying oil and wine as an ointment. Then he hoisted him on his own beast, brought him to an inn, and took care of him. Next day he took out two silver pieces, and gave them to the innkeeper, saying: 'Take care of him, and if you spend anymore I will reimburse you on my return.' Which of these three in your opinion was neighbor to the man who fell into the hands of the robbers?" He answered Him: "The one who treated him with compassion." Jesus said to him: "Go and act like him."

➤ *Creed, p.* 18.

OFFERTORY   Ex. 32, 11. 13. 14   [*Mediator*]

Moses prayed in the sight of the Lord his God, and said, *
  "Why, O Lord, is Your indignation enkindled against Your people? *
Let the anger of Your mind cease; *

remember Abraham, Isaac, and Jacob, *
to whom You swore to give a land flowing
with milk and honey." *
And the Lord was appeased from doing the evil *
which He had spoken of doing against His
people.

➤ *Offertory Prayers, p.* 21.

SECRET [*Honor to God*]

*O Lord, we beseech You, graciously look upon
the offerings which we lay upon Your sacred
altar; so that they may bring us plentiful forgiveness while they give honor to Your Name.
Through our Lord, etc.* People: **Amen.**

➤ *Preface, p.* 26.

COMMUNION Ps. 103, 13. 14. 15 [*God's Favors*]

The earth is replete *
with the fruit of Your works, O Lord; *
You produce bread from the earth, *
and wine to gladden men's hearts, *
So that their faces gleam with oil, *
and bread fortifies the hearts of men.

POSTCOMMUNION [*Pardon through Participation*]

*May the holy reception of this sacrament, we
beseech You, O Lord, restore us to life, and
bestow upon us forgiveness and protection.
Through our Lord, etc.* People: **Amen.**

➤ *Dismissal, p.* 42.

"Stand up . . . your Faith has saved you."

13th SUNDAY AFTER PENTECOST

THOUGHT FOR TODAY: Ten lepers were "made clean." Only one returned to give thanks and glory to God. We send many petitions to heaven, but we often forget our prayers of thanksgiving. A grateful soul may always hope for more and greater blessings.

BIBLE AND LITURGY: We should be thankful for the tremendous favors God has bestowed upon us. The best way to thank God is to join often in the Great Prayer of Thanksgiving and Adoration, which is the very core of the Mass. READ: Num. 15, 13-21; Deut. 4, 9-14 (esp. 9); Acts 4, 23-31; Eph. 5, 1-20 (esp. 19); Phil. 4, 4-9; Matt. 26, 26-29 (esp. 27); Ps. 117.

INTROIT   Ps. 73, 20. 19. 23. 1   [*Be Not Angry, Lord*]

Look to Your covenant, O Lord, *
   forsake not forever the lives of Your afflicted
     ones. *

Arise, O Lord; defend Your cause; *
   be not unmindful of the voices of those who
     ask You.

(Ps.) Why, O God, have You cast us off forever? *
Why does Your anger smolder against the sheep
     of Your pasture? *

Glory be to the Father, etc.

Look to Your covenant, O Lord, *
   **forsake not forever the lives of Your afflicted
      ones.** *

Arise, O Lord; defend Your cause; *
   **be not unmindful of the voices of those who
      ask You.**

➔ *Kyrie and Gloria, pp. 13-14.*

PRAYER   [*Love for God's Command*]

*Almighty, eternal God, grant us an increase of
faith, hope and charity; and make us love what
You command so that we may be made worthy
to attain what You promise. Through our Lord,
etc.* People: **Amen.** ↓

EPISTLE   Gal. 3, 16-22   [*Preparation for Sonship*]

Brethren: The promises were spoken to Abraham "and to his offspring." It is not said:
"and to his offsprings," as applicable to many,
but in a way applicable to one only: "and to
your offspring," that is, Christ. I make a further
point: a covenant formally ratified by God is not
set aside as no longer valid by the Law that
came into being four hundred and thirty years
later, so as to render the Promise null and
void. Clearly if one's inheritance comes by
virtue of the Law it is no longer conferred by
virtue of the Promise. Yet it was by way of
the Promise that God granted Abraham his
privilege.

What, then, is the relevance of the Law? It
was given as a supplement, in view of transgressions of it; it was promulgated by the help

of angels and with the services of a mediator; but it was intended to be valid only until that Offspring came to whom the Promise had been given. Now there can be no mediator when only one person acts, and God is only one. Then is the Law in opposition to God's promises? Impossible! Obviously, if the Law which was given were such as could itself give life, justice would in reality be a consequence of the Law. But in fact Scripture has locked in all things under the restraining force of sin, so that the Promise might be given to those who believe, as a fruit of faith in Jesus Christ. ⋎

GRADUAL   Ps. 73, 20. 19. 22   [Remember Us, Lord]

Look to Your covenant, O Lord, *
   **be not unmindful of the lives of Your afflicted
      ones. ***
Arise, O Lord; defend Your cause; *
   remember the reproach of Your servants.

Alleluia, alleluia. *   Ps. 89, 1   [Ever the Refuge]
Lord, You have been our refuge *
   through all generations. Alleluia.

➔ *Prayer before the Gospel, p. 16.*

GOSPEL   Luke 17, 11-19   [Saving Faith]

At that time on His journey to Jerusalem, Jesus passed along the border of Samaria and Galilee. As He entered a village ten lepers went to meet Him. Keeping their distance they raised their voices and said: "Jesus, Master, have pity on us." When He saw them He said, "Go and show yourselves to the priests." And on their way they were made clean. One of them realizing that he had been made clean, returned praising God in a loud voice. He threw himself face down at the feet of Jesus, thanking Him. And this man was a Samaritan.

Jesus' comment was: "Were not ten of them made clean? Where are the other nine? Was no one found to return and give glory to God except this stranger?" And He said to the man, "Stand up, and go your way; your faith has saved you." ➤ *Creed, p. 18.*

OFFERTORY   Ps. 30, 15. 16   [We Belong to God]

My trust is in You, O Lord; *
  I say, "You are my God."* *
  In Your hands is my destiny.

➤ *Offertory Prayers, p. 21.*

SECRET   [Grant Our Petitions]

Look with favor upon Your people, O Lord; look with favor upon their gifts; so that, appeased by this offering, You will grant us pardon and give us what we ask. Through our Lord, etc. People: **Amen.** ➤ *Preface, p. 26.*

COMMUNION   Wis. 16, 20   [Food from Heaven]

You have given us, O Lord, bread from heaven, *
  endowed with all delights *
  and the sweetness of every taste.

POSTCOMMUNION [Eternal Life through Sacrifice]

Having received Your heavenly sacrament, O Lord, may we make progress, we beseech You, toward our everlasting salvation. Through our Lord, etc. People: **Amen.** ➤ *Dismissal, p. 42.*

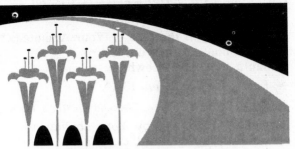

"Learn a lesson from the way the wild lilies grow."

14th SUNDAY AFTER PENTECOST

THOUGHT FOR TODAY: We of "weak Faith" attend with such anxiety to our temporal affairs that we neglect our religious duties. If we seek the supernatural first, we may confidently rely on God's help in our daily affairs.

BIBLE AND LITURGY: A Christian must try so to pass through temporal things, as not to lose those which are eternal. Trying to make a living or finding a way out of trouble should never absorb us so much that we forget God and lose our confidence in Him. We should be known by the fruits of the Spirit we bear! (*Ep.*) READ: Pss. 26; 45; 124; Jer. 17, 5-8; Sir. 11, 20-28.

INTROIT   Ps. 83, 10. 11. 2. 3   [*Courts of the Lord*]

Behold, O God, our Protector, *
   and look upon the face of Your Anointed. *
Better is one day in Your courts *
   than a thousand elsewhere. *

(Ps.) How lovely is Your dwelling place, *
   O Lord of hosts! *
My soul yearns and pines *
   for the courts of the Lord. *

Glory be to the Father, etc.

Behold, O God, our Protector, *
   and look upon the face of Your Anointed. *
Better is one day in Your courts *
   than a thousand elsewhere.

➔ *Kyrie and Gloria, pp.* 13-14.

PRAYER   [*Depend on God's Power*]

Protect Your Church by Your abiding mercy, we beseech You, O Lord, and since all mortals fall without You, may Your help keep them from danger and guide them to salvation. Through our Lord, etc. People: **Amen.** ↓

EPISTLE   Gal. 5, 16-24   [*Flesh and Spirit Compared*]

Brethren: Act according to the spirit; then you will not carry out the desires of the flesh. The desires of the flesh are against the spirit, and those of the spirit are against the flesh; these two are directly opposed to one another. That is why you do not carry out what your will intends. But if you are led by the Spirit, you are not under the Law. Now it is obvious what proceeds from the flesh: fornication, impurity, indecency, idolatry, sorcery, hatreds, contentiousness, jealousy, outbursts of rage, rivalries, dissensions, factions, envy, drunkenness, orgies of debauchery, and the like. I warn you, as I have warned you before: those who do such things will not inherit the kingdom of God! But the fruit of the Spirit is love, joy, peace, patient endurance, kindness, goodness, faith, mildness, self-control. Against such there is no law! Now those who belong to Christ Jesus have crucified their flesh with its passions and desires. ↓

GRADUAL   Ps. 117, 8. 9   [*Trust Not in Man*]

It is better to take refuge in the Lord *
    than to trust in man. *
It is better to take refuge in the Lord *
    than to trust in princes.

Alleluia, alleluia. *   Ps. 94, 1   [*God of Salvation*]

Come, let us sing joyfully to the Lord; *
    let us acclaim the God of our salvation.
    Alleluia.

➔ *Prayer before the Gospel, p. 16.*

GOSPEL Matt. 6, 24-33 [*Confidence in the Lord of Life*]

At that time Jesus said to His disciples: "No man can serve two masters. He will either hate one and love the other, or be attentive to one and despise the other. You cannot devote yourself to God and to money. So I warn you, do not worry about your livelihood, about what you are to eat, or what you are to drink, or how you are to clothe yourselves. Is not life more important than food? Is not the body more important than clothes? Take a look at the birds in the sky: they do not sow; they do not reap; they gather nothing into barns. Yet your heavenly Father feeds them. Aren't you more important than they? Still, which of you by worrying can add a single moment to his allotted span of life? And as for clothes, what are you worrying about? Learn a lesson from the way the wild lilies grow. They do not toil; they do not spin thread. Yet I assure you, not even Solomon in his royal robes was arrayed like one of them. If God can so deck out the wild flowers which bloom today but tomorrow are thrown into the oven, is He not much more likely to provide for you? What weak faith you have! Stop worrying then over questions like 'What are we to eat?' 'What are we to drink?' 'What are we to wear?' That is what pagans are always looking for. Your heavenly Father realizes that you need all this sort of thing. Seek first His kingdom and His will, and everything else will be given to you." ➤ *Creed, p.* 18.

OFFERTORY Ps. 33, 8. 9   [Protection by Angels]

The Angel of the Lord encamps *
   around those who fear Him, and delivers them. *
Taste and see *
   how good the Lord is.

➤ *Offertory Prayers, p.* 21.

SECRET   [Restrain God's Arm]

Grant us, Lord, we beseech You, that this salutary sacrifice may be not only a cleansing from our sins but also a propitiation of Your divine power. Through our Lord, etc. People: **Amen.** ➤ *Preface, p.* 26.

COMMUNION Matt. 6, 33   [Kingdom of God First]

"Seek first the Kingdom of God; *
   and all things shall be given you besides," *
says the Lord.

POSTCOMMUNION   [Purify and Protect]

May Your sacrament, O God, ever cleanse and strengthen us, and bring us to everlasting salvation. Through our Lord, etc. People: **Amen.**

➤ *Dismissal, p.* 42.

"The dead man sat up and began to speak."

15th SUNDAY AFTER PENTECOST

THOUGHT FOR TODAY: Physical and spiritual health are not always found together. If your conscience tells you that you are spiritually dead, do not delay to arise in sincere confession. Life is too short to be wasted. "A man will surely reap whatever he sows," life or death.

BIBLE AND LITURGY: Christian tradition sees in the mother of Naim another Mother, who weeps over the spiritual death of so many of her children. Holy Mother Church prays constantly for those children and keeps urging them to repent. READ: Mark 2, 1-10; Isa. 1, 1-31 (esp. 18); Jer. 9; Phil. 3, 17-21; James 5, 13-18.

INTROIT   Ps. 85, 1. 2. 3. 4   [*Hear My Prayer*]

Incline Your ear, O Lord; answer me; *
  save Your servant, O my God, who trusts in
    You. *
Have pity on me, O Lord, *
  for to You I call all the day. *
(Ps.) Gladden the soul of Your servant, *
  for to You, O Lord, I lift up my soul. *
Glory be to the Father, etc.

Incline Your ear, O Lord; answer me; *
  save Your servant, O my God, who trusts in
    You. *
Have pity on me, O Lord, *
  for to You I call all the day.

> → *Kyrie and Gloria, pp.* 13-14.

PRAYER   [Govern Your Church]

*May Your abiding mercy, O Lord, cleanse and
strengthen Your Church, and, since without You
she cannot exist in safety, let her be ever guided
by Your grace. Through our Lord, etc.* People:
Amen. ↓

EPISTLE   Gal. 5, 25-26; 6, 1-10   [Mutual Love]

Brethren: Since we live by the Spirit, let us in
fact follow the Spirit's lead. Let us never
be boastful, a source of provocation to others,
or jealous of one another. My brothers, if a
person is overtaken by some sin, you who are
spiritual should set him right in a spirit of mildness, looking to yourself to avoid also falling
into temptation. Help carry one another's burdens, and in that way fulfill the law of Christ.
If anyone thinks he is something, when he is
really nothing, he is deceiving himself. Each one
should examine his own conduct, and thus if
he has reason to boast of anything, it will be
on his own account, not on another's, and each
one will bear his own responsibility. He who
is instructed in the word should share with his
instructor all his goods. Make no mistake about
it: God is not made a fool of! A man will surely

reap whatever he sows. If he sows in the field of flesh, he will reap from it a harvest of corruption. But if his seed-ground is the spirit, from the spirit he will reap everlasting life. Let us not grow weary of doing good, for, if we do not relax our efforts, in due time we shall reap our harvest. So while we have the opportunity, let us do good to all men, but especially to those who belong to the household of the faith. ↓

GRADUAL   Ps. 91, 2. 3   [Thanks]

It is good to give thanks to the Lord, *
  to sing to Your Name, Most High. *
To proclaim Your kindness at dawn *
  and Your faithfulness throughout the night.

Alleluia, alleluia. *   Ps. 94, 3   [Great Is the Lord]
For the Lord is a great God, *
  and a great King over all the earth. Alleluia.

➔ *Prayer before the Gospel, p.* 16.

GOSPEL   Luke 7, 11-16   [The Dead Live]

At that time Jesus went to a town called Naim; His disciples and a large crowd accompanied Him. As He approached the gate of the town a man who had died was being carried out, an only son of a widowed mother; and a good-sized crowd of townsfolk were with her. And the Lord, seeing her, was moved with pity for her and said to her: "Do not lament." Then He stepped forward and touched the stretcher, and the bearers halted. And He said: "Young man, I bid you rise up." The dead man sat up and began to speak. Then Jesus gave him back to his mother. Fear seized them all and they began to praise God. "A great prophet," they said, "has risen among us," and "God has visited His people."

➤ *Creed, p. 18.*

OFFERTORY   Ps. 39, 2. 3. 4   [God Hears Me]

I have waited, waited for the Lord; *
  and He stooped toward me and heard my cry. *
And He put a new song into my mouth, *
  a hymn to our God.

➤ *Offertory Prayers, p. 21.*

SECRET   [Protection from Satan]

May Your sacrament, O Lord, always keep us and guard us from the assaults of the devil. Through our Lord, etc. People: **Amen.**

➤ *Preface, p. 26.*

COMMUNION   John 6, 52   [Heavenly Food]
The bread that I will give *
  is My Flesh for the life of the world.

POSTCOMMUNION   [Effects of the Sacrifice]

May the working of the heavenly gift, O Lord, so possess us, mind and body, that the action of the sacrament, rather than our senses, may continually prevail in us. Through our Lord, etc. People: **Amen.**

➤ *Dismissal, p. 42.*

"Everyone who exalts himself shall be humbled . . ."

16th SUNDAY AFTER PENTECOST

THOUGHT FOR TODAY: The supernatural life which we receive in Baptism is like a seed that must be developed. With love the root and foundation of our lives, we pray that God may increase our Faith and hope, and that His grace may stir up in us zeal for good works.

BIBLE AND LITURGY: Human nature will constantly try to seduce us to pride and selfishness. Only when love is the root and foundation of our lives can we avoid it. "Love . . . does not put on airs" (1 Cor. 13, 4). **READ:** Tob. 4, 1-23 (esp. 14); 1 Cor. 13, 1-13; Sir. 10, 6-30; 1 Pet. 5, 5-7; James 4, 11-17.

INTROIT Ps. 85, 3. 5. 1 [*Have Pity*]

Have pity on me, O Lord, *
   for to You I call all the day; *
For You, O Lord, are good and forgiving, *
   abounding in kindness to all who call upon
   You. *

(Ps.) Incline Your ear, O Lord; answer me, *
   for I am afflicted and poor. *

Glory be to the Father, etc.

Have pity on me O Lord, *
   for to You I call all the day; *
For You, O Lord, are good and forgiving, *
   **abounding in kindness to all who call upon
   You.**

➤ *Kyrie and Gloria, pp.* 13-14.

PRAYER   [Good Works]

*May Your grace, we beseech You, O Lord, ever
go before us and follow us, and may it make
us ever intent upon good works. Through our
Lord, etc.* People: **Amen.** ↓

EPISTLE   Eph. 3, 13-21   [Christ Dwelling in Us]

Brethren: I beg you not to be disheartened by
the trials I endure for you; they are your
glory. For this reason I kneel before the Father
from Whom every family in heaven and on
earth takes its name; and I pray that He will
bestow on you gifts corresponding to the richness of His glory. May He strengthen your inner
selves with power through His Spirit. May
Christ dwell in your hearts through faith; and
may love be the root and foundation of your
life. Thus you will be able to grasp fully with
all the saints the breadth and length and height
and depth, and to know that the love of Christ
surpasses all knowledge, so that you will be
filled with all the fullness of God. To Him
Whose power now at work within us is able
to do immeasurably more than all we ask or
imagine, to Him be glory in the Church and in
Christ Jesus through all generations, ages without end. Amen. ↓

GRADUAL   Ps. 101, 16-17   [All Revere the Lord]

The nations shall revere Your Name, O Lord, *
   and all the kings of the earth Your glory. *
For the Lord has rebuilt Sion; *
   and He shall appear in His glory.

Ps. 97, 1

Alleluia, alleluia. *   [God's Wondrous Works]
Sing to the Lord a new song, *
   for the Lord has done wondrous deeds.
      Alleluia.

➤ *Prayer before the Gospel, p.* 16.

GOSPEL   Luke 14, 1-11   [God Spurns the Proud]

At that time when Jesus came on a Sabbath
to eat a meal in the house of one of the
leading Pharisees, they kept Him under observa-
tion. There was a man right there in front of
Him suffering from dropsy. Jesus asked the
lawyers and the Pharisees: "Is it lawful to
cure on the Sabbath or not?" But they kept
silent. And He took the man, healed him, and
sent him away. Then He addressed Himself to
them, saying: "If one of you has a son or an
ox and it falls into a well, will he not immediately retrieve it on the Sabbath day?" This
they were incapable of answering. He then
addressed a parable to the guests, noticing
how they were trying to get the places of
honor at table: "When you are invited by someone to a wedding do not sit in the place of
honor lest some greater dignitary has also been
invited by the host, who will come to you and
say: 'This place is for this man.' And then,
shame-faced, you will proceed to take the low-

est place. On the contrary, when you have been invited, go and sit in the lowest place so that when your host comes to you he will say: 'My friend, come up higher.' Then you will win the esteem of all those at table with you. For everyone who exalts himself shall be humbled, and he who humbles himself, shall be exalted."

➤ *Creed, p.* 18.

OFFERTORY   Ps. 39, 14. 15   [Rescue Me]

Deign, O Lord, to rescue me; *
Let all be put to shame and confusion *
  who seek to snatch away my life. *
Deign, O Lord, to rescue me.

➤ *Offertory Prayers, p.* 21.

SECRET   [Make Us Worthy]

Cleanse us by this sacrifice, we beseech You, O Lord, and by the workings of Your mercy, make us worthy to receive it. Through our Lord, etc. People: **Amen.** ➤ *Preface, p.* 26.

COMMUNION   Ps. 70, 16. 17. 18   [In God's Keeping]

O Lord, I will tell of Your singular justice; *
  O God, You have taught me from my youth; *
And now that I am old and gray, *
  O God, forsake me not.

POSTCOMMUNION   [Restore Even-Our Bodies]

O Lord, we beseech You, graciously cleanse and renew our minds with the heavenly sacrament, so we may thereby also receive bodily help for the present as well as for the future. Through our Lord, etc. People: **Amen.** ➤ *Dismissal, p.* 42.

'You shall love your neighbor as yourself.'

17th SUNDAY AFTER PENTECOST

THOUGHT FOR TODAY: We all have "one Lord, one Faith, one Baptism; one God and Father of all." This supernatural unity encourages us to "avoid the temptations of the devil," and to perform works of charity. By the grace of the sacraments we curb our passions that they may not separate us from our holy union in the Mystical Body of Christ.

BIBLE AND LITURGY: Again charity is emphasized as basic in the Christian Religion. READ: Prov. 10, 12; 1 Cor. 13, 1-13; Gen. 13, 1-13; 1 Kgs. 18, 1-16; 19, 1-7; 20, 1-43; 23, 16-18; Luke 6, 27-28.

INTROIT Ps. 118, 137. 124. 1   [God's Law]

You are just, O Lord, *
   and Your ordinance is right. *
Deal with Your servant according to Your
   kindness. *
(Ps.) Happy are they whose way is blameless, *
   who walk in the law of the Lord. *
Glory be to the Father, etc.

You are just, O Lord, *
   and Your ordinance is right. *
**Deal with Your servant according to Your
   kindness.**

➔ *Kyrie and Gloria, pp. 13-14.*

PRAYER   [*Protection from the Devil*]

*Grant, we beseech You, O Lord, that Your
people may avoid the temptations of the devil,
and with pure minds follow You, the only God.
Through our Lord, etc.* People: **Amen.** ↓

EPISTLE   Eph. 4, 1-6   [*Unity in the Spirit*]

Brethren: I plead with you, I, a prisoner for
the Lord, to live a life worthy of the calling
you have received, with perfect humility and
meekness, and with patience, supporting one
another lovingly. Make every effort to preserve
the unity whose source is the Spirit and whose
bond is peace. There is but one body and one
Spirit, just as there is but one hope given you
by your call. There is but one Lord, one faith,
one baptism; one God and Father of all, Who is
over all, and works through all, and is in us
all, Who is blessed forever. Amen. ↓

GRADUAL   Ps. 32, 12. 6   [*God's People*]

Happy the nation whose God is the Lord, *
   **the people the Lord has chosen for His own
      inheritance.** *
**By the word of the Lord the heavens were
      made;** *
   by the breath of His mouth all their host.

Alleluia, alleluia. *   Ps. 101, 2   [Hear Our Prayer]
O Lord, hear my prayer, *
  and let my cry come to You. Alleluia.

➤ *Prayer before the Gospel, p.* **16.**

GOSPEL   Matt. 22, 34-46   [Law and Lawgiver]

At that time the Pharisees approached Jesus and one of them, a lawyer, in an attempt to trip Him up, asked Him, "Master, which commandment in the Law is the greatest?" So He said to him, " 'You shall love the Lord your God with all your heart, with all your soul, and with all your mind.' This is the greatest and the first commandment. And the second is similar to it, 'You shall love your neighbor as yourself.' On these two commandments, the whole Law is based, and the Prophets as well." In turn, Jesus put a question to the assembled Pharisees, "What is your opinion about the Messiah? Whose Son is He?" "David's," they answered. He said to them, "Then how is it that David, under divine inspiration, calls Him 'Lord,' as he does, 'The Lord said to my Lord, sit at My right hand until I humble your enemies beneath your feet'? If therefore David calls Him 'Lord,' how can He be his Son?" No one was able to give Him an answer, and so no one dared, from that day on, to ask Him any more questions.

➤ *Creed, p.* **18.**

OFFERTORY   Dan. 9, 17. 18. 19   [Look Down on Us]

I, Daniel, prayed to my God, saying, *
  "Hear, O Lord, the prayers of Your servant; *

Show Your face upon Your sanctuary, *
and favorably look down upon this people, *
upon whom Your Name is invoked, O God."

➤ *Offertory Prayers, p. 21.*

SECRET [Free from All Sins]

O Lord, we humbly pray Your Majesty that the holy rite which we are celebrating may free us from past and future sins. Through our Lord, etc. People: **Amen.**

➤ *Preface, p. 26.*

COMMUNION Ps. 75, 12-13 [Acclaim the Great Lord]

**Make vows to the Lord, your God, and fulfill
them;** *
  **let all round about Him bring gifts to the
terrible Lord** *
Who checks the pride of princes, *
  Who is terrible to the kings of the earth.

POSTCOMMUNION [Remedies for Vices]

By the workings of Your sanctifying power, almighty God, may our vices be cured and eternal remedies provided for us. Through our Lord, etc. People: **Amen.**

➤ *Dismissal, p. 42.*

"Stand up, pick up your mat and go home."

18th SUNDAY AFTER PENTECOST

THOUGHT FOR TODAY: "Your sins are forgiven." We also hear the identical words, "I absolve you from your sins," when after due preparation, we humbly confess our sins. Let us be grateful to God for the Sacrament of Penance and use it frequently to restore or to increase the supernatural life of our souls, which is so pleasing to Him.

BIBLE AND LITURGY: God, our Father, approaching us in Christ, is willing to forgive our human weakness over and over again, if we are sorry. Indeed, in everything we have been enriched in Him (*Ep.*). READ: Matt. 18, 21-35; Luke 15, 11-32; Matt. 16, 13-20; John 20, 19-23; Ps. 31.

INTROIT   Sir. 36, 18; Ps. 121, 1   [Peace]

**Give peace, O Lord, to those who have hoped
   in You,** *
   and let Your Prophets be proved true. *
Hear the prayers of Your servant, *
   and of Your people Israel. *

(Ps.) I rejoiced because they said to me, *
   "We will go up to the house of the Lord." *

Glory be to the Father, etc.

**Give peace, O Lord. to those who have hoped
    in You,** *
    and let Your Prophets be proved true. *
Hear the prayers of Your servant, *
    and of Your people Israel.

➜ *Kyrie and Gloria, pp. 13-14.*

PRAYER   [*Pleasing God by His Help*]

*May the working of Your mercy, we beseech
You, O Lord, guide our hearts, for without You,
we cannot please You. Through our Lord, etc.*
People: **Amen.** ⋎

EPISTLE   1 Cor. 1, 4-8   [*Witnessing Christ's Grace*]

Brethren: I keep thanking my God always for
you because of the favor which He gave
you in Christ Jesus, in Whom you have been
enriched in every way, with every gift of speech
and of knowledge. Thus the witness I bore to
Christ has been confirmed among you, and you
lack no spiritual gift as you wait for the revelation of our Lord Jesus Christ. He will strengthen
you to the end, so that you will be blameless on
the day of our Lord Jesus Christ. ⋎

GRADUAL   Ps. 121, 1. 7   [*The House of the Lord*]

I rejoiced because they said to me, *
    "We will go up to the house of the Lord." *
May peace be within your walls, *
    prosperity in your buildings.

Alleluia, alleluia. * Ps. 101, 16 [*Glory from All*]
The nations shall revere Your Name, O Lord, *
  and all the kings of the earth Your glory.
    Alleluia.

➤ *Prayer before the Gospel, p.* 16.

GOSPEL Matt. 9, 1-8 [*Proof of Forgiveness*]

A t that time Jesus got into a boat, made the
  crossing, and came back to His own town.
Just then people came bringing to Him a paralyzed man lying on a mat. When Jesus saw their
faith, He said to the paralyzed man, "Courage,
My son, your sins are forgiven." With that,
some of the scribes said to themselves, "This
fellow is blaspheming!" Aware of what they
were thinking, Jesus said, "What makes you
harbor evil thoughts in your minds? Which is
less trouble—to say, 'Your sins are forgiven,'
or to say, 'Stand up and walk'?—Now, in order
that you people may realize that the Son of
Man possesses authority on earth to forgive
sins..." Then He said to the paralyzed man:
"Stand up, pick up your mat and go home." He
stood up and went home. At the sight, a feeling
of awe came over the crowd, and they praised
God for having bestowed such authority upon
men.

➤ *Creed, p.* 18.

OFFERTORY Ex. 24, 4. 5 [*Evening Sacrifice*]
Moses consecrated an altar to the Lord, *
  offering upon it holocausts, *
  and sacrificing victims: *

He made an evening sacrifice to the Lord God *
for an odor of sweetness, *
in the sight of the Israelites.

➤ *Offertory Prayers, p. 21.*

SECRET   [Life Conforming to Truth]

O God, Who, through the gifts we have ex-
changed with You in this sacrament, have made
us partakers of the supreme Godhead, grant,
we beseech You, that, as we have knowledge of
Your truth, so we may fully live up to it.
Through our Lord, etc. People: **Amen.**

➤ *Preface, p. 26.*

COMMUNION   Ps. 95, 8. 9   [Worship]

Bring gifts and enter His courts; *
worship the Lord in His holy court.

POSTCOMMUNION   [Eucharistic Gift]

Strengthened by Your sacred gift, we thank
You, O Lord, beseeching Your mercy to make
us receive it worthily. Through our Lord, etc.
People: **Amen.**

➤ *Dismissal, p. 42.*

"For while many are called, few are chosen."

19th SUNDAY AFTER PENTECOST

THOUGHT FOR TODAY: Without the garment of sanctifying grace, we cannot enter the kingdom of heaven. To die in the state of grace is a special gift for which we must pray and which God will certainly not deny us if we keep His commandments.

BIBLE AND LITURGY: The Church teaches us to "put on that new man," keeping our baptismal robe unstained and our candle lighted till the Lord comes to His marriage feast (*Rites of Baptism*). READ: Luke 16, 19-31; Matt. 8, 10-12; Luke 13, 22-30; Apoc. 14, 6-11; 2 Thess. 1, 3-10.

INTROIT   Ps. 77, 1   [God, Our Savior]

"I am the salvation of the people," *
   says the Lord, *
"In whatever tribulation they shall cry to Me, *
   I will hear them; *
   and I will be their Lord forever." *

(Ps.) Hearken, My people, to My teaching; *
   incline your ears to the words of My mouth. *

Glory be to the Father, etc.

"I am the salvation of the people," *
   says the Lord, *
"In whatever tribulation they shall cry to Me, *
   I will hear them; *
   and I will be their Lord forever."

➤ *Kyrie and Gloria, pp. 13-14.*

PRAYER   [*God's Will with Free Hearts*]

Almighty and merciful God, graciously keep away from us all misfortune, that, unhampered in soul and body, we may perform with peaceful minds the works that are Yours. Through our Lord, etc. People: **Amen.** ↓

EPISTLE   Eph. 4, 23-28   [*Change of Heart*]

Brethren: Acquire a new, a spiritual way of thinking, and put on that new man who has been created in the image of God with the justice and holiness that come from truth. And so, renouncing falsehood, let everyone speak the truth to his neighbor, for we are members of one another. If you are angry, let it be without sin. The sun must not go down on your anger; and do not give the devil an opening. The man who has been stealing must steal no longer; rather let him work with his hands at honest toil, so as to have something to share with those who are in need. ↓

GRADUAL   Ps. 140, 2   [*Incense of Prayer*]

Let my prayer come like incense before You, O
   Lord, *
   the lifting up of my hands, like the evening
   sacrifice.

Alleluia, alleluia. *   Ps. 104, 1   [*Proclaim the Lord*]
Give thanks to the Lord, invoke His Name; *
   make known among the nations His deeds.
     Alleluia.

➔ *Prayer before the Gospel, p* 16.

GOSPEL   Matt. 22, 1-14   [*The Great Feast*]

A t that time Jesus began to address the chief
priests and the Pharisees, using parables.
"The kingdom of heaven may be compared to
the situation of a king who gave a wedding banquet for his son. He dispatched his slaves to
summon the invited guests to the wedding, but
they refused to come. A second time he dispatched other slaves saying, 'Tell those who
were invited, "Look, I have my dinner prepared;
my bullocks and cornfed cattle have been
butchered, and everything is ready. Come to
the wedding."' Some of them ignored the invitation and went their way, one to his farm,
another to his business. The rest seized his
slaves, insulted them, and killed them. Now the
king became angry, and sent his army which
destroyed those murderers and burnt their city.
Then he said to his slaves, 'The banquet is ready,
but those who were invited proved unworthy.
Therefore, go out to the country roads, and
invite to the wedding anyone you find.' So
those slaves went out on the roads and collected
all the people they found, bad as well as good,
till the wedding hall was filled with guests. But
when the king came in to meet the guests, he
caught sight of a man there who was not
properly dressed for a wedding. 'My friend,'

he said to him, 'how is it you came in here not properly dressed?' But he had nothing to say. Then the king told the attendants, 'Tie him up, hand and foot, and throw him into the darkness outside where he will wail and gnash his teeth.' —For while many are called, few are chosen."

➤ *Creed, p.* 18.

OFFERTORY Ps. 137, 7 [*The Lord Makes Us Fearless*]

Though I walk amid distress, You preserve me, O Lord; *

  against the anger of my enemies You raise Your hand;*

  Your right hand saves me.

➤ *Offertory Prayers, p.* 21.

SECRET   [*Salutary Gifts*]

Grant, we beseech You, O Lord, that these gifts which we offer in the sight of Your Majesty, may be the means of our salvation. Through our Lord, etc. People: **Amen.** ➤ *Preface, p.* 26.

COMMUNION   Ps. 118, 4-5   [*Steadfast Obedience*]

You have commanded that Your precepts *
  be diligently kept. *
Oh, that I might be firm in the ways *
  of keeping Your statutes!

POSTCOMMUNION   [*Loyal to God's Law*]

May Your healing power, O Lord, mercifully deliver us from our waywardness and make us ever keep Your commandments. Through our Lord, etc. People: **Amen.** ➤ *Dismissal, p.* 42.

"Return home; your son is going to live."

20th SUNDAY AFTER PENTECOST

THOUGHT FOR TODAY: "These are evil days." Numberless sins, committed daily on earth, cry to heaven for punishment. Let us appease God by leading a good Christian life. The holy sacraments are the medicine to "expel evil from our hearts."

BIBLE AND LITURGY: The Church deals again with Faith (i.e., the total surrender of ourselves to God, Who reveals Himself to us) and the motives for belief. Faith is a grace of God. Fulfilled prophecies and miracles help those of "weak Faith" to come to the complete surrender of mind and heart, which means "Faith" in the Biblical meaning of the word. READ: John 20, 24-29; Luke 24, 13-35 (esp. 27); Matt. 2, 1-6; 11, 7-19; Luke 1, 67-79 (esp. 70); 18, 31-43; John 20, 30-31.

INTROIT   Dan. 3, 31. 29. 35; Ps. 118, 1

[*Acknowledging Our Guilt*]

All that You have done to us, O Lord, *
   You have done in true judgment; *
Because we have sinned against You, *
   and we have not obeyed Your commandments; *
But give glory to Your Name, *
   and deal with us according to the multitude

of Your mercy. *

(Ps.) **Happy are they whose way is blameless,** *
who walk in the law of the Lord. *

Glory be to the Father, etc.

All that You have done to us, O Lord, *
You have done in true judgment; *
Because we have sinned against You, *
and we have not obeyed Your command-
ments; *
But give glory to Your Name, *
and deal with us according to the multitude
of Your mercy.

→ *Kyrie and Gloria, pp.* 13-14.

PRAYER [*Pardon and Peace*]

O Lord, we beseech You, graciously grant Your
faithful forgiveness and peace, that they may
be cleansed of all sin and serve You with minds
free from care. Through our Lord, etc. People:
Amen. ↓

EPISTLE Eph. 5, 15-21 [*Filled with the Spirit*]

Brethren: Keep careful watch over your conduct. Do not act like fools, but like wise
men make the most of every opportunity, for
these are evil days. Therefore do not be thought-
less, but know how to discern the will of the
Lord. Do not get drunk on wine, for that leads
to debauchery. But be filled with the Spirit,
expressing yourselves in psalms, hymns and
inspired songs, singing and praising the Lord
with all your heart. Give thanks to God the
Father always and for everything in the name
of our Lord Jesus Christ. Defer to one another,
out of reverence for Christ. ↓

GRADUAL   Ps. 144, 15-16   [*Hopeful Eyes*]

The eyes of all look hopefully to You, O Lord, *
  and You give them their food in due season. *
You open Your hand *
  and satisfy the desire of every living thing.

Alleluia, alleluia. *   Ps. 107, 2   [*Steady of Heart*]

My heart is steadfast, O God; my heart is
  steadfast; *
  I will sing and chant praise to You, my glory.
  Alleluia.

➤ *Prayer before the Gospel, p.* 16.

GOSPEL   John 4, 46-53

[*Full Confidence in Christ's Word*]

At that time there was at Capharnaum a royal
official whose son was ill. When he heard
that Jesus had come back from Judea to Galilee,
he went to Him and begged Him to come down
and restore the health of his son who was
near death. Jesus replied, "Unless you people
can see signs and wonders, you will not believe."
"Sir," the royal official pleaded with Him, "come
down before my little boy dies." Jesus told him,
"Return home; your son is going to live." The
man put his trust in the word Jesus had spoken
to him and started for home. And when he was
already on his way back, his servants met him
with the message that his boy was going to live.
When he asked them at what time he had shown
improvement, they told him, "The fever left him
yesterday afternoon about one." Now it was at
that very hour, the father realized, that Jesus

had told him, "Your son is going to live." And he believed and his whole household along with him.

➤ *Creed, p.* 18.

OFFERTORY   Ps. 136, 1   [*Tears for the Fatherland*]

By the streams of Babylon *
we sat and wept *
when we remembered you, O Sion.

➤ *Offertory Prayers, p.* 21.

SECRET   [*Heavenly Remedies*]

May these sacramental rites, O Lord, we beseech You, be our heavenly medicine and expel evil from our hearts. Through our Lord, etc.
People: **Amen.**

➤ *Preface, p.* 26.

COMMUNION   Ps. 118, 49. 50

[*Hope in God's Promises*]

Remember Your word to Your servant, O Lord, *
since You have given me hope. *
This is my comfort in my affliction.

POSTCOMMUNION   [*Worthy by Obedience*]

That we may be made worthy, O Lord, of Your sacred gifts, make us, we beseech You, ever obedient to Your commandments. Through our Lord, etc. People: **Amen.**

➤ *Dismissal, p.* 42.

"My kingdom does not belong to this world."

FEAST OF CHRIST THE KING

THOUGHT FOR TODAY: Jesus came to establish a kingdom of justice and holiness for our will, a kingdom of love and peace for our heart. If we follow Him, He will lead us into His eternal kingdom.

BIBLE AND LITURGY: At the very moment of His incarnation, Christ (i.e., the Anointed One) was anointed by His Father as Eternal High Priest and King. The Church honors today Christ, our King, and His Kingdom, i.e., a spiritualized Israel, the Church. READ: 2 Kgs. 5, 1-5; Luke 1, 30-33; Matt. 21, 1-9; John 6, 14-15; 18, 33-37 (*Gosp.*); Matt 16, 18-19; Heb. 1, 1-14.

INTROIT Apoc. 5, 12; 1, 6; Ps. 71, 1   [*Glory to the King*]

Worthy is the Lamb Who was slain *
   to receive power, and divinity, *
   and wisdom, and strength, and honor. *
To Him belong glory and dominion *
   forever and ever. *

(Ps.) **O God, with Your judgment endow the King,** *
   and with Your justice, the King's son. *
Glory be to the Father, etc.

- 301 -

Worthy is the Lamb Who was slain *
  to receive power, and divinity, *
  and wisdom, and strength, and honor. *
To Him belong glory and dominion *
  forever and ever.

➔ *Kyrie and Gloria, pp. 13-14.*

PRAYER   [*Union in Christ the King*]

Almighty and eternal God, Who willed to restore all things in Your beloved Son, the King of the Universe, graciously grant that the peoples of the earth torn asunder by the wound of sin, may submit to His most gentle rule. Who with You lives, etc. People: **Amen.** ↓

EPISTLE   Col. 1, 12-20 [*Full Power of Christ the King*]

Brethren: Give thanks to the Father for making you worthy to share the lot of the saints in light. For He rescued us from the power of darkness and brought us into the kingdom of His beloved Son, through Whom we have redemption, and the forgiveness of our sins. He is the image of the invisible God, the firstborn of all creatures; for in Him everything was created in heaven and on earth, things visible and invisible, whether Thrones, or Dominations, or Principalities, or Powers; they were all created through Him and for Him. He is before all things, and in Him all things hold together. And He is head of the body, the Church; He is the beginning, the firstborn of the dead, that He may hold first place in everything. For God was pleased to have all fullness abide in Him and through Him to reconcile for Himself all things, making peace through His blood shed on the cross—all things, I say, both on earth and in heaven, in Christ Jesus, our Lord. ↓

GRADUAL   Ps. 71, 8. 11   [*The Ruler*]

He shall rule from sea to sea, *
  and from the River to the ends of the earth. *
All kings shall pay Him homage, *
  all nations shall serve Him.

Alleluia, alleluia. * Dan. 7, 14   [*Everlasting Reign*]
His dominion is an everlasting dominion *
  that shall not be taken away, *
  and His kingdom shall not be destroyed.
  Alleluia.

➤ *Prayer before the Gospel, p. 16.*

GOSPEL   John 18, 33-37   [*Christ's Kingdom*]

At that time Pilate said to Jesus: "Are You the King of the Jews?" Jesus answered, "Are you saying this on your own, or have others been telling you about Me?" "I'm no Jew, am I?" Pilate retorted. "It is Your own nation and the chief priests who handed You over to me. What have You done?" Jesus answered, "My kingdom does not belong to this world. If My kingdom belonged to this world, My subjects would be fighting to save Me from being handed over to the Jews. But, as it is, My kingdom does not belong here." At this, Pilate said to Him, "So then, You are a King?" Jesus replied, "You say that I am a King. The reason why I have been born, the reason I have come into the world, is to testify to the truth.

Everyone who belongs to the truth listens to My voice."

➤ *Creed, p. 18.*

OFFERTORY   Ps. 2, 8   [All Power]

Ask of Me and I will give You *
the nations for an inheritance *
and the ends of the earth for Your possession.

➤ *Offertory Prayers, p. 21.*

SECRET   [Unity and Peace for All]

O Lord, we offer You this sacrificial Victim of mankind's reconciliation with You; grant, we beseech You, that our Lord Jesus Christ, Your Son, Whom we offer in this sacrifice, may bestow upon all peoples the gifts of unity and peace. Who with You lives, etc. People: **Amen.** ⍟

PREFACE OF CHRIST THE KING
[King of a Universal Realm]

Right and worthy it is, fitting and for our good that in every time and place our thanks should rise to You, O Lord, holy Father, almighty and eternal God. With the oil of gladness You anointed Your only Son, our Lord Jesus Christ, making Him Priest forever and King over all. He offered Himself upon the altar of the Cross, a sinless Victim, effecting peace, and working out the holy mysteries of mankind's Redemption. Then, with all creation subject to His sway, He could hand over to Your boundless

Majesty a kingdom unbounded and undying, a kingdom of truth and life, a kingdom of holiness and grace, a kingdom of justice, love and peace. And therefore, with the Angels and Archangels, with the Thrones and Dominations, and all the forces of heaven, we chant the endless hymn of Your glory:

➤ *Sanctus, p. 27.*

COMMUNION Ps. 28, 10. 11 [Enthroned]

The Lord is enthroned as King forever; *
may the Lord bless His people with peace!

POSTCOMMUNION
[Eternal Kingdom for the Loyal]

We have received the food of eternal life, and we beseech You, O Lord, that we who are proud to serve under the flag of Christ the King may forever reign with Him in the Kingdom of heaven. Who with You lives, etc. People: **Amen.**

➤ *Dismissal, p. 42.*

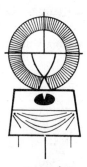

"His lord handed him over to the torturers."

21st SUNDAY AFTER PENTECOST

THOUGHT FOR TODAY: We say in the Our Father: "Forgive us our trespasses as we forgive those who trespass against us." But those who do not forgive think only of revenge, and never forget an offense. They act like the "wicked servant." "Happy the merciful: they shall find mercy."

BIBLE AND LITURGY: To nourish hatred is to go against the very basic laws of our Religion. **READ**: Lev. 19, 17-18; Matt. 5, 1-26; Luke 11, 1-4; 6, 37-38; Matt. 18, 21-22; Luke 23, 33-34.

INTROIT Esther 13, 9. 10. 11;   [*God's Sacred Will*]

In Your will are all things, O Lord *
    and there is none that can resist Your will; *
For You have made all things, heaven and
        earth, *
    and all things that are under the cope of
        heaven. *
    You are Lord of all. *

(Ps.) Happy are they whose way is blameless, *
    who walk in the law of the Lord. *

Glory be to the Father, etc.

In Your will are all things, O Lord, *
   and there is none that can resist Your will; *
**For You have made all things, heaven and
      earth,** *
   **and all things that are under the cope of
      heaven.** *
   You are Lord of all.

➜ *Kyrie and Gloria, pp. 13-14.*

PRAYER   [*Devotion to God's Name*]

*Guard Your household, we beseech You, O
Lord, with unceasing care, that under Your pro-
tection it may be free from all harm and serve
You by good deeds. Through our Lord, etc.*
People: **Amen.** ↓

EPISTLE   Eph. 6, 10-17   [*Bravery of the Christian*]

Brethren: Draw your strength from the Lord
   and from His mighty power. Put on the
armor of God, that you may be able to stand
firm against the wiles of the devil. For our
battle is not against flesh and blood, but against
the Principalities and the Powers, against the
rulers of this world of darkness, against the evil
spirits in regions above. You must take up the
armor of God, if you are to resist on the evil
day, to do your whole duty, and to hold your
ground. So stand fast with the truth as the belt
that girds you, and with justice as your breast-
plate, and with zeal for the gospel of peace on
your feet. In all circumstances take up faith as
your shield; it will enable you to extinguish all

the fiery darts of the evil one. Take also the helmet of salvation and the sword of the Spirit, which is the word of God. ↓

GRADUAL   Ps. 89, 1-2   [*Everlasting God*]

O Lord, You have been our refuge *
   through all generations. *
Before the mountains were begotten *
   and the earth and the world were brought
      forth, *
from everlasting to everlasting You are God.

Alleluia, alleluia. *   Ps. 113, 1   [*Liberator*]
When Israel came forth from Egypt, *
   the house of Jacob from a people of alien
      tongue. Alleluia.

➤ *Prayer before the Gospel, p. 16.*

GOSPEL   Matt. 18, 23-35   [*Forgiveness if We Forgive*]

At that time Jesus told His disciples this parable: "The kingdom of heaven may be compared to the situation of a king who decided to settle accounts with his ministers. When he began the auditing, one was brought in who owed him several million dollars. As he had no means of repaying it, his lord ordered him to be sold together with his wife and children and all his property, in payment of the debt. At that the minister prostrated himself in homage before him and said, 'My lord, be patient with me, and I will pay you back in full.' So his lord, being moved with pity, let the minister go and wrote off the debt. But when that same minister went out, he met one of his fellow officials

who owed him about a hundred dollars. He
seized him and throttled him. 'Pay back what
you owe,' he demanded. His fellow official,
dropping to his knees, began to plead with him,
'Be patient with me, and I will pay you back.'
But he refused. Instead, he went off and had
him put in jail until he could pay back what he
owed. When his other fellow officials saw
what had happened, they were very upset, and
went to their lord and reported the whole incident. So his lord sent for him and said to him,
'You wicked servant! I wrote off the whole of
your debt when you pleaded with me. Shouldn't
you, in turn, have dealt mercifully with your
fellow-servant, as I dealt with you?' Then in
anger, his lord handed him over to the torturers,
until he could pay back all that he owed him.
So will My heavenly Father treat you, unless
each of you forgives his brother with all his
heart."

➤ *Creed, p. 18.*

OFFERTORY   Job 1   [*Trials before Victory*]

There was a man in the land of Us, *
  whose name was Job, *
  simple, and upright, and fearing God, *
Whom Satan besought that he might tempt: *
  and power was given him from the Lord *
  over his possessions and his flesh; *
And he destroyed all his substance and his
    children, *
  and wounded his flesh also with a grievous
    ulcer.

➤ *Offertory Prayers, p. 21.*

SECRET [Restore by Mercy]

Graciously accept these sacrificial gifts, O Lord, with which You have willed us to find favor with You, and, by Your mighty love, restore salvation to us. Through our Lord, etc. People: **Amen.**

➤ *Preface, p. 26.*

COMMUNION Ps. 118, 81. 84. 86 [Plea for Defense]

My soul pines for Your salvation; *
  I hope in Your word. *
When will You do judgment *
  on my persecutors? *
The wicked persecuted me wrongfully; *
  help me, O Lord my God!

POSTCOMMUNION [Purity of Heart]

We who have eaten the Food of eternal life beseech You, O Lord, that what we take by mouth, we may strive after with pure minds. Through our Lord, etc. People: **Amen.**

➤ *Dismissal, p. 42.*

"Then give to the Emperor what is the Emperor's, but to God what is God's."

22nd SUNDAY AFTER PENTECOST

THOUGHT FOR TODAY: Man was made by God and continually needs His sustaining hand. Hence he does not possess absolute dominion over his life. It is our obligation to take reasonable care of our body and to use it in the service of God and our fellowmen, and to cultivate our spiritual life, so that we may practice "blameless conduct right up to the day of Christ."

BIBLE AND LITURGY: "There exists no authority except from God" (Rom. 13, 1). We should give due respect and obedience to all legal authority, except when it commands us to do something that is surely against God's will. READ: Rom. 13, 1-7; Sir. 3, 1-16; Heb. 13, 7-17; Eph. 6, 5-9; Luke 2, 41-52 (esp. 51); Phil. 2, 1-11.

INTROIT Ps. 129, 3. 4. 1. 2   [A Forgiving God]

If You, O Lord, mark iniquities, *
    Lord, who can stand? *
But with You is forgiveness, *
    O God of Israel. *
(Ps.) Out of the depths I cry to You, O Lord; *
    Lord, hear my voice! *

Glory be to the Father, etc.

If You, O Lord, mark iniquities, *
  Lord, who can stand? *

But with You is forgiveness, *
  O God of Israel.

➔ *Kyrie and Gloria, pp. 13-14.*

PRAYER [*Prayer of Faith*]

O God, our refuge and our strength, the very source of holiness, heed the devout prayers of Your Church, and grant that what we seek in Faith we may obtain in fact. Through our Lord, etc. People: **Amen.** ↓

EPISTLE Phil. 1, 6-11 [*Abounding in Charity*]

Brethren: I am sure of this in the Lord Jesus, that He Who has begun in you a noble work will, by the same token, carry it through to completion right up to the day of Christ Jesus. It is only natural that I should entertain such expectations in regard to all of you, since I hold all of you in my heart—you who are one and all sharers with me in this favor of imprisonment and of defense of the gospel and its firm establishment. God Himself can testify how much I long for each of you with the affection of Christ Jesus! This is what I pray for: that your love may abound ever more and more in knowledge and depth of experience, so that you may learn to value those things that are really important, in purity of conscience and in blameless conduct right up to the day of Christ. I want you to be found rich in the harvest of that justice which Jesus Christ has ripened in you, to the glory and praise of God. ↓

GRADUAL Ps. 132, 1-2 [Brotherly Love]

Behold how good it is, and how pleasant, *
where brethren dwell at one! *
**It is as when the precious ointment upon the
head ***
runs down over the beard, the beard of Aaron.

Alleluia, alleluia. * Ps. 113, 11 [Trust in the Lord]
Those who fear the Lord trust in the Lord; *
He is their help and their shield. Alleluia.

➤ *Prayer before the Gospel, p. 16.*

GOSPEL Matt. 22, 15-21 [Seek God, Not the World]

At that time the Pharisees went off and began
to plot how they might trap Jesus in speech.
So they sent their disciples to Him, accompanied by the Herodians, to say, "Master, we
know You are a sincere man and sincerely teach
God's way of life. You are unconcerned about
anybody's opinion, since You don't act out of human respect. Then tell us Your opinion about
this case. Is it lawful to pay the poll tax to the
Emperor, or not?" But Jesus, realizing their bad
faith, said to them, "Why are you trying to
trip Me up, you hypocrites? Show me the coin
used for the poll tax." When they handed Him
a Roman coin, He asked them, "Whose head is
this, and whose inscription?" "The Emperor's,"
they replied. At that He said to them, "Then
give to the Emperor what is the Emperor's, but
to God what is God's."

➤ *Creed, p. 18.*

OFFERTORY Esther 14, 12. 13

[*Put the Right Prayer on My Lips*]

Remember me, O Lord, *

You Who rule above all power: *

And give a well-ordered speech in my mouth, *

**that my words may be pleasing in the sight
of the prince.**

➜ *Offertory Prayers, p. 21.*

SECRET [*Shield Us*]

*Grant, O merciful God, that this saving sacrifice
may always free us from sin, and protect us
from all that works against us. Through our
Lord, etc.* People: **Amen.**

➜ *Preface, p. 26.*

COMMUNION Ps. 16, 6 [*Hear My Words*]

**I call upon You, for You will answer me, O
God;** *

incline Your ear to me; hear my word.

POSTCOMMUNION [*Aid for Our Weakness*]

*We who have received the gift of Your blessed
sacrament, O Lord, humbly pray that what You
have taught us to do in commemoration of You,
may profit and help us in our weakness. Who
live, etc.* People: **Amen.**

➜ *Dismissal, p. 42.*

"He entered, took her by the hand, and the little girl got up."

23rd SUNDAY AFTER PENTECOST

THOUGHT FOR TODAY: The same Jesus Who raised the little girl to life again, will make our body "into an image of His Own glorified Body." Therefore, let us not yield to blind passions, but rather let us consider all that we do in the light of eternity.

BIBLE AND LITURGY: "We are citizens of heaven. And it is from there that we hopefully await the coming of our Savior." (*Ep.*). Waiting for Christ's final coming is a typical Christian attitude. READ: Apoc. 22, 16-21; Luke 12, 35-48; 1 Thess. 5, 1-11; 1 Cor. 1, 4-9; Matt. 24, 36-51; Jude 20-25.

INTROIT   Jer. 29, 11. 12. 14; Ps. 84, 2

The Lord says: *   [*Thoughts of Peace*]
"I think thoughts of peace, and not of affliction. *
You shall call upon Me, *
   and I will hear you; *
   and I will bring back your captivity from all
    places." *

(Ps.) You have favored, O Lord, Your land; *
   You have restored the well-being of Jacob. *
Glory be to the Father, etc.

The Lord says: *
"I think thoughts of peace, and not of affliction. *
You shall call upon Me, *
    and I will hear you; *
    and I will bring back your captivity from all
      places."

➜ *Kyrie and Gloria, pp. 13-14.*

PRAYER   [Absolve from Sin]

*Forgive, we beseech You, O Lord, the sins of
Your faithful people, so that by Your goodness
we may be released from the net of sin in which
we have been caught by our weakness. Through
our Lord, etc.* People: **Amen.** ↓

EPISTLE Phil. 3, 17-21; 4, 1-3 [Our Country is Heaven]

Brethren: Join the others who follow my example, and observe the behavior of those
who conduct themselves according to the pat-
tern you have in us. For alas, many go about
in a manner which shows them to be enemies
of the Cross of Christ, as I have often said to
you and now say again tearfully. These people
will end up in disaster! Their only god is their
stomach; their "glory" is their very shameful-
ness. I mean those people whose sole concern
is things of this world. For, as you know, we
are citizens of heaven. And it is from there that
we hopefully await the coming of our Savior,
the Lord Jesus Christ. He will give a new form
to this lowly body of ours, making it into an
image of His Own glorified Body. This He will
do by the power He has to bring all things into
submission to His will. For these reasons, my
brothers whom I so love and long for, you who

are my joy and my crown, stand firm in the Lord, worthy of love. I plead with Evodia and Synteche: come to a mutual understanding in the Lord. Yes, and I ask you also, my true fellow-worker, go to their aid, for they have struggled at my side in promoting the gospel, along with Clement and my other co-workers, all of whose names are in the Book of Life.

GRADUAL   Ps. 43, 8-9   *[Grateful Praise]*

You saved us, O Lord, from our foes, *
    and those who hated us You put to shame. *
In God we gloried day by day; *
    Your Name we praised always.

Ps. 129, 1. 2

Alleluia, alleluia. *   *[Cry from the Depths]*

Out of the depths I cry to You, O Lord; *
    Lord, hear my prayer. Alleluia.

➤ *Prayer before the Gospel, p. 16.*

GOSPEL   Matt. 9, 18-26   *[Life and More Abundant Life]*

A t that time Jesus had not finished speaking to the crowds when, suddenly, a magistrate came along, did Him reverence, and said, "My daughter has just died. But please come and lay Your hand on her and she will come back to life." Jesus stood up and followed him, and His disciples did likewise. Now a woman who had suffered from hemorrhages for twelve years came along behind Him, and touched the tassel on His cloak. "If only I can touch His cloak," she thought to herself, "I shall get well." Jesus turned around, saw her, and said, "Courage, My daughter! Your faith has made you well." That very moment the woman got well. When Jesus arrived at the magistrate's house and saw the flute-players and the crowd making a dreadful din, He said, "Get out of here. The little girl is not dead. She is asleep." At this, they laughed at Him. But when the crowd had been put out, He entered, took her by the hand, and the little girl got up. News of this circulated around the entire district.

➤ *Creed, p.* 18.

OFFERTORY   Ps. 129, 1. 2   [*Earnest Prayer*]

Out of the depths I cry to You, O Lord; *
   Lord, hear my prayer! *
   Out of the depths I cry to You, O Lord.

➤ *Offertory Prayers, p.* 21.

SECRET   [*Fulfill What You Have Granted*]

We offer You, O Lord, the sacrifice of praise that we may serve You even better, so that You may graciously complete what You have given us, Your undeserving servants. Through our Lord, etc. People: **Amen.** ➤ *Preface, p.* 26.

COMMUNION   Mark 11, 24   [*Power of Prayer*]

Amen I say to you, *
   all things whatever you ask for in prayer, *
Believe that you shall receive, *
   and it shall be done to you.

POSTCOMMUNION   [*Free Us from Dangers*]

We beseech You, almighty God, let not human dangers overcome us to whom You grant joyful participation in things divine. Through our Lord, etc. People: **Amen.** ➤ *Dismissal, p.* 42.

ADDITIONAL MASS NO. 1

INTROIT   Jer. 29, 11. 12. 14; Ps. 84, 2   [*Thoughts of Peace*]

The Lord says: "I think thoughts of peace, *
  and not of affliction. *
You shall call upon Me, *
  and I will hear you; *
  and I will bring back your captivity from all
    places." *

(Ps.) You have favored, O Lord, Your land; *
  You have restored the well-being of Jacob. *

Glory be, etc. — The Lord, etc., as far as (Ps.).

➤ *Kyrie and Gloria*, p. 13. *Prayer and Epistle*, p. 107.

GRADUAL   Ps. 43, 8-9   [*Grateful Praise*]

You saved us, O Lord, from our foes, *
  and those who hated us You put to shame. *
In God we gloried day by day; *
  Your Name we praised always.

Alleluia, alleluia. *   Ps. 129, 1. 2   [*Cry from the Depths*]
Out of the depths I cry to You, O Lord; *
  Lord, hear my prayer! Alleluia.

➤ *Prayer*, p. 16. *Gospel*, p. 108. *Creed*, p. 18.

OFFERTORY   Ps. 129, 1. 2   [*Earnest Prayer*]

Out of the depths I cry to You, O Lord; *
  Lord, hear my prayer! *
Out of the depths I cry to You, O Lord.

➤ *Offertory Prayers*, p. 21. *Secret*, p. 109. *Preface*, p. 26.

COMMUNION   Mark 11, 24   [*Power of Prayer*]

Amen I say to you, *
  all things whatever you ask for in prayer, *
Believe that you shall receive, *
  and it shall be done to you.

• *Postcommunion*, p. 109.   • *Dismissal*, p. 42.

ADDITIONAL MASS NO. 2

INTROIT   Jer. 29, 11. 12. 14; Ps. 84, 2   [*Thoughts of Peace*]

The Lord says: "I think thoughts of peace, *
and not of affliction. *

You shall call upon Me, *
and I will hear you; *
and I will bring back your captivity from all
places." *

(Ps.) You have favored, O Lord, Your land; *
You have restored the well-being of Jacob. *

Glory be, etc. — The Lord, etc., as far as (Ps.).

➤ *Kyrie and Gloria, p. 13. Prayer and Epistle, p. 103.*

GRADUAL   Ps. 43, 8-9   [*Grateful Praise*]

You saved us, O Lord, from our foes, *
and those who hated us You put to shame. *

In God we gloried day by day; *
Your Name we praised always.

Alleluia, alleluia. *   Ps. 129, 1. 2   [*Cry from the Depths*]

Out of the depths I cry to You, O Lord; *
Lord, hear my prayer! Alleluia.

➤ *Prayer, p. 16. Gospel, p. 104. Creed, p. 18.*

OFFERTORY   Ps. 129, 1. 2   [*Earnest Prayer*]

Out of the depths I cry to You, O Lord; *
Lord, hear my prayer! *

Out of the depths I cry to You, O Lord.

➤ *Offertory Prayers, p. 21. Secret, p. 100. Preface, p. 26.*

COMMUNION   Mark 11, 24   [*Power of Prayer*]

Amen I say to you, *
all things whatever you ask for in prayer, *

Believe that you shall receive, *
and it shall be done to you.

• *Postcommunion, p. 105*   • *Dismissal, p. 42.*

ADDITIONAL MASS NO. 3

INTROIT Jer. 29, 11. 12. 14; Ps. 84, 2 [Thoughts of Peace]

The Lord says: "I think thoughts of peace, *
  and not of affliction. *
You shall call upon Me, *
  and I will hear you; *
  and I will bring back your captivity from all
    places." *

(Ps.) You have favored, O Lord, Your land; *
  You have restored the well-being of Jacob. *

Glory be, etc. — The Lord, etc., as far as (Ps.).

➤ *Kyrie and Gloria, p. 13. Prayer and Epistle, p. 99.*

GRADUAL Ps. 43, 8-9 [Grateful Praise]

You saved us, O Lord, from our foes, *
  and those who hated us You put to shame. *
In God we gloried day by day; *
  Your Name we praised always.

Alleluia, alleluia. * Ps. 129, 1. 2 [Cry from the Depths]

Out of the depths I cry to You, O Lord; *
  Lord, hear my prayer! Alleluia.

➤ *Prayer, p. 16. Gospel, p. 100. Creed, p. 18.*

OFFERTORY Ps. 129, 1. 2 [Earnest Prayer]

Out of the depths I cry to You, O Lord; *
  Lord, hear my prayer! *
Out of the depths I cry to You, O Lord.

➤ *Offertory Prayers, p. 21. Secret, p. 105. Preface, p. 26.*

COMMUNION Mark 11, 24 [Power of Prayer]

Amen I say to you, *
  all things whatever you ask for in prayer, *
Believe that you shall receive, *
  and it shall be done to you.

• *Postcommunion, p. 101.* • *Dismissal, p. 42.*

"He will dispatch His angels 'with a mighty trumpet-blast.'"

TWENTY-FOURTH AND LAST SUNDAY AFTER PENTECOST

THOUGHT FOR TODAY: At the end of the ecclesiastical year the Church earnestly reminds us of the judgment that we must pass before the all-knowing God. It is wise to anticipate that judgment in frequent and contrite confession, and always to live in friendly union with Jesus in the Blessed Sacrament Who will be our Judge.

BIBLE AND LITURGY: The History of our Salvation began with the calling of Abraham, our Patriarch, and reached its peak in the death and Resurrection of our Lord and the descent of the Holy Spirit; it will be finished at Jesus' second coming, when He delivers the Kingdom to God the Father. READ: Matt. 25, 31-46; Apoc. 7, 13-17; 1 Cor. 15, 20-28 (esp. 24); Apoc. 21. 1-4.

This Mass is always said on the Last Sunday after Pentecost.

INTROIT   Jer. 29, 11. 12. 14; Ps. 84, 2 [*Thoughts of Peace*]

The Lord says: "I think thoughts of peace, *
   and not of affliction. *
You shall call upon Me, *
   and I will hear you; *

and I will bring back your captivity from all places." *

(Ps.) **You have favored, O Lord, Your land;** * **You have restored the well-being of Jacob.** *

Glory be to the Father, etc.

The Lord says: "I think thoughts of peace, * **and not of affliction.** *

You shall call upon Me, * **and I will hear you;** * **and I will bring back your captivity from all places."**

➔ *Kyrie and Gloria, pp.* 13-14.

PRAYER   [Stirring of Wills]

O Lord, we beseech You, arouse the wills of Your faithful people that, by a more earnest search for the fruit of Your divine work, they may receive more abundantly of the healing effects of Your goodness. Through our Lord, etc. People: **Amen.** ↓

EPISTLE   Col. 1, 9-14   [Brought into the Kingdom]

Brethren: We have been praying for you unceasingly, asking that you may attain full knowledge of God's will through perfect wisdom and spiritual understanding. Thus you will lead a life worthy of the Lord and pleasing to Him in every way; you will be fruitful in every kind of good deed and you will grow in the knowledge of God; by the might of His glory you will be endowed with great power to stand fast and endure joyfully whatever may come; and you will give thanks to the Father for making you worthy to share the lot of the saints in light. For He rescued us from the power of darkness and brought us into the kingdom of His beloved Son, through Whom we have redemption and the forgiveness of our sins. ℣

GRADUAL   Ps. 43, 8-9   [*Grateful Praise*]

You saved us, O Lord, from our foes, *
   and those who hated us You put to shame. *
In God we gloried day by day; *
   Your Name we praised always.   Ps. 129, 1. 2

Alleluia, alleluia.   [*Cry from the Depths*]

Out of the depths I cry to You, O Lord; *
   Lord, hear my prayer! Alleluia.

⟶ *Prayer before the Gospel, p. 16.*

GOSPEL   Matt. 24, 15-35   [*Prophecy of the End*]

At that time Jesus said to His disciples: "When you see the abominable and destructive thing, which the prophet Daniel foretold, standing upon holy ground (the reader will take note!), then those in Judea must flee to the mountains. If a man is on the roof terrace, he must not go down to get anything out of his house. If a man is in the field, he must not turn back to pick up his cloak. Unhappy the women who are pregnant or nursing their children at that period! Keep praying that you will not have to flee in the winter or on a sabbath. For then, there will be great distress surpassing any since the beginning of the world until now, or any that is to come. Indeed if that period had not been shortened, not a human being would have been saved. However, for the sake of the chosen that period will be shortened. Then, if anyone tells you, 'Look, here is the Messiah!' or 'There He is!' don't believe it. False messiahs and false prophets will appear displaying such great signs and wonders as to mislead (were that possible) even the chosen. Remember, I have foretold this to you. So if they tell you, 'Look, He is in the desert!' don't go out there, or, 'Look, He is hidden in the house!' don't believe it. Just as lightning from the east flashes clear to the west, so will be the coming of the Son of Man. It is where the dead body lies that the eagles will gather. Immediately after the distress of that period, 'the sun will be darkened, the moon will not shed her light, the stars will fall out of the sky, the hosts of heaven will be shaken loose.' And then the sign of the Son of Man will appear in the sky, 'while all the clans of earth' will strike their breasts when they see 'the Son of Man coming on the clouds of heaven' with power and great glory. He will dispatch His angels 'with a mighty trumpet-blast and they will assemble His chosen from the four winds, from one horizon to the other.' Learn a lesson from the example of the figtree. Once its branch becomes tender and sprouts leaves, you realize that summer is near. Likewise, when you see all these things, you will realize that He is near, standing at your door. I assure you, the men of today will not pass away before all these things happen. Heaven and earth will pass away, my words will never pass away." → *Creed, p.* 18.

OFFERTORY   Ps. 129, 1. 2   [Earnest Prayer]

Out of the depths I cry to You, O Lord; *
    Lord, hear my prayer! *
    Out of the depths I cry to You, O Lord.

→ *Offertory Prayers, p.* 21.

SECRET   [Convert Us to You]

*Be merciful, O Lord, to our humble requests and
accept the offerings and prayers of Your people:
turn the hearts of all of us to You, that, freed
from earthly cravings, we may pass over to
heavenly yearnings. Through our Lord, etc.*
People: **Amen.**

→ *Preface, p.* 26.

COMMUNION   Mark 11, 24   [Power of Prayer]

Amen I say to you, *
    all things whatever you ask for in prayer, *
Believe that you shall receive, *
    and it shall be done to you.

POSTCOMMUNION   [Restore Us]

*Grant us, we beseech You, O Lord, that all the
evil in our hearts may be cured by the healing
power of the Sacrament we have received.
Through our Lord, etc.* People: **Amen.**

→ *Dismissal, p.* 42.

"I am the Immaculate Conception."

IMMACULATE CONCEPTION

THOUGHT FOR TODAY: Because Mary was chosen to be the Mother of God, the singular privilege was bestowed upon her by which, in the first instant of her Conception, in view of the merits of Jesus Christ, she was preserved from all stain of original sin. Unable to imitate her in her original sinlessness, let us follow her example of loving fidelity to God.

BIBLE AND LITURGY: The Church believes in the preservation of the Blessed Virgin from the stain of original sin from the very moment of her conception. We praise God for this excellent favor which He bestowed upon the Mother of Christ. We learn from the Virgin of virgins about the excellence of virginity and a life entirely dedicated to God. READ: Gen. 3, 14-15; Luke 1, 28; 1 Cor. 7, 25-40; Matt. 19, 10-12; 19, 27-30; Apoc. 14, 1-5.

INTROIT   Isa. 61, 10; Ps. 29, 2   [*Like a Bride*]

I will heartily rejoice in the Lord, *
   in my God is the joy of my soul; *

For he has clothed me with a robe of salvation, *
   and wrapped me in a mantle of justice, *
   like a bride bedecked with her jewels. *

(Ps.) **I will extol you, O Lord, for you drew me clear** *
and did not let my enemies rejoice over me. *
Glory be to the Father, etc.
I will heartily rejoice in the Lord, *
in my God is the joy of my soul; *
For he has clothed me with a robe of salvation, *
and wrapped me in a mantle of justice, *
like a bride bedecked with her jewels.

→ *Kyrie and Gloria, pp. 13-14.*

PRAYER   [Paradise of Our Lord]

O God, Who by the Immaculate Conception of the Virgin, prepared a worthy dwelling for Your Son, and Who, by Your Son's death, foreseen by You, preserved her from all taint, grant, we beseech You, through her intercession, that we too may come to You unstained by sin. Through the same, etc. People: **Amen.** ↓

EPISTLE   Prov. 8, 22-35   [Ever in God's Mind]

"The Lord begot me, the firstborn of His ways, the forerunner of His prodigies of long ago;
From of old I was poured forth,
at the first, before the earth.
When there were no depths I was brought forth,
when there were no fountains or springs of water;
Before the mountains were settled into place,
before the hills, I was brought forth;
While as yet the earth and the fields were not made,
nor the first clods of the world.

When He established the heavens I was there,
> when He marked out the vault over the face
> of the deep;

When He made firm the skies above,
> when He fixed fast the foundations of the
> earth;

When He set for the sea its limit,
> so that the waters should not transgress His
> command;

Then was I beside Him as His craftsman,
> and I was His delight day by day,

Playing before Him all the while,
> playing on the surface of His earth
> and I found delight in the sons of men.

So now, O children, listen to me;
> instruction and wisdom do not reject!

Happy the man who obeys me,
> and happy those who keep my ways,

Happy the man watching daily at my gates,
> waiting at my doorposts;

For he who finds me finds life,
> and wins favor from the Lord." ↓

GRADUAL   Judith 13, 23; 15, 10   [*Our Glory*]

Blessed are you, O Virgin Mary, *
by the Lord the most high God, *
above all women upon the earth. *
You are the glory of Jerusalem, *
you are the joy of Israel, *
you are the honor of our people.

Alleluia, alleluia. *   Cant. 4, 7   [*No Stain*]

You are all-beautiful, O Mary, *
and there is in you no stain of original sin.
Alleluia.

During Paschaltime, the Gradual is omitted and the following Alleluia is said:

Judith 15, 10; Cant. 4, 7

Alleluia, alleluia. *   [*Glory of Beauty*]
You are the glory of Jerusalem, *
   you are the joy of Israel, *
   you are the honor of our people. *
Alleluia. You are all-beautiful, O Mary, *
   and there is in you no stain of original sin.
    Alleluia.

➤ *Prayer before the Gospel, p. 16.*

GOSPEL   Luke 1, 26-28   [*Full of Grace*]

At that time the angel Gabriel was sent from God to a town of Galilee named Nazareth, to a virgin engaged to a man named Joseph, of the house of David, and the virgin's name was Mary.

The angel arrived and said to her: "Hail, full of grace; the Lord is with you. Blessed are you among women."

➤ *Creed, p. 18.*

OFFERTORY   Luke 1, 28   [*Blest amongst Women*]

Hail, Mary, full of grace, *
   the Lord is with you; *
   blessed are you among women. Alleluia.

➤ *Offertory Prayers, p. 21.*

SECRET   [*Free from Sin*]

Accept, O Lord, the sacrifice of salvation which we offer You on the feast of the Immaculate Conception of the blessed Virgin Mary; and grant that as we profess that she was kept from all taint of evil, by Your anticipating grace, so, through her intercession, may we be freed from all sin. Through our Lord, etc. People: **Amen.** ↓

PREFACE OF THE BLESSED VIRGIN

[*Our Prayer of Thanksgiving*]

Right and worthy it is, fitting and for our good that in every time and place our thanks should rise to You, O Lord, holy Father, almighty and eternal God: and fitting it is that on this day which honours the Immaculate Conception *(on the Feast of the Assumption, substitute: Assumption)* of Blessed Mary ever Virgin, we should bless and praise Your goodness. By the overshadowing of the Holy Spirit she conceived Your only Son and, with the glory of her virginity unaltered, gave the world its eternal Light, Jesus Christ our Lord. Through Him the Angels praise Your Majesty, while Dominations adore and all the Powers stand in awe. In one great voice, the heavens, all the hosts of heaven, and the Blessed Seraphim, cry out their praise. In our turn we pray that our voices now may be joined with theirs as in humble witness we sing: ➤ *Sanctus, p. 27.*

COMMUNION
[*Mighty Lord*]

Glorious things are said of you, O Mary, *** **because He Who is mighty has done great things for you.**

POSTCOMMUNION
[*Heal Our Wounds*]

May the sacrament we have received, O Lord our God, heal in us the wounds of that sin from which by a singular privilege, You kept Immaculate the Conception of Blessed Mary. Through our Lord, etc. People: **Amen.** ➤ *Dismissal, p. 42.*

"Alleluia, Alleluia. Mary has been taken up into heaven."

THE ASSUMPTION of the BLESSED VIRGIN MARY

THOUGHT FOR TODAY: This feast celebrates the privilege of Mary, solemnly defined by the Church, proclaiming that the body of the Blessed Virgin Mary was gloriously assumed into heaven. "He Who is mighty has done great things for" her in the first instant of her Conception. He also preserved her body from corruption in imitation of the Body of her Son which was formed in her womb.

BIBLE AND LITURGY: The most outstanding of all saints in heaven is Mary, the Mother of Christ. Honoring her, we are in good company. The Angel Gabriel, sent by God, and Elizabeth, filled with the Holy Spirit, taught us how to honor Mary. God honored the Blessed Virgin by taking her up into heaven both soul and body. READ: Luke 1, 26-56; 2; Matt. 2, 13-23; John 19, 25-30; Acts 1, 12-14.

INTROIT   Apoc. 12, 1; Ps. 97, 1   [*The Sign in Heaven*]

A great sign appeared in heaven: *
     a woman clothed with the sun, *
And the moon was under her feet, *
     and upon her head a crown of twelve stars. *

(Ps.) **Sing to the Lord a new song,** *
  for He has done wondrous deeds. *

Glory be to the Father, etc.

A great sign appeared in heaven: *
  a woman clothed with the sun, *
And the moon was under her feet, *
  and upon her head a crown of twelve stars.

PRAYER   [*Share Her Glory*]

*Almighty, everlasting God, Who took up, body
and soul, the immaculate Virgin Mary, Mother
of Your Son, into heavenly glory, grant, we beseech You, that, always devoting ourselves to
heavenly things, we may be found worthy to
share in her glory. Through the same, etc.*
People: **Amen.** ↓

EPISTLE   Judith 13, 22-25; 15, 10   [*Blessed beyond All*]

The Lord has blessed you with His power
because through you He has today brought
to nought the enemies of your people. Blessed
are you, daughter, by the Most High God, of
all the women on the earth; and blessed be the
Lord God, the creator of heaven and earth, Who
guided your blow at the head of the chief of
our enemies. Your deed of hope will never be
forgotten by those who tell of the might of
God. May God make this redound to your
everlasting honor, rewarding you with blessings,
because you risked your life when your people
were being oppressed, and you averted our disaster in the sight of our God. You are the glory

of Jerusalem, the surpassing joy of Israel; you are the splendid boast of our people. ♥

GRADUAL Ps. 44, 11-12. 14   [Her Beauty]

Hear, O daughter, and see; turn your ear; *
for the King shall desire your beauty. *
All glorious is the King's daughter as she
enters; *
her raiment is threaded with spun gold.

Alleluia, alleluia. *   [Rejoice]
Mary has been taken up into heaven; *
the choirs of the angels rejoice. Alleluia.

➔ *Prayer before the Gospel, p.* 16.

GOSPEL Luke 1, 41 50   [Magnificat]

At that time Elizabeth was filled with the Holy Spirit, and cried out in a loud voice: "Blessed are you among women, and blessed is the fruit of your womb. And who am I, that the mother of my Lord should come to me? For the moment that your salutation sounded in my ears the infant stirred in my womb with joy. Happy is she who has believed that the Lord's words to her will be fulfilled."

And Mary said:

"My soul magnifies the Lord,
    and my spirit rejoices in God my Savior,
Because He has regarded the lowliness of His
        handmaid,
    for behold, henceforth all generations shall
        call me blessed,

Because He Who is mighty has done great
  things for me,
    and holy is His Name;
And His mercy is from generation to generation
  toward those who fear Him." ➤ *Creed, p.* 18.

OFFERTORY   Gen. 3, 15   [Protectress]

I will put enmity between you and the Woman, *
between your seed and her seed.

➤ *Offertory Prayers, p.* 21.

SECRET   [Long for God]

*May the offering of our devotion rise unto You,
O Lord, and by the intercession of the most
Blessed Virgin Mary, who was taken up into
heaven, may our hearts, on fire with love, strive
ever upward to You. Through our Lord, etc.*
People: **Amen.** ➤ *Preface of the Blessed Virgin,*
p. 331.

COMMUNION   Luke 1, 48-49   [Great Things]

All generations shall call me blessed; *
**because He Who is mighty has done great
    things for me.**

POSTCOMMUNION   [Risen Glory]

*Having partaken, O Lord, of the sacrament of
salvation, grant, we beseech You, that through
the merits and intercession of the Blessed Virgin
Mary, who was taken up into heaven, we may
be brought to the glory of the resurrection.
Through our Lord, etc.* People: **Amen.**

➤ *Dismissal, p.* 42.

————————

"Happy the sincere of heart: they shall behold God."

FEAST OF ALL SAINTS

THOUGHT FOR TODAY: We celebrate today the feast of all servants of God who reached their eternal goal. With their help we hope to share their joy in heaven.

BIBLE AND LITURGY: We believe in the Communion of Saints. We pray with them, ask their help, honor them as God's friends, and imitate their virtues. READ: Apoc. 4, 1-11; 6, 9-11; 14, 12-13; Heb. 12, 18-24; Apoc. 5, 1-14 (esp. 8); 2 Mach. 15, 1-16 (esp. 12-15).

INTROIT Ps. 32, 1   [*Glory of the Saints*]

Let us all rejoice in the Lord, *
    celebrating a feast day in honor of all the saints, *
On whose solemnity the angels rejoice, *
    and join in praising the Son of God. *

(Ps.) Exult, you just, in the Lord; *
    praise from the upright is fitting. *

Glory be, etc.—Repeat: Let us, etc.

➤ *Kyrie and Gloria, pp. 13-14.*

PRAYER   [Abundance of Mercy]

Almighty, eternal God, Who granted us to honor the merits of all Your Saints in a single solemn festival, bestow on us, we beseech You, through their manifold intercession, that abundance of Your

mercy for which we yearn. Through our Lord, etc.
People: **Amen.** ✟

EPISTLE   Apoc. 7, 2-12   [*The Redeemed*]

In those days I, John, saw another angel come up from the east; he held the seal of the living God, and with mighty voice he cried out to the four angels who had been given power to ravage land and sea: "Do not ravage land or sea or trees until we have marked with this seal the foreheads of the servants of our God." (I heard that the number of those thus marked with the seal was one hundred forty-four thousand from every tribe of the Israelites: twelve thousand sealed from the tribe of Juda, twelve thousand from the tribe of Gad, twelve thousand from the tribe of Aser, twelve thousand from the tribe of Nephthali, twelve thousand from the tribe of Manasse, twelve thousand from the tribe of Simeon, twelve thousand from the tribe of Levi, twelve thousand from the tribe of Issachar, twelve thousand from the tribe of Zabulon, twelve thousand from the tribe of Joseph, twelve thousand sealed from the tribe of Benjamin.)

After this I saw in vision a great throng which no one could count, from every nation—from all tribes, peoples, and tongues—standing before the throne and before the Lamb; they wore white robes and held palm branches in their hands. With mighty voice they cried: "Salvation is from our God Who is seated upon His throne, and from the Lamb." At this all the angels who stood around the throne, outside the circle of the elders and the four living creatures, fell face down before the throne, worshiping God, as they sang: "Amen! Praise, glory and wisdom, thanksgiving, honor, power, and might be to our God forever and ever. Amen." ✟

GRADUAL   Ps. 33, 10. 11   [*The Lord, Our Reward*]
Fear the Lord, you His holy ones, *
  for nought is lacking to those who fear Him. *

But those who seek the Lord want for no good thing.

Alleluia, alleluia. * Matt. 11, 28   [Refreshment]
Come to Me, all you who labor and are burdened, *
and I will give you rest. Alleluia.

➤ *Prayer before the Gospel, p. 16.*

GOSPEL   Matt. 5, 1-12   [The Way to Heaven]

At that time, when Jesus saw the crowds, He went up on the mountain, and after He had sat down, His disciples gathered around. Then He began to teach them, "Happy the poor in spirit: theirs is the kingdom of heaven. Happy those who mourn: they shall be consoled. Happy the humble: they shall inherit the land. Happy those who hunger and thirst for holiness: they shall be satisfied. Happy the merciful: they shall find mercy. Happy the sincere of heart: they shall behold God. Happy the peacemakers: they shall be called God's children. Happy those who suffer persecution for religion: theirs is the kingdom of heaven. Happy are you when they insult you and persecute you and utter every kind of slander against you on My account. Be glad! Yes, be overjoyed: your reward in heaven is great." ➤ *Creed, p. 18.*

OFFERTORY   Wis. 3, 1-2. 3   [Peace at Last]
The souls of the just are in the hand of God, *
and no torment shall touch them. *
They seemed, in the view of the foolish, to be dead; *
but they are in peace. Alleluia. ➤ *Off. Pr., p. 21.*

SECRET   [Salvation]
We offer You, O Lord, the gifts of our service; may they be pleasing to You for the honor of Your just ones and, through Your mercy, bring us salvation. Through our Lord, etc. People: **Amen.** ▼

PREFACE FOR ALL SAINTS
[*Our Prayer of Thanksgiving*]

Right and worthy it is, fitting and for our good that in every time and place our thanks should rise to You, O Lord, holy Father, almighty and eternal God. You are made glorious in the assembly of the saints for in crowning their merit You crown Your own gift. You offer us their way of life as an example, communion with them for fellowship, their intercession to strengthen us. Such a mighty throng of witnesses has been set before us that in joy and patience we enter upon the struggle to which we are called, and so with them achieve the unfading crown of glory, through Christ our Lord. Through Him the Angels praise Your Majesty, while Dominations adore and all the Powers stand in awe. In one great voice, the heavens, all the hosts of heaven, and the Blessed Seraphim, cry out their praise. In our turn we pray that our voices now may be joined with theirs, as in humble witness we sing:

➔ *Sanctus. p.* 27.

COMMUNION   Matt. 5, 8-10   [*The Kingdom*]

Blessed are the pure of heart, *
  for they shall see God. *
Blessed are the peacemakers, *
  for they shall be called children of God. *
**Blessed are they who suffer persecution for justice'
    sake,** *
  for theirs is the kingdom of heaven.

POSTCOMMUNION   [*Unceasing Prayers*]

Grant Your faithful people, we beseech You, O Lord, ever to rejoice in the veneration of all the Saints, and to be protected by their unceasing prayers. Through our Lord, etc. People: **Amen.**

➔ *Dismissal, p.* 42.

"Man must not separate what God has joined together."

THE NUPTIAL MASS

THOUGHT FOR TODAY: For Christians, marriage is not only a very important contract, a source of life, but is the most intimate and sublime union between husband and wife. This union of love and confidence has been raised by our Lord to the dignity of a great sacrament.

BIBLE AND LITURGY: In the Old Testament, the love of God for His Chosen People was compared to the love of a husband and wife. In the New Testament, Christ is called the Spouse of the Church (the New Jerusalem). And the love of Christ for His Church is given as the model for the love of husband and wife. READ: Osee 1-2; Ps. 44; Ezech. 16, 1-63; Isa. 54, 5-9; John 3, 28-30; Apoc. 19, 7-8; 21, 1-2; Eph. 5, 22-33 (*Ep.*).

INTROIT   Tob. 7, 15; 8, 19; Ps. 127, 1   [*May God Join You*]

May the God of Israel join you together; *
   and may He be with you, *
Who was merciful to two only children: *
   and now, O Lord, make them bless you more
      fully. (P.T. Alleluia, alleluia.) *

(Ps.) Blessed are all who fear the Lord, *
   who walk in His ways. *

Glory be to the Father, etc.

May the God of Israel join you together; *
   and may He be with you, *

Who was merciful to two only children: *
and now, O Lord, make them bless You more
fully. (P.T. Alleluia, alleluia.)

➔ *Kyrie and Gloria, pp.* 13-14.

PRAYER   [*Ratify the Union*]

Graciously hear us, O Almighty God, that what is
done by our ministry may be abundantly fulfilled
by Your blessing. Through, etc. People: **Amen.** ▼

EPISTLE Eph. 5, 22-23 [*Love as Christ Loves the Church*]

Brethren: Wives should be submissive to their
husbands as though to the Lord; because the
husband is head of the wife just as Christ is head
of the Church, His body, of which He is also the
Savior. Just as the Church submits to Christ, so
should wives submit in everything to their husbands. Husbands, love your wives, just as Christ
loved the Church and gave Himself up for her to
make her holy, purifying her in the bath of water
by the power of the word, so as to present to Himself a glorious Church, holy and immaculate, without
stain or wrinkle or anything of that sort. In the
same way husbands, too, should love their wives
as they do their own bodies. He who loves his wife
loves himself. Now no one ever hates his own·flesh;
no, he nourishes and takes care of it, just as Christ
does for the Church,· because we are members of
His body. "For this reason a man shall leave his
father and mother, and shall cling to his wife, and
the two shall become one flesh." This is a great
foreshadowing: I mean to say it refers to Christ
and the Church. But in any case, each one of you
should love his wife just as he loves himself; and
the wife should revere her husband. ▼

GRADUAL Ps. 127, 3   [*Fruitful Union*]

Your wife shall be like a fruitful vine *
in the recesses of your home. *

Your children like olive plants *
   around your table.

Alleluia, alleluia. * Ps. 19, 3   [*Help from God*]

May the Lord send you help from the sanctuary, *
   from Sion may He sustain you. Alleluia.

After Septuagesima, omit Alleluia, and say:

TRACT Ps. 127, 4-6   [*Prosperity*]

Behold, thus is the man blessed *
   who fears the Lord. *

The Lord bless you from Sion: *
   may you see the prosperity of Jerusalem *
   all the days of your life. *

May you see your children's children. *
   Peace be upon Israel!

During Paschaltime, omit Gradual and say:

Alleluia, alleluia. * Ps. 19, 3   [*Help from God*]

May the Lord send you help from the sanctuary, *
   from Sion may He sustain you. *

Alleluia. May the Lord bless you from Sion, *
   the Maker of heaven and earth. Alleluia.

➤ *Prayer before the Gospel, p. 16.*

GOSPEL Matt. 19, 3-6   [*Not Two But One*]

At that time some Pharisees came up to Jesus
and as a test said to Him, "Is it permissible
for a man to divorce his wife for any reason whatever?" In reply He said, "Have you not read that
the Creator at the beginning made them male and
female, and declared, 'For this reason a man shall
leave his father and mother, and shall cling to his
wife, and the two shall become one flesh'? So they
are no longer two but one flesh. Therefore man
must not separate what God has joined together." ∀

After the Gospel and homily all stand.

THE RITE OF MATRIMONY

The Priest asks the bridegroom, who stands at the right side of the bride: [The Solemn Contract]

N . . . , do you take N . . . , here present, for your lawful wife according to the rite of our holy Mother, the Church? *Response:* I do.

Then the Priest asks the bride:

N . . . , do you take N . . . , here present, for your lawful husband, according to the rite of our holy Mother, the Church? *Response:* I do.

After the mutual consent of the contractants has been given, the Priest directs them:

Now join your right hands and say after me:

Groom:

I, N.N., . . . take you, N.N., . . . for my lawful wife, to have and to hold, from this day forward, for better, for worse, for richer, for poorer, in sickness and in health, until death do us part.

Bride:

I, N.N., . . . take you, N.N., . . . for my lawful husband, to have and to hold, from this day forward, for better, for worse, for richer, for poorer, in sickness and in health, until death do us part.

Then the Priest says: [Pronounced Man and Wife]

By the authority of the Church I ratify and bless the bond of marriage you have contracted. In the name of the Father, and of the Son, ✠ and of the Holy Spirit. ℟. **Amen.**

I call upon all of you here present to be witnesses of this holy union which I have now blessed. "Man must not separate what God has joined together."

Next the Priest blesses the ring or rings.

℣. Our help ✠ is in the name of the Lord. ℟. **Who made heaven and earth.** ℣. O Lord, hear my prayer. ℞. **And let my cry come to You.** ℣. The Lord be with you. ℞. **And with your spirit.**

Let us pray. (for two rings) [Ring of Fidelity]

Bless, ✠ O Lord, these rings, which we are blessing ✠ in Your name, so that they who wear them, keeping faith with each other in unbroken loyalty, may ever remain at peace with You according to Your will, and may live together always in mutual love. Through Christ our Lord. ℞. **Amen.**

Let us pray. (for one ring)

Bless, ✠ O Lord, this ring, which we are blessing ✠ in Your name, so that she who wears it, keeping faith with her husband in unbroken loyalty, may ever remain at peace with You according to Your will, and may live with him always in mutual love. Through Christ our Lord. ℞. **Amen.**

Now that you have sealed a truly Christian marriage, give these wedding rings to each other (this wedding ring to your bride) saying after me:

The groom places the bride's ring on the bride's ring finger saying after the Priest:

In the name of the Father, and of the Son, and of the Holy Spirit. Take and wear this ring as a sign of our marriage vows.

The bride places the groom's ring on the groom's ring finger saying the same words after the Priest.

Priest: In the name of the Father, and of the Son, ✠ and of the Holy Spirit. Amen.

℣. Strengthen, O God, what You have wrought in us. ℞. **From Your holy temple, which is in Jerusalem.**

Lord, have mercy. **Christ, have mercy. Lord, have mercy.**

Our Father *(silently as far as):*

℣. And lead us not into temptation. ℞. **But deliver us from evil.** ℣. Save Your servants. ℞. **Who trust**

in You, my God. ℣. Send them help, O Lord, from
Your sanctuary. ℟. **And sustain them from Sion.**
℣. Be a tower of strength for them, O Lord. ℟.
Against the attack of the enemy. ℣. O Lord, hear
my prayer. ℟. **And let my cry come to You.** ℣. The
Lord be with you. ℟. **And with your spirit.**

Let us pray.   [Remain True]

We beg You, Lord, to look on these Your serv-
ants, and graciously to uphold the institution of
marriage established by You for the continuation
of the human race, so that they who have been
joined together by Your authority may remain
faithful together by Your help. Through Christ our
Lord. ℟. **Amen.**

May almighty God bless you by the Word of His
mouth, and unite your hearts in the enduring bond
of pure love. ℟. **Amen.**

The following blessing may be omitted if the spouses
are too old to expect children. The Priest says:

May you be blessed in your children, and may
the love that you lavish on them be returned a
hundredfold. ℟. **Amen.**

May the peace of Christ dwell always in your
hearts and in your home; may you have true friends
to stand by you, both in joy and in sorrow. May
you be ready with help and consolation for all those
who come to you in need; and may the blessings
promised to the compassionate descend in abun-
dance on your house. ℟. **Amen.**

May you be blessed in your work and enjoy its
fruits. May cares never cause you distress, nor the
desire for earthly possessions lead you astray; but
may your hearts' concern be always for the treasures
laid up for you in the life of heaven. ℟. **Amen.**

May the Lord grant you fullness of years, so that
you may reap the harvest of a good life, and, after
you have served Him with loyalty in His kingdom

on earth, may He take you up into His eternal dominions in heaven.

Through our Lord Jesus Christ, His Son, Who lives and reigns with Him in the unity of the Holy Spirit, God, forever and ever. ℟. **Amen.**

Then the Priest continues the Nuptial Mass.

OFFERTORY   Ps. 30, 15. 16   [*Future in God's Keeping*]

My trust is in You, O Lord; *
 I say, "You are my God." *
 In Your hands is my destiny. (P.T. Alleluia.)

➜ *Offertory Prayers, p. 21.*

SECRET   [*Guard the Union*]

Accept, we beseech You, O Lord, the offering we make in behalf of the holy bond of wedlock: and further the work which You have bountifully brought about. Through our Lord, etc. People: **Amen.** ☩

PREFACE FOR WEEKDAYS

Right and worthy it is, fitting and for our good that in every time and place our thanks should rise to you, O Lord, holy Father, almighty and eternal God: through Christ our Lord. Through Him the Angels praise Your Majesty, while Dominations adore and all the Powers stand in awe. In one great voice, the heavens, all the hosts of heaven, and the Blessed Seraphim, cry out Your praise. In our turn we pray that our voices now may be joined with theirs as in humble witness we sing:
➜ *Sanctus, p. 27.*

NUPTIAL BLESSING

After the "Our Father," p. 35, the Priest says the following prayers over the spouses:

   Let us pray   [*Preserve Mutual Love*]

   Listen with favor, O Lord, to our prayers, and graciously uphold the institution of marriage es-

tablished by You for the continuation of the human race, so that they who have been joined together by Your authority may remain faithful together by Your help. Through our Lord, etc. ℞. **Amen.**

Let us pray. [*The Nuptial Blessing*]

O God, by Your mighty power You made all things where before there was nothing; You put in order the beginnings of the universe and formed for man, made to Your image, an inseparable help-mate, woman. You gave woman's body its origin from man's flesh, to teach that it is never right to separate her from the one being from whom it has pleased You to take her.

O God, You consecrated the union of marriage, making it a sign so profound as to prefigure in the marriage covenant the mystery of Christ and the Church.

O God, You join woman to man and give to that society, the first to be established, the blessing which alone was not taken away in punishment for original sin or in the doom of the Flood:

Look with kindness on this Your servant who is to be joined to her husband in the companionship of marriage and who seeks to be made secure by Your protection.

May this yoke that she is taking on herself be one of love and peace. May she be faithful and chaste, marrying in Christ, and may she always imitate the holy women: may she be the beloved of her husband, as was Rachel; wise, as was Rebecca; long-lived and loyal, as was Sara.

May the author of sin have no mastery over her because of her acts. May she hold firm to the Faith and the Commandments. Faithful to one embrace, may she flee from unlawful companionship. By firm discipline may she fortify herself against her *weakness. May she be grave in her modesty, honorable in her chastity, learned in the teaching of heaven.*

May she be rich in children, may she prove worthy and blameless, and may she attain in the end to the peace of the blessed, the kingdom of heaven.

*May she and her husband together see their children's children to the third and fourth generation and enjoy the long life that will fulfill their desires. Through the same, etc. ℞. **Amen.**

The Priest then continues as usual with the Prayer: "Deliver us, we beseech You," p. 36.

COMMUNION   Ps. 127, 4. 6   [Blessing]

Behold, thus is the man blessed *
  who fears the Lord; *
May you see your children's children. *
  Peace be upon Israel! (P.T. Alleluia.)

POSTCOMMUNION   [Everlasting Peace]

We beseech You, Almighty God, to accompany with Your holy approval this institution of Your providence, that You will preserve in long-lived peace those who are joined in legitimate union. Through our Lord, etc. People: **Amen.**

The Priest, before giving the blessing, turns toward the bridegroom and bride, saying:
                                        [Long Life]

May the God of Abraham, the God of Isaac, the God of Jacob be with you, and may He fulfill in you His blessing, so that you may see your children's children to the third and fourth generation and afterward possess everlasting and boundless life. Through the help of our Lord Jesus Christ, Who with the Father and the Holy Spirit lives and reigns, God, forever and ever. ℞. **Amen.**

➤ *Dismissal, p. 42.*

"Eternal rest grant unto them, O Lord: and let perpetual light shine upon them."

THE FUNERAL MASS

THOUGHT FOR TODAY: According to the doctrine and practice of the Church, based on the words of Holy Scripture, "It is therefore a holy and wholesome thought to pray for the dead, that they may be loosed from their sins" (2 Mach, 12, 46), we pray and offer the holy Sacrifice for the relief and release of the souls detained in purgatory.

BIBLE AND LITURGY: We believe in the Communion of Saints, which also means that we can help our beloved deceased who are perhaps still going through that process of final cleansing in purgatory. READ: 1 Cor. 3, 10-17; 2 Mach. 12, 43-46.

RESPONSORY   [*Receive This Soul*]

Come to his (her) aid, *
  O saints of God; *
Hasten to meet him (her), *
  Angels of the Lord; *
Taking up his (her) soul, *
  presenting it in the sight of the Most High. *
May you be received by Christ, Who has called
    you: *

and may the Angels bring you into the bosom of
   Abraham. *
Taking up his (her) soul, *
   presenting it in the sight of the Most High. *
Eternal rest grant unto him (her), O Lord: *
   and let perpetual light shine upon him (her). *
Presenting his (her) soul in the sight of the Most
   High.

INTROIT   4 Esdras 2, 34. 35   [*Light and Rest*]

Eternal rest grant unto them, O Lord: *
   and let perpetual light shine upon them. *
(Ps.) To You we owe our hymn of praise, *
   O God, in Sion; *
To You must vows be fulfilled *
   in Jerusalem. *
Hear my prayer; *
   to You all flesh must come. *
Repeat: **Eternal rest,** etc., as far as (Ps.).

➜ *Kyrie, p.* 13. *Omit Gloria.*

PRAYER   [*Bring Them to Their True Home*]

*O God, Whose property is ever to pity and·to spare,
we humbly pray for the soul of Your servant (handmaid) N., whom at this time You have called forth
from this world; abandon him (her) not into the
hands of the enemy, forget him (her) not forever
but rather, bid him (her) to be received by the holy
Angels and borne to the realm of Paradise, so that
he (she) who has hoped and believed in You may
not suffer the punishments of hell, but come into
possession of everlasting happiness. Through our
Lord, etc.* ℟. **Amen.** ⅴ

EPISTLE   1 Thess. 4, 13-18 [*The Dead in Christ Shall Rise*]

Brethren: We would not have you lack understanding concerning those in the sleep of
death, lest you yield to grief like the others, who

have no hope. For if we believe that Jesus died and yet rose, so also will God bring forth with Him those who have fallen asleep believing in Jesus. This we say to you as the Lord's own word, that we who live, who survive till the Lord's coming, will in no way have an advantage over those who have fallen asleep. No, for the Lord Himself, when the order is given, at the sound of Archangel's voice and of God's trumpet, will come down from heaven and the dead in Christ will first rise; then we the living, the survivors, will be caught up together with them in the clouds to meet the Lord in the air; and thus we shall be with the Lord always. Therefore, console one another with these words. ℣

GRADUAL   4 Esdras 2, 34. 35; Ps. 111, 7

[*Just Are Not Forgotten*]

Eternal rest grant unto them, O Lord: *
   and let perpetual light shine upon them. *
The just man shall be in everlasting remem-
   brance; *
   an evil report he shall not fear. ℣

TRACT   [*Forgive and Grant Bliss*]

Absolve, O Lord, the souls of all the faithful de-
   parted *
   from every bond of sin. *
And by the help of Your grace *
   may they deserve to escape the judgment of
   vengeance. *
   And to enjoy the blessedness of light eternal. ℣

SEQUENCE   [*Song of Judgment*]

Day of wrath! O day of mourning! *
See fulfilled the prophets' warning, *
Heav'n and earth in ashes burning! *

O what fear man's bosom rendeth *
When from heav'n the Judge descendeth, *
On Whose sentence all dependeth! *

Wondrous sound the trumpet flingeth; *
Through earth's sepulchers it ringeth; *
All before the throne it bringeth. *

Death is struck, and nature quaking, *
All creation is awaking, *
To its Judge an answer making. *

Lo! the book, exactly worded, *
Wherein all hath been recorded: *
Thence shall judgment be awarded. *

When the Judge His seat attaineth *
And each hidden deed arraigneth, *
Nothing unavenged remaineth. *

What shall I, frail man, be pleading? *
Who for me be interceding, *
When the just are mercy needing? *

King of majesty tremendous, *
Who dost free salvation send us, *
Fount of pity, then befriend us! *

Think, good Jesus, my salvation *
Cost Thy wondrous Incarnation; *
Leave me not to reprobation! *

Faint and weary, Thou hast sought me, *
On the Cross of suff'ring bought me. *
Shall such grace be vainly brought me? *

Righteous Judge! for sin's pollution *
Grant Thy gift of absolution, *
Ere the day of retribution. *

Guilty, now I pour my moaning, *
All my shame with anguish owning; *
Spare, O God, Thy suppliant groaning! *

Thou the sinful woman savedst; *
Thou the dying thief forgavest; *
And to me a hope vouchsafest. *

Worthless are my prayers and sighing, *
Yet, good Lord, in grace complying, *
Rescue me from fires undying! *

With Thy favored sheep, O place me *
Nor among the goats abase me, *
But to Thy right hand upraise me. *

While the wicked are confounded, *
Doomed to flames of woe unbounded, *
Call me with Thy Saints surrounded. *

Low I kneel, with heart submission: *
See, like ashes, my contrition; *
Help me in my last condition. *

Ah! that day of tears and mourning! *
From the dust of earth returning, *
Man for judgment must prepare him; *
Spare, O God, in mercy spare him! *

Lord, all pitying, Jesus blest, *
Grant them Thine eternal rest. Amen.

➤ Prayer before the Gospel, p. 16.

GOSPEL John 11, 21-27 [Christ, Resurrection and Life]

At that time Martha said to Jesus, "Lord, if You had been here, my brother would never have died. Even now, I am sure that whatever You ask of God, God will give You." "Your brother will rise again," Jesus told her. "I know he will rise again," Martha replied, "in the resurrection on the last day." Jesus told her, "I am the Resurrection and the Life; he who believes in Me, even if he dies, will come to life. And everyone who is alive and believes in Me will never die at all.—Do you believe this?" "Yes, Lord," she replied. "I have learned to believe that You are the Messiah, the Son of God, He Who is to come into the world." ⱱ

OFFERTORY   [*Deliver the Souls of the Faithful*]

Lord Jesus Christ, King of glory, *
  deliver the souls of all the faithful departed *
  from the pains of hell and the deep pit; *
Deliver them from the lion's mouth, *
  may hell not swallow them up, *
  nor may they fall into darkness, *
But may Michael, the holy standard-bearer, *
  bring them into the holy light: *
  **Which You once promised to Abraham and to
    his seed.** *
We offer You, O Lord, *
  sacrifices and prayers of praise; *
Receive them for the souls *
  whom we remember this day. *
**Grant, O Lord, that they may pass from death to
    life.** *
  **Which You once promised to Abraham and to
    his seed.**

➤ *Offertory Prayers, p. 21.*

SECRET   [*Atonement*]

*Be merciful, we beseech You, O Lord, to the soul
of Your servant (handmaid) N., for whom we offer
to You the sacrifice of praise, humbly beseeching
Your Majesty that, through this propitiatory rite,
he (she) may be worthy to enter into everlasting
rest. Through our Lord, etc.* ℟. **Amen.** ℣

PREFACE FOR THE DEAD

[*Our Prayer of Thanksgiving*]

Right and worthy it is, fitting and for our good
that in every time and place our thanks should rise

to You, O Lord, holy Father, almighty and eternal God: through Christ our Lord. Through Him there lives in us the hope of a blessed resurrection, so that the very hearts which are saddened at the thought of certain death find comfort in the promise of the life to come. For Your faithful, O Lord, life is changed but not ended; and, when the dwelling which was theirs on earth has fallen to dust, an eternal home stands ready for them in heaven. And therefore, with the Angels and Archangels, with the Thrones and Dominations, and all the forces of heaven, we chant the endless hymn of Your glory: ➤ *Sanctus, p. 27.*

COMMUNION   4 Esdras 2, 35. 34   [*Perpetual Light*]

May light eternal shine upon them, O Lord: *
   With Your saints forever, for You are merciful. *
Eternal rest grant unto them, O Lord; *
   and let perpetual light shine upon them. *
   With Your saints forever, for You are merciful.

POSTCOMMUNION   [*Forgiveness and Rest*]

Grant, we beseech You, almighty God, that the soul of Your servant (handmaid) N., who has now departed this life, having been cleansed by this sacrificial rite and released from his (her) sins, may enjoy everlasting rest. Through our Lord, etc. ℟. **Amen.**

➤ *Dismissal, p. 42.*

THE ABSOLUTION AND BURIAL

PRAYER   [*Mercy*]

O Lord, do not bring Your servant to trial, for no man becomes holy in Your sight unless You grant him forgiveness of all his sins. We implore You therefore, do not let the verdict of Your judgment go against him (her), whom the loyal prayer of Christian Faith is commending to Your mercy. Rather, by the help of Your grace, may he (she) escape the sentence which he (she) deserves, for during his (her) earthly life, he (she) was signed with the seal of the Holy Trinity. You Who live and reign forever and ever. ℞. **Amen.**

RESPONSORY [Save Them from Eternal Death]

Deliver me, O Lord, from everlasting death on that day of terror: *

When the heavens and the earth will be shaken. *
  As You come to judge the world by fire. *

I am in fear and trembling *
  at the judgment and the wrath that is to come. *

When the heavens and the earth will be shaken. *

That day will be a day of wrath, of misery, and of ruin: *
  a day of grandeur and great horror: *
  As You come to judge the world by fire. *

Eternal rest grant unto them, O Lord, *
  and let perpetual light shine upon them. *

Deliver me, O Lord, from everlasting death on that day of terror: *

When the heavens and the earth will be shaken. *
  As You come to judge the world by fire.

Lord, have mercy.

Christ, have mercy.

Then all together:

Lord, have mercy.

Next the Priest says in a high voice:

Our Father, etc. (continued silently).

He walks twice around the bier, first sprinkling it with holy water, and then incensing it. He continues:

℣. And lead us not into temptation. ℟. **But deliver us from evil.** ℣. From the gate of hell. ℟. **Rescue his (her) soul, O Lord.** ℣. May he (she) rest in peace. ℟. **Amen.** ℣. O Lord, hear my prayer. ℟. **And let my cry come to You.** ℣. The Lord be with you. ℟. **And with your spirit.** ℣. Let us pray.

PRAYER   [Bring Them to Their True Home]

O God, Who alone are ever merciful and sparing of punishment, humbly we pray You in behalf of the soul of Your servant, N., whom You have commanded to go forth today from this world. Do not hand him (her) over to the power of the enemy and do not forget him (her) forever; but command that this soul be taken up by the Holy Angels and brought home to paradise, so that, since he (she) hoped and believed in You, he (she) may not undergo the punishments of hell, but rather possess everlasting joys. Through Christ our Lord. ℟. **Amen.**

While the body is being carried to the grave, either at the grave or in the church, the following is said or sung:

ANTIPHON   [May Heaven Welcome You]

May the Angels take you into paradise; *
    may the Martyrs come to welcome you on your
        way, *
    and lead you into the holy city, Jerusalem.
May the choir of Angels welcome you, *
    and with Lazarus who once was poor may you
        have everlasting rest.

PSALM 114

I love the Lord because He has heard *
    my voice in supplication, *

Because He has inclined His ear to me *
   the day I called. *

The cords of death encompassed me; the snares of
      the nether world seized upon me; *
   I fell into distress and sorrow. *

And I called upon the Name of the Lord, *
   "O Lord, save my life!" *

Gracious is the Lord and just; *
   yes, our God is merciful. *

The Lord keeps the little ones; *
   I was brought low and He saved me. *

Return, O my soul, to your tranquillity, *
   for the Lord has been good to you. *

For He has freed my soul from death, *
   my eyes from tears, my feet from stumbling. *

I shall walk before the Lord, *
   in the lands of the living. *

Eternal rest grant unto him (her), O Lord. *

And let perpetual light shine upon him (her).

Repeat Antiphon, "May the Angels," etc., as above.

ANTIPHON   [Christ Speaks]

I am the Resurrection and the Life; he who believes
in Me, even if he die, shall live, and whoever lives
and believes in Me, shall never die.

CANTICLE   Luke 1, 68-79   [Zachary's Canticle of Hope]

Blessed be the Lord, the God of Israel, *
   because He has visited and wrought Redemption
      for His people, *

And has raised up a horn of salvation for us *
   in the house of David His servant, *

As He promised through the mouths of His holy
      ones, *
   the Prophets from of old: *

Salvation from our enemies *
   and from the hands of all our foes. *
He has fulfilled His kindness to our fathers, *
   and been mindful of His Holy Covenant *
   in the oath to Abraham our father, *
   by which He swore to grant us *
That, delivered from the hands of our enemies, *
   we should serve Him without fear *
In holiness and justice before Him *
   all our days. *
And you, O child, shall be called *
   the prophet of the Most High; *
For you shall go before the Lord *
   to prepare His ways, *
To grant His people knowledge of salvation *
   through forgiveness of their sins, *
Because of the compassionate kindness of our God *
   with which the Orient from on high will visit us, *
To shine on those who sit in darkness and the
     shadow of death *
   to guide our feet into the way of peace. *
Eternal rest *
   grant unto him (her), O Lord. *
And let perpetual light *
   shine upon him (her).

Repeat Antiphon, "I am," etc., as above.

*When the procession comes to the grave, if it is not
blessed, the Priest says:*
         [Bless This Grave]

*Let us pray. O God, by Whose mercy rest is given
to the souls of the faithful, in Your kindness bless
✠ this grave. Entrust it to the care of Your holy
Angel, and set free from all the chains of sin the
souls of those whose bodies are buried here, so
that with all Your saints they may rejoice in You
forever. Through Christ our Lord.* ℟. **Amen.**

If the grave will serve for one person only, the following is said: the soul of him (her) whose body is buried here, so that with all Your saints he (she) may rejoice in You forever.

Priest: [Loving Remembrance]

Dearest brothers, let us faithfully and lovingly remember our brother (sister) whom God has taken from the trials of this world.

℣. Lord, have mercy.

℟. **Christ, have mercy. Lord, have mercy.**

Priest:

Our Father, etc.

Meanwhile he sprinkles the body, without going around it.

℣. And lead us not into temptation. ℟. **But deliver us from evil.** ℣. From the gate of hell. ℟. **Rescue his (her) soul, O Lord.** ℣. May he (she) rest in peace. ℟. **Amen.** ℣. O Lord, hear my prayer. ℟. **And let my cry come to You.** ℣. The Lord be with you. ℟. **And with your spirit.**

[Spare Your Faithful Servant]

Let us pray. O Lord, we implore You to grant this mercy to Your dead servant, that he (she) who held fast to Your will by his (her) intentions, may not receive punishment in return for his (her) deeds; so that, as the true Faith united him (her) with the throng of the faithful on earth, Your mercy may unite him (her) with the company of the choirs of Angels in heaven. Through Christ our Lord. ℟. **Amen.**

℣. Eternal rest grant unto him (her), O Lord. ℟. **And let perpetual light shine upon him (her).** ℣. May he (she) rest in peace. ℟. **Amen.** ℣. May his (her) soul and the souls of all the faithful departed through the mercy of God rest in peace. ℟. **Amen.**

The Priest says one of the Prayers for the Dead.

PRAYERS FOR THE BYSTANDERS AT THE GRAVE

[Grace to Be Ready]

Let us pray. Grant, O Lord, we pray You, that while we lament the departure of our brother (sister), Your servant, out of this life, we may bear in mind that we are most certainly to follow him (her). Give us the grace to make ready for that last hour by a devout and holy life, and protect us against a sudden and unprovided death. Teach us how to watch and pray that when Your summons comes, we may go forth to meet the Bridegroom and enter with Him into life everlasting. Through Christ our Lord. ℞. **Amen.**

[Consolation]

Let us pray. Almighty and most merciful Father, You know the weakness of our nature. Bow down Your ear in pity to Your servants, upon whom You have laid the heavy burden of sorrow. Take away out of their hearts the spirit of rebellion, and teach them to see Your good and gracious purpose working in all the trials which You send upon them. Grant that they may not languish in fruitless and unavailing grief, nor sorrow as those who have no hope, but through their tears look meekly up to You, the God of all consolation. Through Christ our Lord, etc. ℞. **Amen.**

℣. Eternal rest grant to him (her), O Lord. ℞. **And let perpetual light shine upon him (her).** ℣. May he (she) rest in peace. ℞. **Amen.** ℣. May his (her) soul and the souls of all the faithful departed through the mercy of God rest in peace. ℞. **Amen.**

SUPPLEMENT

(People's parts of Additional Feasts that displace the Sunday Mass when they fall on Sundays.)

Feb. 2 — PURIFICATION OF THE B.V.M.

INTROIT   Ps. 47, 10-11. 2   [*Pondering God's Love*]

O God, we ponder Your kindness *
  within Your temple. *
As Your Name, O God, so also Your praise *
  reaches to the ends of the earth. *
Of justice Your right hand is full. *

(Ps.) Great is the Lord, and wholly to be praised *
  in the city of our God, His holy mountain. *

Glory be to the Father, etc.

Repeat: O God, etc., as far as (Ps.).

GRADUAL   Ps. 47, 10-1. 9   [*The Expected Has Come*]

O God, we ponder Your kindness *
  within Your temple. *
As Your Name, O God, so also Your praise *
  reaches to the ends of the earth. *
As we have heard, so have we seen, *
  in the city of our God, in His holy mountain.

Alleluia, alleluia. *   [*The Mighty Child*]
The old man carried the Child: *
  but the Child governed the old man. Alleluia.

After Septuagesima, the Alleluia and versicle are omitted and the following Tract is said:

TRACT   Luke 2, 29-32   [*Salvation Is Hers*]

Now You dismiss Your servants, O Lord, *
  according to Your word, in peace. *
Because my eyes have seen Your salvation. *
  Which You have prepared before the face of all
    peoples. *

- 362 -

A light of revelation to the Gentiles, *
and a glory for Your people Israel.

OFFERTORY   Ps. 44, 3   [Blessed Forever]

Grace is poured out upon your lips; *
thus God has blessed you forever and ever.

COMMUNION   Luke 2, 26   [Seeing the Lord]

It was revealed to Simeon *
by the Holy Spirit *
That he should not see death *
before he had seen the Christ of the Lord.

May 1 — ST. JOSEPH THE WORKER
Spouse of the Blessed Virgin Mary, Confessor

INTROIT   Wis. 10, 17; Ps. 126, 1   [The Reward of Labor]

Wisdom gave the holy ones the recompense of their
labors, *
and conducted them by a wondrous road, *
And became a shelter for them by day *
and a starry flame by night. (P.T. Alleluia, alleluia.) *

(Ps.) Unless the Lord build the house, *
they labor in vain who build it. *

Glory be to the Father, etc.

Repeat: **Wisdom,** etc., as far as (Ps.).

In Paschaltime:

Alleluia, alleluia. *   [Joseph's Patronage]
In whatever trouble they shall call upon me, *
I will hear them, *
and I will always be their protector. *

Alleluia. Obtain for us grace to lead an innocent
life, O Joseph; *
and may it ever be secure under your protection.
Alleluia.

In Votive Masses in September:

GRADUAL   Ps. 127, 1-2   [Glory of Work]

Happy are you who fear the Lord, *
  who walk in His ways! *
You shall eat the fruit of your handiwork *
  and you shall be favored.

Alleluia, alleluia. *   [Patronage]
Obtain for us grace to lead an innocent life, O
  Joseph; *
  and may it ever be secure under your protection.
  Alleluia.

OFFERTORY   Ps. 89, 17   [Prosper Us]

May the gracious care of the Lord our God be ours; *
  prosper the work of our hands for us! *
  Prosper the work of our hands! (P.T. Alleluia.)

COMMUNION   Matt. 13, 54, 55   [Family of Jesus]

Where did He get this wisdom and these miracles? *
Is not this the carpenter's Son? *
  Is not His Mother called Mary? (P.T. Alleluia.)

June 29 — STS. PETER AND PAUL,
Apostles

INTROIT   Acts 12, 11; Ps. 138, 1-2   [Rescue]

Now I know for certain *
  that the Lord has sent His angel *
And rescued me from the power of Herod *
  and from all that the Jewish people were expect-
  ing. *
(Ps.) O Lord, You have probed me and You know
  me; *
  You know when I sit and when I stand. *

Glory be to the Father, etc.

Repeat: **Now I know,** etc., as far as (Ps.).

GRADUAL   Ps. 44, 17-18   [Princes]

You shall make them princes through all the land; *
    they shall remember Your Name, O Lord. *
The place of Your fathers Your sons shall have; *
    therefore shall nations praise Yon.

Alleluia, alleluia.   * Matt. 16, 18   [Rock]

You are Peter, *
    and upon this rock I will build My Church. Alleluia.

OFFERTORY   Ps. 44, 17-18   [Unforgettable Name of God]

You shall make them princes through all the land; *
    they shall remember Your Name, O Lord, *
    through all generations.

COMMUNION   Matt. 16, 18   [Foundation]

You are Peter, *
    and upon this rock I will build My Church.

Aug. 6 — TRANSFIGURATION OF OUR LORD

INTROIT   Ps. 76, 19; 83, 2-3   [Light]

Your lightning illumined the world; *
    the earth quivered and quaked.
(Ps.) How lovely is Your dwelling place, *
    O Lord of Hosts! *
My soul yearns and pines *
    for the courts of the Lord. *

Glory be to the Father, etc.

Repeat: **Your lightning,** etc., as far as (Ps.).

GRADUAL   Ps. 44, 3. 2   [Full of Beauty]

Fairer in beauty are You than the sons of men; *
    grace is poured out upon Your lips. *
My heart overflows with a goodly theme; *
    as I sing my ode to the King.

Alleluia, alleluia. *   Wis. 7, 26   [Spotless Image]

He is the refulgence of eternal light, *
    the spotless mirror, *
    and the image of His goodness. Alleluia.

OFFERTORY   Ps. 111, 3   [Spiritual Wealth]

Glory and wealth are in His house; *
    His generosity shall endure forever. Alleluia.

COMMUNION   Matt. 17, 9   [Prevue]

Tell the vision you have seen to no one, *
    till the Son of Man has risen from the dead.

Sept. 14 — EXALTATION OF THE HOLY CROSS

INTROIT   Gal. 6, 14; Ps. 66, 2   [Glory in the Cross]

But it behooves us to glory *
    in the Cross of our Lord Jesus Christ; *
In Whom is our salvation, life, and resurrection; *
    by Whom we are saved and delivered. *

(Ps.) May God have pity on us and bless us; *
    may He let His face shine upon us; *
    and may He have pity on us. *

Glory be to the Father, etc.

Repeat: But it behooves, etc., as far as (Ps.).

GRADUAL   Phil. 2, 8. 9   [Obedient to Death]

Christ became obedient for us to death, *
    even to death on a cross. *
Therefore God has also exalted Him, *
    and has bestowed upon Him *
    the Name that is above every name.

Alleluia, alleluia. *   [Blessed Cross]

Sweet the wood, sweet the nails, *
    sweet the load that hangs on you! *

You alone were worthy *
   to bear up the King and Lord of heaven. Alleluia.

OFFERTORY   [The Cross, Our Protection]

Protect Your people, O Lord, *
   through the sign of the Holy Cross, *
   from the snares of their enemies, *
That we may pay You a pleasing service, *
   and our sacrifice may be acceptable to You.
   Alleluia.

COMMUNION   [Sign of the Cross]

O our God, through the sign of the Cross, *
   deliver us from our enemies.

Sept. 29 — DEDICATION OF
ST. MICHAEL THE ARCHANGEL

INTROIT   Ps. 102, 20. 1   [God's Angels]

Bless the Lord, all you His angels, *
   you mighty in strength, who do His bidding, *
   obeying His spoken word. *

(Ps.) Bless the Lord, O my soul; *
   and all my being, bless His holy Name. *

Glory be to the Father, etc.

Repeat: Bless the Lord, etc., as far as (Ps.).

GRADUAL   Ps. 102, 20. 1   [Angelic Servants]

Bless the Lord, all you His angels, *
   you mighty in strength, who do His bidding. *
Bless the Lord, O my soul; *
   and all my being, bless His holy Name.

Alleluia, alleluia. *   [Defend Us in Battle]
St. Michael the Archangel, defend us in battle, *
   that we may not perish in the dreadful judgment.
   Alleluia.

OFFERTORY   Apoc. 8, 3. 4   [Angelic Ministers]

An Angel stood before the altar of the temple, *
   having a golden censer in his hand, *
And there was given to him much incense; *
   and the smoke of the spices ascended before God.
   Alleluia.

COMMUNION   Dan. 3, 58   [All Angels, Bless the Lord]

All you angels of the Lord, *
   bless the Lord, *
Sing a hymn, *
   and exalt Him above all forever.

Nov. 9 — DEDICATION OF THE BASILICA OF OUR SAVIOR

INTROIT   Gen. 28, 17; Ps. 83, 2-3   [House of the Lord]

How awesome is this place! *
   This is none other than the house of God; *
This is the gate of heaven; *
   and it shall be called the court of God. (P.T.
   Alleluia, alleluia.) *
(Ps.) How lovely is Your dwelling place, *
   O Lord of Hosts! *
My soul yearns and pines *
   for the courts of the Lord. *
Glory be to the Father, etc.
Repeat: **How awesome,** etc., as far as (Ps.).

GRADUAL   [Priceless Mystery]

This place was made by God, a priceless mystery; *
   it is without reproof. *
O God, before Whom stands the choir of angels, *
   hear the prayers of Your servants.

Alleluia, alleluia. * Ps. 137, 2   [Worship]

I will worship at Your holy temple *
   and give thanks to Your Name. Alleluia.

OFFERTORY   1 Par. 29, 17. 18   [Total Offering]

O Lord God, in the simplicity of my heart *
    I have joyfully offered all these things; *
And I have seen with great joy Your people *
    which is here present: *
O God of Israel, * keep this will. Alleluia.

COMMUNION   Matt. 21, 13   [House of Prayer]

"My house shall be called a house of prayer," *
    says the Lord; *
"In it everyone who asks receives: *
    and he who seeks finds, *
And to him who knocks, *
    it shall be opened." (P.T. Alleluia.)

VOTIVE MASS OF THE BLESSED SACRAMENT

Mass as on p. 211, omitting Sequence and (outside Paschaltime) the word "Alleluia," and substituting the following:

From Pentecost to Septuagesima omit Alleluia and say:

GRADUAL   Ps. 144, 15-16   [Hope]

The eyes of all look hopefully to You, O Lord; *
    and You give them their food in due season. *
You open Your hand; *
    and satisfy the desire of every living thing.

Alleluia, alleluia. *   John 6, 56. 57   [The Heavenly Food]

My Flesh is food indeed, *
He who eats My flesh, and drinks My Blood, *
    abides in Me and I in him. Alleluia.

From Septuagesima to Easter omit Alleluia and say:

TRACT   Mal. 1, 11; Prov. 9, 5   [Perpetual Sacrifice]

From the rising of the sun, even to its setting, *
    My Name is great among the nations. *
And everywhere they bring sacrifice to My Name, *
    and a pure offering; *

For great is My Name among the nations. *
Come, eat of my bread, *
   and drink of the wine I have mixed for you.

VOTIVE MASS FOR PEACE

Introit, p. 116 (adding "Alleluia, alleluia" before (Ps.) *in Paschaltime).*

GRADUAL Ps. 121, 6-7   [Peace]
Pray for the peace of Jerusalem! *
   May those who love You prosper! *
May peace be within your walls, *
   prosperity in your buildings.

Alleluia, alleluia. * Ps. 147, 12   [Glorify God]
Glorify the Lord, O Jerusalem; *
   praise your God, O Sion. Alleluia.

After Septuagesima, omit Alleluia and versicle and say:

TRACT Ps. 75, 2-4   [City of Peace]
God is renowned in Juda; *
   in Israel great is His Name. *
In the city of peace is His abode; *
   His dwelling is in Sion. *
There He shattered the flashing shafts of the bow, *
   shield and sword, and weapons of war.

During Paschaltime, omit Gradual and say:

Alleluia, alleluia. * Ps. 147, 12 *   [Spiritual food]
Glorify the Lord, O Jerusalem; *
   praise your God, O Sion. Alleluia.

Alleluia. He has granted peace in your borders; *
   with the best of wheat he fills you. Alleluia.

➤ *Offertory, p. 146.*

COMMUNION John 14, 27   [My Peace]
"Peace I leave with you, *
   My peace I give to you," says the Lord. (P.T.
   Alleluia.)

Dec. 24 — VIGIL OF CHRISTMAS

INTROIT   Ex. 16, 6. 7; Ps. 23, 1   [*Great Glory of Tomorrow*]

This day you shall know *
> that the Lord will come and save us: *
> and in the morning you shall see His glory. *

(Ps.) The Lord's are the earth and its fullness; *
> the world and those who dwell in it. *

Glory be to the Father, etc.

Repeat: **This day you**, etc., as far as (Ps.).

GRADUAL   Ex. 16, 6. 7; Ps. 79, 2-3
[*Salvation Made Known Today*]

This day you shall know *
> that the Lord will come, and save us: *
> and in the morning you shall see His glory. *

O Shepherd of Israel, hearken, *
> O guide of the flock of Joseph! *

From Your throne upon the Cherubim, shine forth *
> before Ephraim, Benjamin and Manasse.

The following Alleluia and its versicle are said only when the Vigil falls on a Sunday.

Alleluia, alleluia. *   [*Tomorrow the Victor*]

Tomorrow shall the wickedness of the earth be
> abolished: *
> and the Savior of the world shall reign over us.
> Alleluia.

OFFERTORY   Ps. 23, 7   [*The Great Welcome*]

Lift up, O gates, your lintels; *
> reach up, you ancient portals, *
> that the King of Glory may come in.

COMMUNION   Isa. 40, 5   [*Glory for All*]

The glory of the Lord shall be revealed, *
> and all mankind shall see the salvation of our
> God.

HYMNS AND PSALMODY

"Liturgical worship is given a more noble form when the divine offices are celebrated solemnly in song, with the assistance of sacred ministers and the active participation of the people . . . ."

1

PRAISE TO THE LORD

Based on Ps. 103 and 150

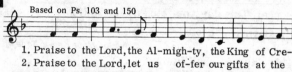

1. Praise to the Lord, the Al-migh-ty, the King of Cre-
2. Praise to the Lord, let us of-fer our gifts at the
3. Praise to the Lord, O let all that is in us a-

a - tion! O my soul, praise Him for
al - tar. Let not our sins and of -
dore Him. All that has life and breath

He is our health and sal - va - tion.
fen - ses now cause us to fal - ter.
come now re - joic - ing be - fore Him.

All you who hear, now to the al - tar draw
Christ, the High-Priest, bids us all join in His
Let the A - men sound from His peo - ple a -

near; Join in pro-found a - do - ra - tion.
feast, Vic-tims with Him on the al - tar.
gain, As we here wor-ship be - fore Him.

WE PRAISE THEE O GOD OUR REDEEMER

2

Ps. 26:12
Tr. Julia B. Cady

E. Kremser

1. We praise Thee, O God, our Redeemer, Creator, In grateful devotion our tribute we bring; We lay it before Thee, we kneel and adore Thee, We bless Thy holy name, glad praises we sing.

2. We worship Thee, God of our fathers, we bless Thee; Thro' trouble and tempest our Guide hast Thou been; When perils o'er-take us, escape Thou wilt make us, And with Thy help, O Lord, our battles we win.

3. With voices united our praises we offer, To Thee, great Jehovah, glad anthems we raise. Thy strong arm will guide us, our God is beside us, To Thee, our great Redeemer forever be praise. A-men.

3

TO THE NAME

DOWN IN ADORATION FALLING

J. M. Neale, Tr.

C. Ett

1. To the name that brings sal-va-tion Hon-or wor-ship
2. 'Tis the name for ad-o-ra-tion 'Tis the name of

1. Down in ad-o-ra-tion fall-ing Lo! the sa-cred
2. To the ev-er-last-ing Fa-ther And the Son who

1. let us pay, Which for man-y a ge-ner-a-tion
2. vic-to-ry 'Tis the name for med-i-ta-tion

1. Host we hail! Lo! O'er an-cient forms de-part-ing
2. reigns on high, With the Spir-it blest pro-ceed-ing

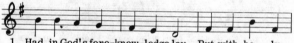

1. Had in God's fore-know-ledge lay, But with ho-ly
2. In this vale of mis-e-ry, 'Tis the name for

1. New-er rites of grace pre-vail; Faith for all de-
2. Forth from each e-ter-nal-ly, Be sal-va-tion

1. ex-ul-ta-tion We may sing a-loud to-day.
2. ven-er-a-tion By the cit-i-zens on high.

1. fects sup-ply-ing Where the fee-ble sen-ses fail.
2. hon-or, bless-ing, Might, and end-less maj-es-ty. A-men.

HOLY, HOLY, HOLY

Reginald Heber, 1826   John B. Dykes, 1861

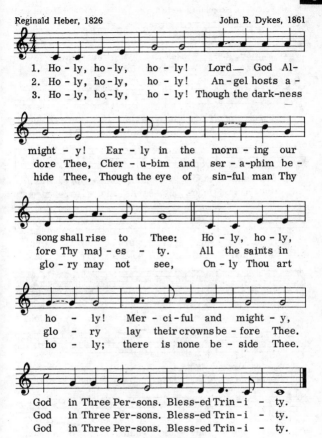

1. Ho - ly, ho - ly, ho - ly! Lord— God Al- might - y! Ear - ly in the morn - ing our song shall rise to Thee: Ho - ly, ho - ly, ho - ly! Mer - ci - ful and might - y, God in Three Per - sons. Bless-ed Trin - i - ty.

2. Ho - ly, ho - ly, ho - ly! An - gel hosts a - dore Thee, Cher - u - bim and ser - a - phim be - fore Thy maj - es - ty. All the saints in glo - ry lay their crowns be - fore Thee. God in Three Per - sons. Bless-ed Trin - i - ty.

3. Ho - ly, ho - ly, ho - ly! Though the dark-ness hide Thee, Though the eye of sin - ful man Thy glo - ry may not see, On - ly Thou art ho - ly; there is none be - side Thee. God in Three Per - sons. Bless-ed Trin - i - ty.

5

PRAISE THE LORD YE HEAVENS

Ps. 148 Foundling Hospital Collection

Rowland H. Prichard

1. Praise the Lord,___ ye heav'ns, a-dore Him; Praise him, an-gels in___ the height;
Sun and moon re-joice be-fore___ him; Praise him, all ye stars of light.
Praise the Lord, for he has spo-ken; Worlds his might-y voice o-beyed;
Laws, which nev-er shall be bro-ken, For their guid-ance he has made.

2. Praise the Lord,___ for he is glo-rious, Nev-er shall his prom-ise fall;
God has made his saints vic-to-rious, Sin and death shall not___ pre-vail.
Praise the God of our sal-va-tion; Hosts on high, his power pro-claim;
Heav'n and earth and all cre-a-tion, Praise and mag-ni-fy his name.

CROWN HIM WITH MANY CROWNS

M. Bridges
J. Thring

G. J. Elvey

1. Crown Him with many crowns, The Lamb up-on His
2. Crown Him the Lord of heav'n, En-throned in worlds a-

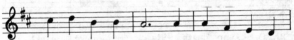

1. throne; Hark how the heav'n-ly an-them drowns All
2. bove; Crown Him the King to whom is giv'n The

1. mu-sic but its own; A - wake my soul, and
2. won-drous name of love; Crown Him with man - y

1. sing Of Him Who died for thee, And hail Him
2. crowns, As thrones be-fore Him fall, Crown Him, ye

1. as thy match-less King Through all e -ter-ni- ty.
2. Kings, with man - y crowns, For He is King of all.

7

ON THIS DAY, THE FIRST OF DAYS

Le Mans Breviary, 1748
Tr. Henry W. Baker

Freylinghausen's
Gesangbuch, 1704

1. On this day, the first of days,
2. On this day th'e - ter - nal Son
3. Fa - ther, Who didst fash - ion me
4. Ho - ly Je - sus, may I be
5. God, the one God of my heart,

1. God the Fa - ther's name we praise,
2. O - ver death His tri - umph won;
3. I - mage of Thy - self to be,
4. Dead and ris - en, here with Thee,
5. I am Thine, and mine Thou art;

1. Who, cre - a - tion's Lord and spring,
2. On this day the Spir - it came
3. Fill me with Thy love di - vine,
4. And up - on love's fire a - rise,
5. Take me, bless - ed One in Three,

1. Did the world from dark - ness bring.
2. With His gifts of liv - ing flame.
3. Let my ev - 'ry thought be Thine.
4. Un - to Thee a sac - ri - fice.
5. Here I give my - self to Thee.

ACCEPT ALMIGHTY FATHER

8

Anonymous

J. Mohr

1. Ac - cept, Al-might - y Fa - ther, This
   gift of bread and wine Which now thy priest
   does of - fer To thee, O God be - nign,
   In hum - ble rep - a - ra - tion For sins
   and fail - ings dread, To win life ev - er -
   last - ing For liv - ing and for dead.

2. O God, by this com - ming - ling Of
   wa - ter and of wine, May he who took
   our na - ture Give us his life di - vine.
   Come, thou who mak - est ho - ly, And bless
   this sac - ri - fice; Then shall our gift be
   pleas - ing To thee a - bove the skies.

LORD ACCEPT THE GIFTS

9

1. Lord, ac-cept the gifts we of-fer
2. May our souls be pure and spot-less
3. Take our gifts, Al-might-y Fa-ther,

At this Eu-char-is-tic Feast.
As the Host of wheat so fine;
Liv-ing God, e-ter-nal, true,

Bread and wine to be trans-formed now
May all stain of sin be crushed out
Which we give through Christ, our Sav-ior,

Through the ac-tion of Thy priest.
Like the grape that forms the wine,
Plead-ing here for us a-new.

Take us, too, O Lord, trans-form us;
As we, too, be-come par-tak-ers
Grant sal-va-tion to all pres-ent

Be thy grace in us in-creased.
In this Sa-cri-fice di-vine.
And our faith and love re-new.

O KING OF MIGHT AND SPLENDOR

"Rex Summae Maiestatis"
Tr. A. Gregory Murray, O.S.B.

S. Somerville

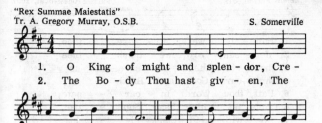

1. O King of might and splen - dor, Cre -
2. The Bo - dy Thou hast giv - en, The

a - tor most a-dored, This sac - ri - fice we render To
Blood Thou hast out-poured, The sin might be for-giv-en, O

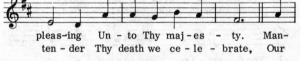

Thee, our sov'-reign Lord. May these, our gifts, be
Je - sus, lov - ing Lord. As now, with love most

pleas-ing Un - to Thy maj - es - ty. Man-
ten - der Thy death we ce - le - brate, Our

kind from sin re - leas - ing Which has of-fend-ed Thee.
lives in self sur - ren - der To Thee we con-se-crate.

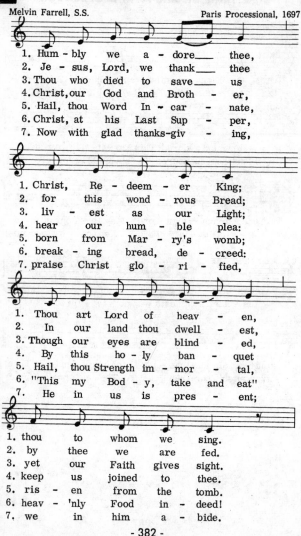

11 HUMBLY WE ADORE THEE

Melvin Farrell, S.S.

Paris Processional, 1697

1. Hum - bly we a - dore thee, Christ, Re - deem - er King; Thou art Lord of heav - en, thou to whom we sing.
2. Je - sus, Lord, we thank thee for this wond - rous Bread; In our land thou dwell - est, by thee we are fed.
3. Thou who died to save us liv - est as our Light; Though our eyes are blind - ed, yet our Faith gives sight.
4. Christ, our God and Broth - er, hear our hum - ble plea: By this ho - ly ban - quet keep us joined to thee.
5. Hail, thou Word In - car - nate, born from Mar - y's womb; Hail, thou Strength im - mor - tal, ris - en from the tomb.
6. Christ, at his Last Sup - per, break - ing bread, de - creed: "This my Bod - y, take and eat" heav - 'nly Food in - deed!
7. Now with glad thanks-giv - ing, praise Christ glo - ri - fied, He in us is pres - ent; we in him a - bide.

- 382 -

HUMBLY WE ADORE THEE (Continued)

1. God, the Might - y, thou hast come,
2. We who share this Mys - te - ry
3. Christ, do thou be mer - ci - ful,
4. Make us one in lov - ing thee,
5. Share with us thy vic - tor - y,
6. Then he blessed the cup of wine -
7. Mem - bers of his Bod - - y,

1. bear - ing gifts of grace;
2. in thee are made one!
3. Lamb for sin - ners slain,
4. one in mind and heart,
5. Sav - ior ev - er blest:
6. "Take ye this," he said:
7. we in him are One;

1. Son of Ad - am still thou art:
2. Ev - 'ry act we of - fer thee
3. We in grief con - fess our guilt:
4. Till in heav - en we are thine,
5. Live more ful - ly in our hearts;
6. "Drink the chal - ice of my Blood,
7. Hail this sa - cred Un - - ion,

1. Sav - ior to our race.
2. in thy Name is done.
3. cleanse our souls of stain.
4. nev - er - more to part.
5. be our con - stant Guest.
6. soon for sin - ners shed."
7. heav'n on earth be - gun!

12 SOUL OF MY SAVIOR

1. Soul of my Savior, sanctify my breast!
   Body of Christ, be Thou my saving guest!
   Blood of my Savior, bathe me in Thy tide!
   Wash me, ye waters, gushing from His side!

2. Strength and protection may His passion be;
   O blessed Jesus, hear and answer me!
   Deep in Thy wounds, Lord, hide and shelter me;
   So shall I never, never part from Thee.

3. Guard and defend me from the foe malign;
   In death's drear moments make me only Thine;
   Call me, and bid me come to Thee on high,
   Where I may praise Thee with Thy saints for aye.

13 O FOOD THAT WEARY PILGRIMS LOVE

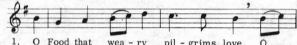

1. O Food that wea-ry pil-grims love, O___
2. O fount of love,— O cleans-ing tide, Which
3. Lord Je-sus, Whom_ by pow'r di-vine, Now_

Bread of an-gel hosts a-bove, O Man-na of the
from the Sav-ior's pierc-ed side, And Sa-cred Heart does
hid-den 'neath the out-ward sign, We wor-ship and a-

saints! The hun-gry soul_ would feed on Thee, Ne'er
flow! Be ours to drink_ from Thy pure rill, Which
dore; Grant, when the veil_ a-way is rolled, With

may the heart un-sol-aced be Which for_ Thy sweet-ness faints.
on-ly can our spir-its fill, And all_ we need be-stow.
o-pen face we may be-hold Thy-self for ev-er-more.

1. At that first Eu-char-ist be-
2. For all Your Church, O Lord, we
3. So, Lord, at length when Sac-ra-

fore You died, O Lord, You
in-ter-cede; O make our
ments shall cease, May we be

prayed that all be one in You;
lack of char-i-ty to cease;
one with all thy Church a-bove,

At this our Eu-char-ist a-
Draw us the near-er each to
One with the saints in one un-

gain pre-side, And in our hearts Your
each, we plead, By draw-ing all to
end-ing peace, One with the saints in

Chorus: All

law of love re-new. Thus may we
You, O Prince of Peace.
one un-bound-ed love.

all one Bread, one Bo-dy be, Through

this blest Sac-ra-ment of U-ni-ty.

15 NOW THANK WE ALL OUR GOD

Martin Rinkart, d. 1649
Tr. Catherine Winkworth, alt.

Johann Cruger

1. Now thank we all our God, With
heart and hands and voi - ces, Who
won - drous things hath done, In
Whom His world re - joi - ces; Who
from our moth - er's arms Hath
blessed us on our way With
count - less gifts of love, And
still is ours to - day.

3. All praise and thanks to God, The
Fa - ther now be giv - en, The
Son, and Him Who reigns With
Them in high - est heav - en, The
one e - ter - nal God Whom
earth and heav'n a - dore; For
thus it was, is now, And
shall be ev - er - more.

O GOD OF LOVELINESS

Rev. E. Vaughan, C. SS. R., Tr.

Andante Maestoso

1. O God of love-li-ness, O Lord of
2. Thou are blest Three in One, Yet un-di-
3. O love-li-ness su-preme, And Beau-ty

Heav'n a-bove, How worth-y to pos-sess My
vi-ded still; Thou art that One a-lone Whose
in-fi-nite; O ev-er-flow-ing Stream, And

heart's de-vo-ted love! So sweet Thy Coun-te-nance,
love my heart can fill. The heav'ns and earth be-low,
O-cean of de-light; O Life by which I live,

So gra-cious to be-hold, That one, one
Were fash-ioned by Thy Word; How a-mia-
My tru-est life a-bove, To You a-

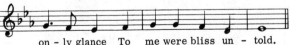

on-ly glance To me were bliss un-told.
ble are Thou, My ev-er-dear-est Lord!
lone I give My un-di-vi-ded love.

17 FAITH OF OUR FATHERS

Frederick W. Faber

Henri F. Hemy
and James G. Walton

1. Faith of our fa - thers! liv - ing still,
2. Faith of our fa - thers! We will love
3. Faith of our fa - thers! Ma - ry's prayers

In spite of dun - geon, fire,___ and sword:
Both friend and foe in all ___ our strife,
Shall keep our coun - try close___ to thee;

O how our hearts beat high with joy,
And preach thee too, as love knows how,
And through the truth that comes from God,

When-e'er we hear that glo - rious word!
By kind - ly words and vir - tuous life.
O we shall pros - per and be free.

Faith of our fa - thers ho - ly faith,

We will be true to thee till death.

O GOD, ALMIGHTY FATHER

1. O God, Al-might-y Fa-ther, Cre-a-tor of all things, The heav-ens stand in won-der, While earth Thy glo-ry sings. O most ho-ly Tri-ni-ty, Un-di-vid-ed U-ni-ty, Ho-ly God Might-y God, God im-mor-tal be a-dored!

2. O Je-sus Word In-car-nate, Re-deem-er most a-dored, All glo-ry, praise and hon-or be Thine, our Sov-'reign Lord.

3. O God the Ho-ly Spir-it, Who lives with-in our soul, Send forth Thy light and lead us To our e-ter-nal goal.

O GOD OUR HELP IN AGES PAST

1. Watts

Traditional

1. O God our help in a-ges past, Our
2. Un-der the sha-dow of Thy throne, Thy

1. aid for years to come. Our shel-ter from the
2. saints have dwelt se-cure, Suf-fi-cient is Thine

1. stor-my blast, And our e-ter-nal home.
2. arm a-lone, And our de-fence is sure.

3. A thousand ages in Thy sight,
   Are like an evening gone:
   Short as the watch that ends the night,
   Before the rising sun.

4. O God, our help in ages past,
   Our hope for years to come,
   Be Thou our guide while troubles last
   And our eternal home.

PRAISE GOD FROM WHOM ALL BLESSING FLOW 20

All People That On Earth Do Dwell

v. 1. Thomas Ken
v. v. 2-4. William Kethe

Louis Bourgeois

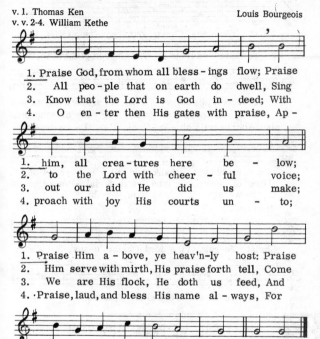

1. Praise God, from whom all bless - ings flow; Praise
2. All peo - ple that on earth do dwell, Sing
3. Know that the Lord is God in - deed; With
4. O en - ter then His gates with praise, Ap -

1. him, all crea - tures here be - low;
2. to the Lord with cheer - ful voice;
3. out our aid He did us make;
4. proach with joy His courts un - to;

1. Praise Him a - bove, ye heav'n-ly host: Praise
2. Him serve with mirth, His praise forth tell, Come
3. We are His flock, He doth us feed, And
4. Praise, laud, and bless His name al - ways, For

1. Fa-ther, Son, and Ho - ly Ghost. A - men.
2. ye be-fore Him and re - joice.
3. for His sheep He doth us take.
4. it is seem - ly so to do.

21   TO JESUS CHRIST OUR SOVEREIGN KING

Martin B. Hellriegel   Mainz, 1870

1. To Je-sus Christ, our sov-'reign King, Who
2. Thy reign ex-tend, O King be-nign, To
3. To thee and to Thy Church, great King, We

is the world's sal-va-tion, All praise and hom-age
ev-'ry land and na-tion; For in thy king-dom
pledge our heart's ob-la-tion; Un-til be-fore thy

do we bring And thanks and ad-o-ra-tion.
Lord di-vine, A-lone we find sal-va-tion.
throne we sing In end-less ju-bi-la-tion.

Refrain

Christ Je-sus, Vic-tor! Christ Je-sus, Rul-er!

Christ Je-sus, Lord and Re-deem-er!

22   HOLY GOD, WE PRAISE THY NAME

Holy God, we praise Thy Name!
    Lord of all, we bow before Thee!
All on earth Thy sceptre claim,
    All in heaven above adore Thee.
Infinite Thy vast domain,
    Everlasting is Thy reign. *Repeat last two lines*

2. Hark! the loud celestial hymn,
    Angel choirs above are raising;
Cherubim and seraphim,
    In unceasing chorus praising,
Fill the heavens with sweet accord;
    Holy, holy, holy Lord! *Repeat last two lines*

O COME, O COME EMMANUEL

23

Melody adapted

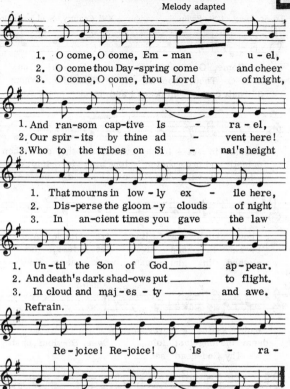

1. O come, O come, Em-man - u-el,
2. O come thou Day-spring come and cheer
3. O come, O come, thou Lord of might,

1. And ran-som cap-tive Is - ra-el,
2. Our spir-its by thine ad - vent here!
3. Who to the tribes on Si - nai's height

1. That mourns in low-ly ex - ile here,
2. Dis-perse the gloom-y clouds of night
3. In an-cient times you gave the law

1. Un-til the Son of God_____ ap-pear.
2. And death's dark shad-ows put _____ to flight.
3. In cloud and maj-es-ty _____ and awe.

Refrain.

Re-joice! Re-joice! O Is - ra-

el, To thee shall come Em-ma - nu-el.

4. O come, thou Rod of Jesse free
   Thy own from Satan's tyranny
   From depths of hell thy people save,
   And give them vict'ry o'er the grave.—*Refrain.*

5. O come, thou Key of David, come,
   And open wide our heavn'ly home;
   Make safe the way that leads on high,
   And close the path to misery.—*Refrain.*

24 COME, O DIVINE MESSIAH

Tr. Sr. Mary of St. Philip   XVI Century, Noel populaire

1. Come, O di-vine Mes - si - ah! The
2. O Thou, Whom na - tions sighed for, Whom
3. Shalt come in peace and meek - ness, And

world in si - lence waits___ the day, When
priests and pro - phets long___ fore-told, Will
low - ly will Thy cra - dle be: All

hope shall sing its tri - umph, And
break the cap - tive fet - ters, Re -
clothed in hu - man weak - ness Shall

Fine **Refrain**

sad-ness flee a - way.___
deem the long-lost fold.___ Sweet Sa-viour, haste;
we Thy God-head see.___

Come, come to earth; Dis-pel the night and show Thy

D. C. al Fine

face, And bid us hail the dawn of grace.___ Come,

DEAR MAKER OF THE STARRY SKIES

Tr. Rev. E. Caswall

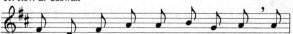

1. Dear Ma - ker of the star - ry skies! Light
2. When man was sunk in sin and death, Lost
3. Thou for the sake of guilt - y men Per -
4. So great the glo - ry of Thy might, If
5. Great judge of all in that last day, When
6. To God the Fa - ther, with the Son, And

1. of be - liev - ers ev - er - more! Je -
2. in the depth of Sa - tan's snare, Love
3. mit - ting Thy pure Blood to flow, Didst
4. we but chance Thy name to sound, At
5. friends shall fail and foes com - bine, Be
6. Ho - ly Spir - it, One in Three, Be

1. su, Re - deem - er of man - kind! Be
2. brought Thee down to cure our ills, By
3. is - sue from Thy Vir - gin shrine And
4. once all Heav'n and Hell u - nite In
5. pres - ent then with us, we pray, To
6. hon - or, glo - ry, bless - ing, praise, All

1. near us who Thine aid im - plore.
2. tak - ing of those ills a share.
3. to the Cross a Vic - tim go.
4. bend - ing low with awe pro - found.
5. guard us with Thy arm di - vine.
6. through the long e - ter - ni - ty. A - men.

THE ADVENT OF OUR KING

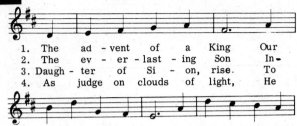

1. The ad-vent of a King Our
2. The ev-er-last-ing Son In-
3. Daugh-ter of Si-on, rise. To
4. As judge on clouds of light, He

1. prayers must now em-ploy, And we must hymns of
2. car-nate deigns to be; Him-self a ser-vants
3. meet the low-ly King; Nor let thy faith-less
4. soon will come a-gain, And his true mem-bers

1. wel-come sing In strains of ho-ly joy.
2. form puts on, To set his ser-vants free.
3. heart de-spise The peace he comes to bring.
4. all u-nite With Him in heav'n to reign. A-men.

COME THOU LONG-EXPECTED SAVIOR

1. Come, thou long-expected Savior,
   Born to set thy people free;
   From our fears and sins release us;
   Let us find our rest in thee.
   Israel's strength and consolation,
   Hope of all the earth thou art;
   Fond desire of ev'ry nation,
   Joy of ev'ry longing heart.

2. Born thy people to deliver
   Born a child, and yet the King,
   Born to reign in us forever,
   Now thy gracious kingdom bring.
   By thine own eternal Spirit
   Rule in all our hearts alone;
   By thine all-sufficient merit
   Raise us to thy glorious throne.

Melody as on page 376.

HOW BRIGHT APPEARS THE MORNING STAR

1. How bright ap-pears the Morn-ing Star, With
2. Re - joice, ye heav'ns; thou earth re-ply; With

mer - cy beam - ing from a - far; The
praise, ye sin - ners, fill the sky, For

host of heav'n re - joic - es; O
this his In - car - na - tion. In-

Right-eous Branch, O Jes - se's Rod! Thou
car - nate God, put forth your power, Ride

Son of Man and Son of God! We,
on, ride on, great Con - quer - or, Till

too, will lift our voic - es: Je - sus,
all know your sal - va - tion. A - men,

Je - sus! Ho - ly, ho - ly, yet most low - ly,
A - men! Al - le - lu - ia! Al - le - lu - ia!

Draw thou near us; Great Em - man - uel,
Praise be giv - en Ev - er - more, by

come and hear us.
earth and heav - en. A - men.

29   HARK! THE HERALD ANGELS SING

Hark! The herald angels sing,
  "Glory to the new-born King,
Peace on earth, and mercy mild
  God and sinners reconciled."
Joyful all ye nations rise,
  Join the triumph of the skies.
With th' angelic host th' proclaim,
  "Christ is born in Bethlehem."

— *Refrain:* Hark! The herald angels sing,
  "Glory to the new-born King."

2. Christ, by highest heaven adored,
  Christ, the everlasting Lord.
Late in time behold Him come,
  Off-spring of a virgin's womb.
Veiled in flesh, the God-head see;
  Hail th' incarnate Deity!
Pleased as Man with men to appear,
  Jesus, our Immanuel here! — *Refrain:*

30   O COME ALL YE FAITHFUL

O come, all ye faithful, joyful and triumphant,
O come ye, O come ye to Bethlehem;
  Come and behold Him, born, the King of angels;

— *Refrain:* O come, let us adore Him,
  O come, let us adore Him,
O come, let us adore Him, Christ the Lord.

2. Sing, Choirs of angels, sing in exultation,
Sing, all ye citizens of heav'n above;
  Glory to God, in the highest: — *Refrain:*

31   THE FIRST NOEL

The first Noel the angel did say,
  Was to three poor shepherds in fields as they lay;
In fields where they lay keeping their sheep
  On a cold winter's night that was so deep.

— *Refrain:* Noel, Noel, Noel, Noel,
  Born is the King of Israel.

2. They looked up and saw a star,
  Shining in the east, beyond them far,
And to the earth it gave great light,
  And so it continued both day and night — *Refrain:*

GOOD CHRISTIAN MEN REJOICE

In Dulci Jubilo
Tr. John Mason Neale

German, 14th cent.

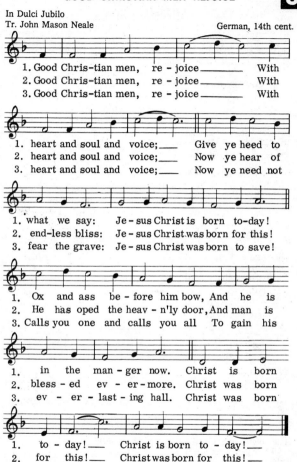

1. Good Chris-tian men, re - joice_____ With
2. Good Chris-tian men, re - joice_____ With
3. Good Chris-tian men, re - joice_____ With

1. heart and soul and voice;___ Give ye heed to
2. heart and soul and voice;___ Now ye hear of
3. heart and soul and voice;___ Now ye need not

1. what we say: Je - sus Christ is born to-day!
2. end-less bliss: Je - sus Christ was born for this!
3. fear the grave: Je - sus Christ was born to save!

1. Ox and ass be - fore him bow, And he is
2. He has oped the heav - n'ly door, And man is
3. Calls you one and calls you all To gain his

1. in the man-ger now. Christ is born
2. bless-ed ev - er-more. Christ was born
3. ev - er - last - ing hall. Christ was born

1. to - day! ___ Christ is born to - day! ___
2. for this! ___ Christ was born for this! ___
3. to save! ___ Christ was born to save! ___

33

A CHILD IS BORN IN BETHLEHEM
THE MAGI KINGS

Verses: Choir

1. A Child is born in Beth-le-hem, al-
2. Our Broth-er in the Flesh is He, al-
3. By grace this Child is born a-gain, al-

1. The Ma-gi Kings come from a-far, al-
2. Gold, in-cense, myrrh they of-fer Him, al-

1. le-lu-ia; Re-joice, re-joice Je-ru-
2. le-lu-ia; Our King for all e-ter-
3. le-lu-ia; In ev-'ry heart He frees

1. le-lu-ia; Led on by faith in heav-
2. le-lu-ia; And bend-ing low they wor-

1. sa-lem, al-le-lu-ia, al-le-lu-ia.
2. ni-ty, al-le-lu-ia, al-le-lu-ia.
3. from sin, al-le-lu-ia, al-le-lu-ia.

1. en's star, al-le-lu-ia, al-le-lu-ia.
2. ship Him, al-le-lu-ia, al-le-lu-ia.

Responsory: All

Let grate-ful hearts now sing, A song

of joy and ho-ly praise to Christ the new-born King.

34

SILENT NIGHT

Silent night, holy night!
  All is calm, all is bright.
'Round yon Virgin Mother and
    Child,
  Holy Infant so tender and mild:
Sleep in heavenly peace,
  Sleep in heavenly peace!

Silent night, holy night!
  Shepherds quake at the sight!
Glories stream from heaven afar,
  Heav'nly hosts sing Alleluia:
Christ, the Savior is born,
  Christ, the Savior is born!

AS WITH GLADNESS MEN OF OLD

W. C. Dix, alt.

C. Kocher

1. As with gladness men of old
2. As with joy-ful steps they sped
3. As they of-fered gifts most rare

Did the guid-ing star be-hold,
To that low-ly man-ger-bed,
At that man-ger, rude and bare,

As with joy they hailed its light,
There to bend the knee be-fore
So may we with hum-ble heart

Lead-ing on-ward, beam-ing bright,
him, Whom heav'n and earth a-dore,
And the joy that you im-part,

So, most gra-cious Lord, may we
So may we, O Lord, this day
All our cost-ly treas-ures bring,

Ev-er-more be led to thee.
Un-to thee our hom-age pay.
Christ, to thee, our heav'n-ly King.

36
ALL GLORY, LAUD, AND HONOR

1. All glo-ry, laud, and hon-or To
3. The com-pa-ny of an-gels Are
5. To thee be-fore thy Pas-sion They

1. thee, Re-deem-er, King! 1. To whom the lips of
3. prais-ing thee on high; 3. And mor-tal men and
5. sang their hymns of praise: 5. To thee, now high ex-

1. chil-dren Made loud ho-san-nas ring. ★
3. all things Cre-a-ted make re-ply. ✱
5. alt-ed, Our mel-o-dy we raise. ★

2. Thou art the King of Is-rael, Thou
4. The peo-ple of the He-brews With
6. Thou didst ac-cept their prais-es; Ac-

2. Da-vid's roy-al Son, Who in the Lord's Name
4. palms be-fore thee went: Our praise and prayer and
6. cept the praise we bring, Who in all good de-

2. com-est, The King and Bless-ed One. ✱
4. an-thems Be-fore thee we pre-sent. ★
6. light-est, thou good and gra-cious King. ★

★ The first stanza is repeated wherever the star occurs.

AT THE CROSS HER STATION KEEPING

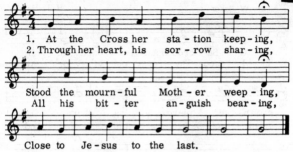

1. At the Cross her sta-tion keep-ing,
Stood the mourn-ful Moth-er weep-ing,
Close to Je-sus to the last.

2. Through her heart, his sor-row shar-ing,
All his bit-ter an-guish bear-ing,
Now at length the sword has passed. A-men.

3 Oh, how sad and sore distressed
Was that Mother highly blessed
of the sole begotten One!

4 Christ above in torment hangs,
She beneath beholds the pangs
Of her dying, glorious Son.

5 Is there one who would not weep
'Whelmed in miseries so deep
Christ's dear Mother to behold?

6 Can the human heart refrain
From partaking in her pain,
In that mother's pain unto'd?

7 Bruised, derided, cursed, defiled,
She beheld her tender Child,
All with bloody scourges rent.

8 For the sins of His own nation
Saw Him hang in desolation
Till His spirit forth He sent.

9 O sweet Mother! fount of love,
Touch my spirit from above,
Make my heart with yours accord.

10 Make me feel as you have felt:
Make my soul to glow and melt
With the love of Christ, my Lord.

11 Holy Mother, pierce me through,
In my heart each wound renew
Of my Savior crucified.

12 Let me share with you His pain,
Who for all our sins was slain,
Who for me in torments died.

13 Let me mingle tears with you
Mourning Him Who mourned for
me,
All the days that I may live.

14 By the Cross with you to stay,
There with you to weep and pray,
Is all I ask of you to give.

15 Virgin of all virgins blest!
Listen to my fond request:
Let me share your grief divine.

16 Let me, to my latest breath
In my body bear the death
Of that dying Son of yours.

17 Wounded with His every wound,
Steep my soul till it has swooned
In His very blood away.

18 Be to me, O Virgin, nigh,
Lest in flames I burn and die,
In His awful judgment day.

19 Christ, when You shall call me
hence,
Be Your Mother my defense,
Be Your Cross my victory.

20 While my body here decays,
May my soul Your goodness
praise,
Safe in heaven eternally.
Amen. Alleluia.

38 O SACRED HEAD SURROUNDED

Tr. Henry W. Baker

H. L. Hassler

1. O Sa - cred Head sur - round - ed By
crown of pierc - ing thorn! O
bleed - ing Head, so wound - ed, Re -
viled, and put to scorn! Death's
pal - lid hue comes o'er Thee, The
glow of life de - cays, Yet
an - gel - hosts a - dore Thee, And
trem - ble as they gaze.

2. I see Thy strength and vig - or All
fad - ing in the strife, And
death with cru - el rig - or, Be -
reav - ing Thee of life; O
ag - o - ny and dy - ing! O
love to sin - ners free! Je -
sus, all grace sup - ply - ing, O
turn Thy face on me.

INCLINE THINE EAR, O LORD

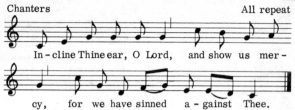

39

Chanters   All repeat

In - cline Thine ear, O Lord, and show us mer -
cy, for we have sinned a - gainst Thee.

LORD WHO THROUGHOUT THESE FORTY DAYS

40

Moderately   English Psalter,

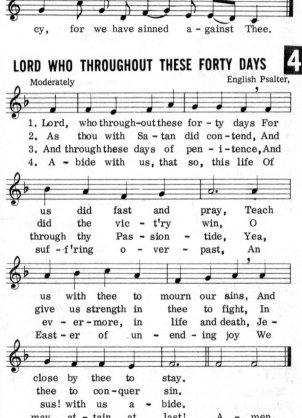

1. Lord, who through-out these for - ty days For
2. As thou with Sa - tan did con - tend, And
3. And through these days of pen - i - tence, And
4. A - bide with us, that so, this life Of

us did fast and pray, Teach
did the vic - t'ry win, O
through thy Pas - sion - tide, Yea,
suf - f'ring o - ver - past, An

us with thee to mourn our sins, And
give us strength in thee to fight, In
ev - er - more, in life and death, Je -
East - er of un - end - ing joy We

close by thee to stay.
thee to con - quer sin.
sus! with us a - bide.
may at - tain at last! A - men.

41 JESUS CHRIST IS RISEN TODAY

Tate and Brady C. Wesley

Lyra Davidica, 1708

1. Je - sus Christ is ris'n to - day, ____
2. Hymns of praise then let us sing, ____
3. But the pains which He en - dured, ____
4. Sing we to our God a - bove, ____

1. Our tri - um - phant
2. Un - to Christ our
3. Our sal - va - tion
4. Praise e - ter - nal

Al - le - lu - ia!

1. ho - ly day, ____
2. heav'n - ly King, ____
3. have se - cured, ____
4. as His love, ____

Al - - le -

1. Who did once up - on the cross,
2. Who en - dured the cross and grave,
3. Now in heav - en Christ our King,
4. Praise Him, all ye heav'n - ly host,

lu - ia!

1. Suf - fer to re -
2. Sin - ners to re -
3. Where the an - gels
4. Fa - ther, Son and

Al - le - lu - ia!

deem our loss,
deem and save,
ev - er sing,
Ho - ly Ghost,

Al - le - lu - ia!

YE SONS AND DAUGHTERS

Jean Tisserand,
Tr. John Mason Neale

1623

Refrain

Al-le-lu-ia, al-le-lu-ia, al-le-lu-ia.

Repeat refrain after each verse.

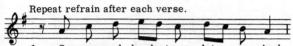

1. O sons and daugh-ters, let us sing!
2. On Eas-ter morn, at break of day,
3. An an-gel clothed in white they see,
4. On this most ho-ly day of days,
5. Glo-ry to Fa-ther and to Son,

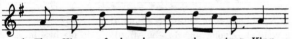

1. The King of heav'n, our glo-rious King.
2. The faith-ful wo-men went their way
3. Who sat and spoke un-to the three,
4. To you our hearts and voice we raise,
5. Who has for us the vic-t'ry won.

1. To-day is ris'n and tri-umph-ing. Al-le-lu-ia.
2. To seek the tomb where Je-sus lay. Al-le-lu-ia.
3. "Your Lord has gone to Gal-i-lee." Al-le-lu-ia.
4. In laud and ju-bi-lee and praise. Al-le-lu-ia.
5. And Ho-ly Ghost; blest Three in One. Al-le-lu-ia.

43 SINGERS, SING

Michael Gannon   12th cent.

1. Sing - ers, sing, and trumpets, play! Christ has conquered
2. An - gels, sing, and swell our hymns! Join with us, ye
3. Ho - ly, ho - ly, ris - en Lord; Man-kind ral-lies

1. death to - day. Think what he has done for men:
2. ser - a - phim. Christ has ris - en where he died;
3. to thy sword; Thou art our tri - umph - ant King,

1. Made them sons and heirs a - gain!
2. Walked a - mong us glo - ri - fied! Al - le - lu - ia.
3. And thy joy - ful sub - jects sing!

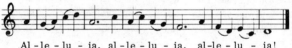

Al - le - lu - ia, al - le - lu - ia, al - le - lu - ia!

1. Let hymns of joy to grief suc - ceed. We
2. The morn had spread her crim-son rays, When
3. To God the Fa - ther let us sing: To

know that Christ is ris'n in - deed: Al - le -
rang the skies with shouts of praise: Al - le -
God the Son, our ris - en King: Al - le -

lu - ia, al - le - lu - ia. We hear His white-robed
lu - ia, al - le - lu - ia. Earth joined the joy - ful
lu - ia, al - le - lu - ia. And e - qual - ly let

an - gel's voice, And in our ris-en Lord re - joice.
hymn to swell That brought de-spair to van-quished hell.
us a - dore The Ho - ly Spir-it ev-er - more.

Al - le - lu - ia, al - le - lu - ia, al - le -

lu - ia, al - le - lu - ia, al - le - lu - ia!

THE STRIFE IS O'ER

F. Pott, Tr.

Melchior Vulpius

1. The strife is o'er, the bat - tle done! The vic - to - ry of life is won! The song of tri - umph has be - gun!
2. The powers of death have done their worst, But Christ their le - gions hath dis - persed; Let shouts of ho - ly joy out - burst!
3. The three sad days are quick - ly sped, He ris - es glo - rious from the dead; All glo - ry to our ris - en Head!
4. He closed the yawn - ing gates of hell; The bars from heaven's high por - tals fell; Let hymns of praise His tri - umph tell!

Refrain

Al - le - lu - ia, _____ al - le - lu - ia, _____ al - le - lu - ia!

BE JOYFUL MARY

Symphonia Sirenum, 1695

1. Be joy-ful, Ma-ry, heav'n-ly Queen,
2. Whom thou didst bear by Hea-ven's grace,
3. The Lord has ri-sen from the dead,
4. O pray to God, thou Vir-gin fair,

Gau-de Ma-ri-

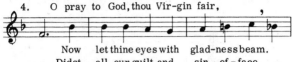

Now let thine eyes with glad-ness beam.
Didst all our guilt and sin ef-face,
He rose with might as He had said,
That He our souls to Hea-ven bear.

a,
Al-

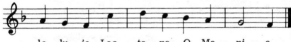

le - lu - ia, Lae - ta - re, O Ma - ri - a.

SING WE TRIUMPHANT HYMNS OF PRAISE   **47**

1. Sing we triumphant hymns of praise
   To greet our Lord these festive days.
   Alleluia, alleluia!
   Who by a road before untrod
   Ascended to the throne of God.
   Alleluia, alleluia, alleluia, alleluia.

2. In wond'ring awe His faithful band
   Upon the Mount of Olives stand.
   Alleluia, alleluia!
   And with the Virgin Mother see
   Their Lord ascend in majesty.
   Alleluia, alleluia, alleluia, alleluia.

(For music see Hymn No. 39).

48 HOLY SPIRIT, LORD OF LIGHT

Tr. Rev. E. Caswall

Samuel Webbe

1. Ho - ly Spir - it, Lord of Light,
2. Thou, of all con - sol - ers best,
3. Light im - mor - tal, Light di - vine,
4. Heal our wounds, our strength re - new;

1. From thy clear ce - les - tial height,
2. Thou the souls most wel - come Guest,
3. Vis - it Thou these hearts of Thine,
4. On our dry - ness pour Thy dew;

1. Thy pure beam - ing ra - diance give.
2. Dost re - fresh - ing peace be - stow.
3. And our in - most be - ing fill.
4. Wash the stains of guilt a - way.

1. Come, Thou Fa - ther of the poor;
2. Thou in toil art com - fort sweet;
3. If Thou take Thy grace a - way,
4. Bend the stub - born heart and will;

1. Come, with treas - ures which en - dure;
2. Plea - sant cool - ness in the heat;
3. Noth - ing pure in man will stay;
4. Melt the fro - zen, warm the chill;

1. Come, Thou Light of all that live.
2. So - lace in the midst of woe.
3. All his good is turned to ill.
4. Guide the steps that go a - stray.

- 412 -

COME HOLY GHOST, CREATOR BLEST

Louis Lambillotte, S.J.

1. Come, Holy Ghost, Creator blest, And in our hearts take up Thy rest; Come with Thy grace and heav'n-ly aid To fill the hearts which Thou hast made, To fill the hearts which Thou hast made.

2. O Comforter, to Thee we cry, Thou heav'n-ly Gift of God most high; Thou fount of life and fire of love And sweet a-noint-ing from a-bove, And sweet a-noint-ing from a-bove.

3. O Holy Ghost, through Thee alone Know we the Father and the Son; Be this our firm un-chang-ing creed: That Thou dost from Them both pro-ceed, That Thou dost from Them both pro-ceed.

4. Praise we the Father and the Son, And the blest Spirit with Them one; And may the Son on us be-stow The gifts that from the Spir-it flow, The gifts that from the Spir-it flow.

50 COME, O CREATOR SPIRIT BLEST

E. Caswall

S. Webbe

1. Come, O Cre-a-tor Spri-it blest, And in our souls take up thy rest; Come with Thy grace and heav'n-ly aid, To fill the hearts that Thou hast made.

2. Our sens-es kin-dle from a-bove, And make our hearts o'er flow with love; With pa-tience firm, and vir-tue high, The weak-ness of our flesh sup-ply.

3. O may Thy grace on us be-stow The Fa-ther and the Son to know, And Thee through end-less times con-fessed O both the heav'n-ly Spir-it blest.

4. All glo-ry while the a-ges run, Be to the Fa-ther and the Son. Who rose from death; the same to Thee, O Ho-ly Ghost e-ter-nal-ly. A - men.

LET ALL MORTAL FLESH KEEP SILENCE

51

Gerald Moultrie

French, Traditional

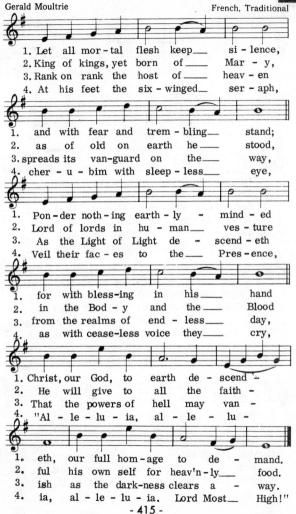

1. Let all mor-tal flesh keep si-lence,
2. King of kings, yet born of Mar-y,
3. Rank on rank the host of heav-en
4. At his feet the six-winged ser-aph,

1. and with fear and trem-bling stand;
2. as of old on earth he stood,
3. spreads its van-guard on the way,
4. cher-u-bim with sleep-less eye,

1. Pon-der noth-ing earth-ly-mind-ed
2. Lord of lords in hu-man ves-ture
3. As the Light of Light de-scend-eth
4. Veil their fac-es to the Pres-ence,

1. for with bless-ing in his hand
2. in the Bod-y and the Blood
3. from the realms of end-less day,
4. as with cease-less voice they cry,

1. Christ, our God, to earth de-scend-
2. He will give to all the faith-
3. That the powers of hell may van-
4. "Al-le-lu-ia, al-le-lu-

1. eth, our full hom-age to de-mand.
2. ful his own self for heav'n-ly food.
3. ish as the dark-ness clears a-way.
4. ia, al-le-lu-ia. Lord Most High!"

- 415 -

St. Thomas Aquinas
Tr. Rev. E. Caswall

Gregorian Chant

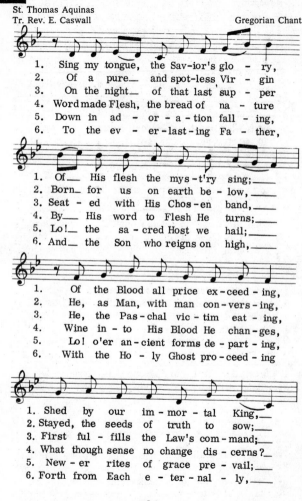

1. Sing my tongue, the Sav-ior's glo - ry,
2. Of a pure and spot-less Vir - gin
3. On the night of that last sup - per
4. Word made Flesh, the bread of na - ture
5. Down in ad - or - a - tion fall - ing,
6. To the ev - er-last-ing Fa - ther,

1. Of His flesh the mys-t'ry sing;
2. Born for us on earth be - low,
3. Seat - ed with His Chos-en band,
4. By His word to Flesh He turns;
5. Lo! the sa - cred Host we hail;
6. And the Son who reigns on high,

1. Of the Blood all price ex - ceed - ing,
2. He, as Man, with man con - vers-ing,
3. He, the Pas-chal vic - tim eat - ing,
4. Wine in - to His Blood He chan-ges,
5. Lo! o'er an-cient forms de - part - ing,
6. With the Ho - ly Ghost pro - ceed - ing

1. Shed by our im - mor - tal King,
2. Stayed, the seeds of truth to sow;
3. First ful - fills the Law's com - mand;
4. What though sense no change dis - cerns?
5. New - er rites of grace pre - vail;
6. Forth from Each e - ter - nal - ly,

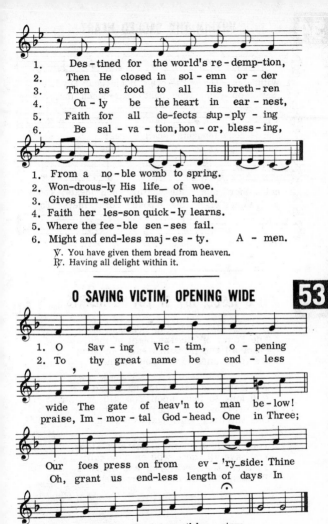

1. Des-tined for the world's re-demp-tion,
2. Then He closed in sol-emn or-der
3. Then as food to all His breth-ren
4. On-ly be the heart in ear-nest,
5. Faith for all de-fects sup-ply-ing
6. Be sal-va-tion, hon-or, bless-ing,

1. From a no-ble womb to spring.
2. Won-drous-ly His life_ of woe.
3. Gives Him-self with His own hand.
4. Faith her les-son quick-ly learns.
5. Where the fee-ble sen-ses fail.
6. Might and end-less maj-es-ty.   A - men.

℣. You have given them bread from heaven.
℟. Having all delight within it.

O SAVING VICTIM, OPENING WIDE   53

1. O Sav-ing Vic-tim, o-pening
2. To thy great name be end-less

wide The gate of heav'n to man be-low!
praise, Im-mor-tal God-head, One in Three;

Our foes press on from ev-'ry_side: Thine
Oh, grant us end-less length of days In

aid sup-ply, thy strength be-stow.
our true na-tive land with thee.   A - men.

54. WITHIN THY SACRED HEART

1. With - in Thy Sa - cred Heart, dear Lord, My
   anx - ious thoughts shall rest I
   nei - ther ask for life nor death, Thou
   know - est what is best.

2. Say on - ly Thou hast par - doned me, Say
   on - ly I am Thine In
   all things else dis - pose of me, Thy
   Ho - ly Will is mine.

55. O JESUS, JOY OF LOVING HEARTS

50

O Jesus, Joy of loving hearts,
The Fount of life, the Light of men,
From all the pleasures earth imparts
We turn, unfilled, to You again.

We taste and eat, O Living Bread,
And long to feast upon You still;
We drink of You, the Fountainhead
Our thirsting souls again You fill.

Your truth unchanged has ever stood,
You save all those who on You call;
To them that seek, You are all good
To them that find, You are their all.

THE GOD WHOM EARTH AND SEA AND SKY

56

Venantius Fortunatus, 609
Tr. J. M. Neale, alt.

J. S. Bach

1. The God whom earth and sea and sky A-
2. O Moth-er blest! the chos-en shrine Where-
3. Blest in the mes-sage Gab-riel brought; Blest
4. O Lord, the Vir-gin born, to thee E-

dore and laud and mag-ni-fy, Whose
in the Ar-chi-tect di-vine, Whose
by the work the Spir-it wrought; Most
ter-nal praise and glo-ry be, Whom

might they own, whose praise they tell, In
hand con-tains the earth and sky, Vouch-
blest, to bring to hu-man birth The
with the Fa-ther we a-dore And

Ma-ry's bo-dy deigned to dwell.
safed in hid-den guise to lie.
long de-sired of all the earth.
Ho-ly Ghost for ev-er-more.

57 IMMACULATE MARY

Immaculate Mary, thy praises we sing,
    Who reignest in splendor with Jesus, our King.
        — *Refrain:*
Ave, ave, ave, Maria! Ave, ave, Maria!

2. In heaven, the blessed thy glory proclaim,
    On earth, we thy children invoke thy fair name.
        — *Refrain:*

3. Thy name is our power, thy virtues our light,
    Thy love is our comfort, thy pleading our might.
        — *Refrain:*

4. We pray for our mother, the Church upon earth;
    And bless, dearest Lady, the land of our birth.
        — *Refrain:*

58 HAIL HOLY QUEEN ENTHRONED ABOVE

Hail, holy Queen, enthroned above, O Maria!
    Hail, Mother of mercy and of love, O Maria!
        — *Refrain:*
Triumph, all ye cherubim,
    Sing with us, ye seraphim,
Heav'n and earth resound the hymn.
    Salve, salve, salve Regina.

2. Our life, our sweetness here below, O Maria!
    Our hope in sorrow and in woe, O Maria!
        — *Refrain:*

3. To thee we cry, poor sons of Eve, O Maria!
    To thee we sigh, we mourn, we grieve, O Maria!
        — *Refrain:*

4. Turn, then, most gracious Advocate, O Maria!
    Toward us thine eyes compassionate, O Maria!
        — *Refrain:*

5. When this our exile's time is o'er, O Maria!
    Show us thy Son for evermore, O Maria!
        — *Refrain:*

GREAT ST. JOSEPH SON OF DAVID

Tr. Louis C. Casartelli

A. Stein,

1. Great Saint Jo - seph, son of Da - vid,
Fos - ter - fa - ther___ of our Lord,
Spouse of Ma - ry, ev - er vir - gin,
Keep - ing o'er them watch and ward:
In the sta - ble thou didst guard them
With a fa - ther's lov-ing care; Thou by God's com-
mand didst save them From the cru - el Her-od's snare.

2. Three long days in grief and an - guish,
With that moth - er___ sweet and mild,
Ma - ry, Vig - gin, didst thou wan - der,
Seek - ing her be - lov - ed Child.
In the tem - ple thou didst find Him:
Oh, what joy then filled thy heart! In thy sor-rows,
in thy glad-ness, Grant us, Jo-seph, to have part.

3. Clasped in Je - sus' arms and Mar - ry's
When death gent - ly___ came at last,
Thy pure spir - it, sweet - ly sigh - ing,
From its earth - ly dwell - ing passed.
Dear Saint Jo - seph, be that pass - ing
May our death be like to thine, And with Je - sus,
Ma - ry, Jo-seph, May our souls for - ev - er shine.

HAIL, HOLY JOSEPH, HAIL!

F. W. Faber

R. L. de Pearsall

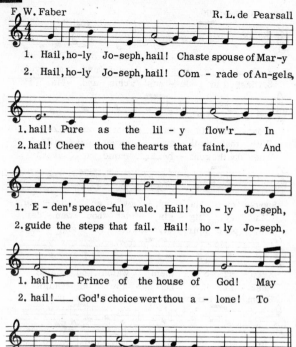

1. Hail, ho-ly Jo-seph, hail! Chaste spouse of Mar-y
2. Hail, ho-ly Jo-seph, hail! Com - rade of An-gels,

1. hail! Pure as the lil - y flow'r___ In
2. hail! Cheer thou the hearts that faint,___ And

1. E - den's peace-ful vale. Hail! ho - ly Jo-seph,
2. guide the steps that fail. Hail! ho - ly Jo-seph,

1. hail!___ Prince of the house of God! May
2. hail!___ God's choice wert thou a - lone! To

1. His best grac-es be___ By thy sweet hands be-stowed.
2. thee the Word made flesh Was sub-ject as a son.

FOR ALL THE SAINTS

William W. How
Moderately, in unison
R. Vaughan Williams, 1872-1958

1. For all the saints, who from their la-bors rest, Who Thee by faith be-fore the world con-fessed, Thy Name, O Je-sus, be for ev-er____ blest. Al-
2. O blest com-mu-nion! fel-low-ship di-vine! We fee-bly strug-gle, they in glo-ry shine; Yet all are one in Thee, for all are____ Thine.
3. But lo! there breaks a yet more glo-rious day; The saints tri-umph-ant rise in bright ar-ray; The King of glo-ry pass-es on His____ way.
4. From earth's wide bounds, from o-cean's far-thest coast, Through gates of pearl streams in the count-less host, ____ Sing-ing to Fa-ther, Son and Ho-ly____ Ghost,

____ le-lu-ia, al-le-lu-ia!

62 THAT ALL BE ONE

(S. Somerville - J. Ritchie),

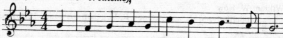

1. That all be one in you, O Lord, we pray,
2. When we are gath-ered for the Eu - char - ist,

That Christ-ians all be joined in one true fold; O
Re - mind us of the words you ut - tered then-Your

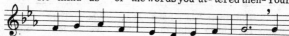

heal the sad di - vis-ions in your Church, Re-
prayer of u - ni - ty and peace and love, The

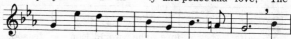

store the Faith kept by your saints of old, Good
one-ness sym-bo-lized by bread and wine. So

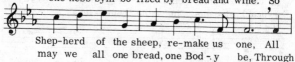

Shep-herd of the sheep, re-make us one, All
may we all one bread, one Bod - y be, Through

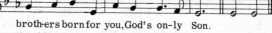

broth-ers born for you, God's on-ly Son.
this blest sac-ra ment of u - ni -ty. A-men.

3. Let charity direct our thoughts and deeds,
Let your love for all men be in our heart;
So Shall we truly your disciples be,
So for our sep'rate brethren do our part.
Teach us our common Father all to own,
Your holy people in one only home.

4. Then praise we God the Father, God the Son,
And God the Holy Spirit, three in one,
That one in him and one together, we
In unity may praise the Trinity.
Till all the ransomed fall before his throne
And give all glory to our God alone. Amen.

PRAISE THE LORD, ALL YOU NATIONS
PSALM 116

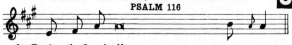

1. Praise the Lord, all you na - tions;
2. For steadfast is his kindness toward us,
3. Glory be to the Father, and to the Son,
4. As it was in the begin- ning, is now and ever shall be,

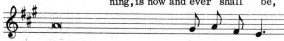

1. glorify him, all you peo-ples!
2. and the fidelity of the Lord en - dures for - ev - er.
3. and to the Ho - ly Spir - it.
4. world with — — out end. A - men.

64

O PERFECT LOVE

Gurney   Barnby

1. O per-fect Love, all hu-man thought tran-scend-ing,
2. O per-fect Life, be thou their full as-sur-ance

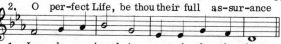

1. Low - ly we kneel in prayer be-fore thy throne,
2. Of ten-der cha - ri - ty and stead-fast faith,

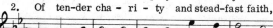

1. That theirs may be the love that knows no end-ing,
2. Of pa-tient hope, and qui-et, brave en - dur-ance,

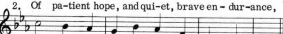

1. Whom thou for ev - er - more dost join in one.
2. With child-like trust that fears nor pain nor death.

- 425 -

65 O WORSHIP THE KING

R. Grant

W. Croft

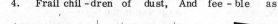

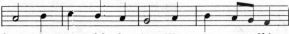

1.   O wor-ship the King, All glo-r'ous a-
2.   O tell of His might, O sing of His
3.   Thy boun-ti-ful care What tongue can re-
4.   Frail chil-dren of dust, And fee-ble as

bove; O grate-ful-ly sing His pow-er and his
grace, Whose robe is the light, Whose can-o-py
cite It breaths in the air, It shines in the
frail, In thee do we trust, Nor find thee to

love; Our Shield and De-fend-er, The An-cient of
space; His char-iots of wrath the deep thun-der clouds
light; It streams from the hills, It de-scends to the
fail; Thy mer-cies how ten-der How firm to the

Days, Pa-vil-ioned in splen-dor, And gird-ed with praise.
form, And dark is His path on the wings of the storm.
plain, And sweet-ly di-stils in the dew and the rain.
end, Our Mak-er, De-fend-er, Re-deem-er and Friend.

S. J. Stone   S. S. Wesley

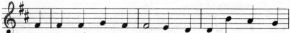

1. The Church's one foun-da-tion Is Je-sus Christ her
2. E - lect from ev'ry na-tion, Yet one o'er all the
3. Mid toil and trib - u -la-tion, and tu-mult of her
4. Yet she on earth has un-ion with God, the Three in

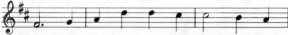

1. Lord. She is his new cre - a - tion, By
2. earth. Her char-ter of sal - va-tion, One
3. war. She waits the con-sum-ma-tion, Of
4. One, And mys - tic sweet com - mu - ion with

1. wa - ter and the Word; From heav'n he came and
2. Lord, one faith, one birth; One ho - ly Name she
3. peace for ev - er-more; Till with the vi-sion
4. those whose rest is won. O hap - py ones and

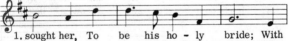

1. sought her, To be his ho - ly bride; With
2. bless-es, Par - takes one ho-ly food; And
3. glor - ious, Her long-ing eyes are blest; And
4. ho - ly! Lord give us grace that we like

1. his own blood he bought her, And for her life he died.
2. to one hope she press-es, With ev-'ry grace en-dued.
3. the great Church Vic-torious Shall be the Church at rest.
4. them the meek and low - ly, On high may dwell with thee.

67 FOR THE BEAUTY OF THE EARTH

F. S. Pierpont

Conrad Kocher

In moderate time

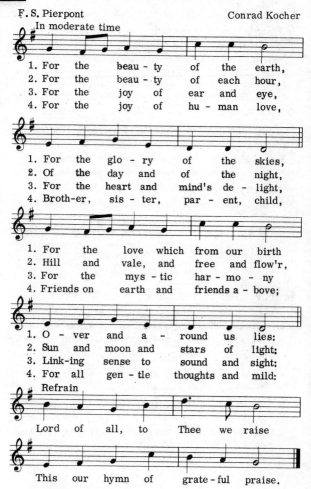

1. For the beau - ty of the earth,
2. For the beau - ty of each hour,
3. For the joy of ear and eye,
4. For the joy of hu - man love,

1. For the glo - ry of the skies,
2. Of the day and of the night,
3. For the heart and mind's de - light,
4. Broth-er, sis - ter, par - ent, child,

1. For the love which from our birth
2. Hill and vale, and free and flow'r,
3. For the mys - tic har - mo - ny
4. Friends on earth and friends a - bove;

1. O - ver and a - round us lies:
2. Sun and moon and stars of light:
3. Link-ing sense to sound and sight:
4. For all gen - tle thoughts and mild:

Refrain

Lord of all, to Thee we raise

This our hymn of grate - ful praise.

PRAISE, MY SOUL, THE KING OF HEAVEN

F. Lyte, alt.   John Goss

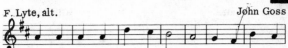

1. Praise my soul, the King of hea-ven; To his feet thy
2. Praise him for his grace and fa-vor To his children
3. Fa-ther-like he tends and spares us; Well our feeble
4. An-gels help us to a-dore him; You be-hold him

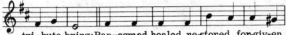

1. tri-bute bring; Ran-somed healed, re-stored, for-giv-en,
2. in dis-tress; Praise him still the same as ev-er,
3. frame he knows; In his hand he gen-tly bears us,
4. face to face; Sun and moon, bow down be-fore him,

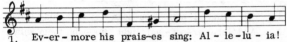

1. Ev-er-more his prais-es sing: Al-le-lu-ia!
2. Slow to chide, and swift to bless: Al-le-lu-ia!
3. Res-cues us from all our foes: Al-le-lu-ia!
4. Dwell-ers all in time and space. Al-le-lu-ia!

1. Al-le-lu-ia! Praise the ev-er-last-ing King.
2. Al-le-lu-ia! Glo-rious in his faith-ful-ness.
3. Al-le-lu-ia! Wide-ly yet his mer-cy flows.
4. Al-le-lu-ia! Praise with us the God of grace.

OUT OF THE DEPTHS TO THEE

Anom., alt. Gibbions, alt.

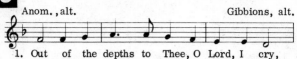

1. Out of the depths to Thee, O Lord, I cry,
2. Oh, hear our pray'rs and sighs, Re-deem-er blest,
3. This God Him-self shall come from Heav'n a-bove,

1. Lord! Gra-cious turn Thine ear to sup-pliant sigh;
2. And grant Thy ho-ly souls e-ter-nal-rest.
3. The Christ! the God of mer-cy and of love!

1. If sins of man Thou scan who may stand
2. And let per-pet-ual light up-on them shine;
3. He comes, He comes! The God in-car-nate He!

1. That search-ing eye of Thine, and chast'ning hand?
2. For tho' not spot-less, still these souls are Thine.
3. This is Thy law, our hope and stead-fast stay.

WHERE ABIDETH CHARITY AND LOVE

Antiphon

Where a - bid - eth char - i - ty

and love God is ev - er there.

1. All to - gether one in
   love of Christ our Bless-ed Lord,
2. Live we in holy
   fear and gentle love our life in God,
3. And whenever we
   come to-geth-er in mind and heart,
4. Cease all angry thoughts
   and bitter words all e-vils end,
5. And when we shall see the
   saints in heav-en,our broth-ers too,
6. O joy that knows
   no fear of end-ing at love so true;

1. let us sing in exaltation of one ac - cord.
2. and give we to one anoth-er our hearts in truth.
3. there is no fear of quar-
   reling among us to drive a - part
4. and Christ our brother
   comes to live among us, our guest and friend.
5. there will Christ in glory
   shine among us our life a - new.
6. through all the ages
   of eternity world with-out end. A - men.

OUR FATHER

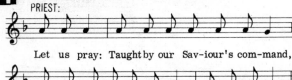

PRIEST:

Let us pray: Taught by our Sav-iour's com-mand,

and formed by the word of God, we dare to say:

PEOPLE:

Our fa-ther who art in heav-en, hal-lowed be thy name,

thy king-dom come, thy will be done on earth

as it is in heav-en. Give us this day

our dai-ly bread; and for-give us our tress-pass-

es as we for-give those who tress-pass a-

gainst us; And lead us not in-to temp-

ta-tion, but de-liv-er us from e-vil.

Stephen Somerville

Lord, have mer - cy. Lord, have mer - cy.

Lord, have mer - cy. Christ have mer-cy.

Christ, have mer - cy. Christ, have mer - cy.

Lord, have mer - cy. Lord, have

mer - cy. Lord, have mer - cy.

THE GLORIA

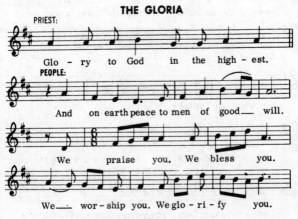

PRIEST:

Glo - ry to God in the high - est.

PEOPLE:

And on earth peace to men of good__ will.

We praise you. We bless you.

We__ wor - ship you. We glo - ri - fy you.

We give you thanks for your great glo-ry.

Lord God, heav-en-ly King, God the Fa-ther al-

might-y. Lord Je-sus Christ, the on-ly be-got-ten Son.

Lord God, Lamb of God, Son of the Fa-ther.

You who take a-way the sins of the world, have

mer-cy on us. You, who take a-way the

sins of the world, re - ceive our prayer.

You, who sit at the right hand of the Fa-ther, have

mer-cy on us. For you a-lone are ho-ly.

You a-lone are Lord. You a-lone, O Je-sus Christ, are

most high, with the Ho-ly Spir - it in the

glo - ry of God the Fa - ther.

A - men, a - men, a - men.

THE CREED

T. B. Armstrong

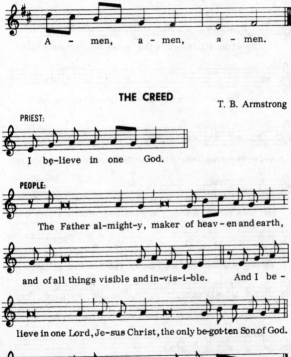

PRIEST:

I be-lieve in one God.

PEOPLE:

The Father al-might-y, maker of heav - en and earth,

and of all things visible and in-vis-i-ble. And I be -

lieve in one Lord, Je-sus Christ, the only be-got-ten Son of God.

Born of the Father be - fore all a - ges.

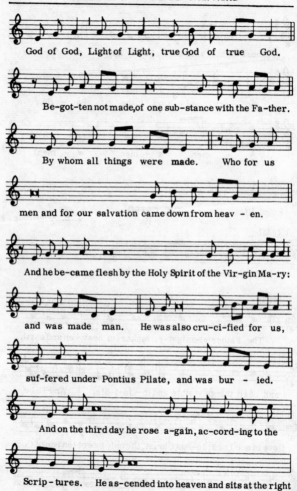

God of God, Light of Light, true God of true God.

Be-got-ten not made, of one sub-stance with the Fa-ther.

By whom all things were made.   Who for us

men and for our salvation came down from heav - en.

And he be-came flesh by the Holy Spirit of the Vir-gin Ma-ry:

and was made man.   He was also cru-ci-fied for us,

suf-fered under Pontius Pilate, and was bur - ied.

And on the third day he rose a-gain, ac-cord-ing to the

Scrip - tures.   He as-cended into heaven and sits at the right

hand of the Fa - ther. He will come again in glory to judge

the liv-ing and the dead. And of his king-dom there will be no end.

And I be-lieve in the Holy Spir - it, the Lord and Giv -

er of life, who pro-ceeds from the Fa-ther and the Son.

Who to-gether with the Father and the Son is a-dored and

glo - ri - fied, and who spoke through the proph-ets.

And one holy, Catholic, and Ap - os - tol - ic Church.
I con-fess one baptism for the for-give - ness of sins;

And I a -wait the res - ur - rec-tion of the dead.

And the life of the world to __ come. A - men.

THE SANCTUS

Ho-ly, ho-ly, ho-ly, Lord___ God of hosts.

Heav — en and earth are filled with your

glo - ry. Ho - san - na in__ the high-est.

Bless-ed is he who comes in the name of the

Lord.___ Ho - san - na in__ the high-est.

THE LAMB OF GOD

Lamb of God, who take a - way the

sins of the world, have mer - cy on us.

Lamb of God, who take a - way the

sins of the world, have mer - cy on

us. Lamb of God, who take a - way the

sins of the world, grant us ___ peace.

A MASS FOR GOD'S PEOPLE

J. Hutton

Lord, have mer-cy. Christ, have mer-cy.

Lord, have mer-cy. Lord, have mer-cy._____

GLORY TO GOD

PRIEST:

PEOPLE: Quickly

Glo-ry to God in the high-est. And on earth peace to

men of good will. We praise you. We bless you. We

wor-ship you. We glo-ri-fy you. We give you thanks for

your great glo-ry. Lord, God, heav-en-ly King,

God the Fa-ther al-might-y. Lord Je-sus

Christ, the on-ly-be-got-ten Son. Lord, God, Lamb of God,

Not as fast

Son of the Fa-ther. You, who take a-

way the sins of the world, have mer-cy on us. You, who

take a-way the sins of the world, re-ceive our prayer.

You, who sit at the right hand of the Fa - ther, have

Quickly

mer-cy on us. For you a-lone are ho - ly.

You a-lone are Lord. — You a-lone O Je-sus Christ

are most high. With the Ho-ly Spi-rit in the

glo-ry of God the Fa-ther. A - men.

HOLY, HOLY, HOLY

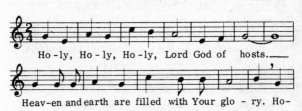

Ho-ly, Ho-ly, Ho-ly, Lord God of hosts.

Heav-en and earth are filled with Your glo-ry. Ho-

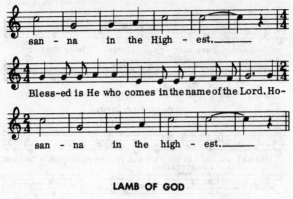

san - na in the High - est.____

Bless-ed is He who comes in the name of the Lord. Ho-

san - na in the high - est.____

LAMB OF GOD

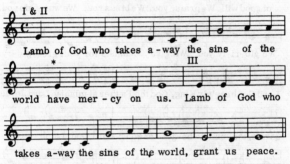

I & II

Lamb of God who takes a - way the sins of the

*

III

world have mer - cy on us. Lamb of God who

takes a - way the sins of the world, grant us peace.

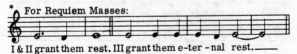

* For Requiem Masses:

I & II grant them rest. III grant them e - ter - nal rest.____

Jules Martel, O.M.I.

Slow (3 times) (3 times)

Lord, have mer - cy. Christ, have mer - cy.
(twice)
Lord, have mer - cy. Lord, have mer - cy.

GLORY TO GOD

Choir

Glo - ry to God in the high-est. And on earth peace to men
Congregation
of good will. We praise you. We bless you. We wor-ship you.
We glo-ri-fy you. We give you thanks for your great glo-ry.
Lord God heav'nly King, God the Fa-ther al-might-y. Lord Je-sus
Christ, the on-ly-be-got-ten Son. Lord God, Lamb of God,
Son of the Fa-ther. You, who take a-way the sins of the
world, have mer-cy on us. You, who take a-way the sins
of the world, re-ceive our pray'r. You, who sit at
the right hand of the Fa-ther, have mer-cy on us.

For you a-lone are ho-ly. You a-lone are Lord.

You a-lone, O Je-sus Christ, are most high. with the Ho-ly

Spi-rit. In the glo-ry of God the Fa-ther.   A-men.

THE CREED

Choir

I be-lieve in one God.   The Fa-ther al-might-y,

Ma-ker of heav-en and earth and of all things vi-si-ble

Congregation

and in-vi-si-ble. And I be-lieve in one Lord, Je-sus

Christ, the on-ly-be-got-ten Son of God, born of the

Fa-ther be-fore all a-ges. God of God, Light of Light,

true God of true God. Be-got-ten, not made, of one subs-

tance with the Fa-ther, by whom all things were made.

Who, for us men, and for our sal-va-tion came down from

heav-en. And he be-came flesh by the Ho-ly

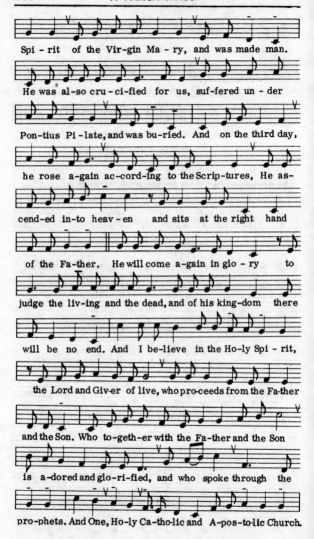

Spi - rit of the Vir-gin Ma - ry, and was made man.

He was al-so cru-ci-fied for us, suf-fered un - der

Pon-tius Pi -late, and was bu-ried. And on the third day,

he rose a-gain ac-cord-ing to the Scrip-tures, He as-

cend-ed in-to heav - en and sits at the right hand

of the Fa-ther. He will come a-gain in glo - ry to

judge the liv-ing and the dead, and of his king-dom there

will be no end. And I be-lieve in the Ho-ly Spi - rit,

the Lord and Giv-er of live, who pro-ceeds from the Fa-ther

and the Son. Who to-geth-er with the Fa-ther and the Son

is a-dored and glo-ri-fied, and who spoke through the

pro-phets. And One, Ho-ly Ca-tho-lic and A-pos-to-lic Church.

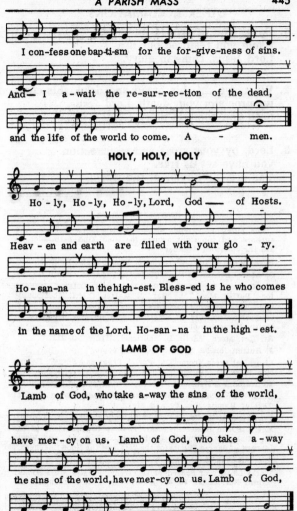

I con-fess one bap-ti-sm for the for-give-ness of sins.

And I a-wait the re-sur-rec-tion of the dead,

and the life of the world to come. A - men.

HOLY, HOLY, HOLY

Ho - ly, Ho - ly, Ho - ly, Lord, God of Hosts.

Heav - en and earth are filled with your glo - ry.

Ho - san-na in the high-est. Bless-ed is he who comes

in the name of the Lord. Ho-san - na in the high - est.

LAMB OF GOD

Lamb of God, who take a-way the sins of the world,

have mer-cy on us. Lamb of God, who take a - way

the sins of the world, have mer-cy on us. Lamb of God,

who take a-way the sins of the world, grant us peace.

OTHER ACCLAMATIONS

1. Dying you destroyed our death,
   rising you restored our life,
   Lord Jesus, come in glory.

   or

2. When we eat this bread and drink this cup,
   we proclaim your death, Lord Jesus,
   until you come in glory.

   or

3. Lord, by your cross and resurrection
   you have set us free.
   You are the Savior of the world.

ACKNOWLEDGMENTS

The publisher extends sincere gratitude to the following authors and copyright owners for their kind permission to use the following hymns:

Burns & Oates, Ltd., *Westminster Hymnal 1940*: Hymn No. 10.

Cathedral Schola Editions (Toronto, Canada): Hymn No. 10.

The Catholic Centre of St. Paul University (Ottawa, Canada) for "Parish Mass," by Rev. J. Martel, O.M.I. Accompaniment and recordings available.

Gregorian Institute of America, from *Hymnal of Christian Unity*: Hymn No. 56

Rt. Rev. Msgr. Martin B. Hellriegel: Hymn No. 21.

J. Hutton for "A Mass for God's People."

Liturgical Press, from *"Our Parish Prays and Sings"*: Hymns Nos. 9, 14, 33, 33A, 39.

McLaughlin & Reilly Co., from *Alverno Hymnal*: Hymn No. 8.

Oxford Univ. Press, from *English Hymnal*: Hymn No. 61; Text of Hymns Nos. 64 and 67.

Frederick Pustet Co., Inc., from *Catholic Hymnal*: Text No. 57.

Rev. Stephen Somerville, Rev. Thomas B. Armstrong of the St. Michael's Cathedral Choir School, Toronto, and World Library of Sacred Music, for the "Mass of the Good Shepherd,"

Rev. Stephen Somerville: Text revised Hymn No. 62.

World Library of Sacred Music, from *"Peoples Mass Book"*: Hymns Nos. 11, 23, 35, 43, 70.

EUCHARISTIC PRAYER No. 2

(This Eucharistic Prayer is particularly suitable on Weekdays or for special circumstances)

Priest: The Lord be with you.
People: **And with your spirit.**
Priest: Lift up your hearts.
People: **We have lifted them up to the Lord.**
Priest: Let us give thanks to the Lord our God.
People: **It is right and just.**

[Praise to the Father]

Father, it is our duty and our salvation,
always and everywhere
to give you thanks
through your beloved Son, Jesus Christ.
He is the Word through whom you made the
  universe,
the Savior you sent to redeem us.
By the power of the Holy Spirit
he took flesh and was born of the Virgin Mary.
For our sake he opened his arms on the cross;
he put an end to death
and revealed the resurrection.
In this he fulfilled your will
and won for you a holy people.
And so we join the angels and the saints
in proclaiming your glory
as we sing (say):

[First Acclamation of the People]

People: **Holy, holy, holy Lord God of hosts. ***
Heaven and earth are filled with your glory. *
Hosanna in the highest. *
**Blessed is he who comes in the name of the
  Lord. ***
Hosanna in the highest.

447

[*Invocation of the Holy Spirit*]

Lord, you are holy indeed,
the fountain of all holiness.
Let your Spirit come upon these gifts to make
    them holy,
so that they may become for us
the body and blood of our Lord, Jesus Christ.

[*The Lord's Supper*]

Before he was given up to death,
a death he freely accepted,
he took bread and gave you thanks.
He broke the bread,
gave it to his disciples, and said:
Take this, all of you, and eat it:
this is my body which will be given up for you.
When supper was ended, he took the cup.
Again he gave you thanks and praise,
gave the cup to his disciples, and said:
Take this, all of you, and drink from it:
this is the cup of my blood,
the blood of the new and everlasting covenant.
It will be shed for you and for all men
so that sins may be forgiven.
Do this in memory of me.

Priest: Let us proclaim the mystery of faith:

People: [*Memorial Acclamation of the People*]

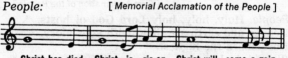

Christ has died. Christ is—ris-en. Christ will come a-gain.

For other acclamations, see **p. 446**

[*The Memorial Prayer*]

In memory of his death and resurrection,
we offer you, Father, this life-giving bread,
this saving cup.
We thank you for counting us worthy
to stand in your presence and serve you.

[*Invocation of the Holy Spirit*]

May all of us who share in the body and blood of
    Christ
be brought together in unity by the Holy Spirit.

[*Intercessions: For the Church*]

Lord, remember your Church throughout the
    world;
make us grow in love,
together with N. our Pope,
N. our bishop, and all the clergy. *

[*For the Dead*]

Remember our brothers and sisters
who have gone to their rest
in the hope of rising again;
bring them and all the departed
into the light of your presence.

[*In Communion with the Saints*]

Have mercy on us all;
make us worthy to share eternal life
with Mary, the virgin Mother of God,

---

* *In Masses for the Dead the following may be added:*

Remember N., whom you have called from this
    life.
In baptism he (she) died with Christ:
may he (she) also share his resurrection.

with the apostles,
and with all the saints who have done your will
   throughout the ages.
May we praise you in union with them,
and give you glory
through your Son, Jesus Christ.

Through him,   [*Concluding Doxology*]
with him,
in him,
in the unity of the Holy Spirit,
all glory and honor is yours,
almighty Father,
for ever and ever.
All reply: **Amen.**

EUCHARISTIC PRAYER No. 3

---

*(This Eucharistic Prayer may be used with any Preface
and preferably on Sundays and feast days)*

[Priest: The Lord be with you, etc.

               [*First Acclamation of the People*]

People: Holy, holy, holy, etc.]

               [*Praise to the Father*]

Father, you are holy indeed,
and all creation rightly gives you praise.
All life, all holiness comes from you
through your Son, Jesus Christ our Lord,
by the working of the Holy Spirit.
From age to age you gather a people to yourself,
so that from east to west
a perfect offering may be made
to the glory of your name.

         [*Invocation of the Holy Spirit*]

And so, Father, we bring you these gifts.

We ask you to make them holy by the power of
   your Spirit,
that they may become the body and blood
of your Son, our Lord Jesus Christ,
at whose command we celebrate this eucharist.

[The Lord's Supper]

On the night he was betrayed,
he took bread and gave you thanks and praise.
He broke the bread, gave it to his disciples, and
   said:
Take this, all of you, and eat it:
this is my body which will be given up for you.
When supper was ended, he took the cup.
Again he gave you thanks and praise,
gave the cup to his disciples, and said:
Take this, all of you, and drink from it:
this is the cup of my blood,
the blood of the new and everlasting covenant.
It will be shed for you and for all men
so that sins may be forgiven.
Do this in memory of me.

Priest: Let us proclaim the mystery of faith:

People: *[Memorial Acclamation of the People]*

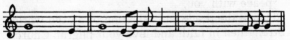

Christ has died. Christ is—ris-en. Christ will come a-gain.

For other acclamations, see p. 446

[The Memorial Prayer]

Father, calling to mind the death your Son en-
   dured for our salvation,
his glorious resurrection and ascension into heav-
   en,

and ready to greet him when he comes again,
we offer you in thanksgiving this holy and living
　　sacrifice.
Look with favor on your Church's offering,
and see the Victim whose death has reconciled
　　us to yourself.

[*Invocation of the Holy Spirit*]

Grant that we, who are nourished by his body
　　and blood,
may be filled with his Holy Spirit,
and become one body, one spirit in Christ.

[*Intercessions: In Communion with the Saints*]

May he make us an everlasting gift to you
and enable us to share in the inheritance of your
　　saints,
with Mary, the virgin Mother of God;
with the apostles, the martyrs,
(Saint N.) and all your saints,
on whose constant intercession we rely for help.

[*For the Church*]

Lord, may this sacrifice, which has made our
　　peace with you,
advance the peace and salvation of all the world.
Strengthen in faith and love your pilgrim Church
　　on earth:
your servant, Pope N., our bishop N.,
and all the bishops,
with the clergy and the entire people your Son
　　has gained for you.
Father, hear the prayers of the family you have
　　gathered here before you.
In mercy and love unite all your children

wherever they may be. *   [*For the Dead*]

Welcome into your kingdom our departed brothers and sisters,
and all who have left this world in your friendship.
We hope to enjoy for ever the vision of your
   glory,
through Christ our Lord, from whom all good
   things come.

Through him,   [*Concluding Doxology*]
with him,
in him,
in the unity of the Holy Spirit,
all glory and honor is yours,
almighty Father,
for ever and ever.
All reply: **Amen.**

---

* *In Masses for the Dead the following is added:*

Remember N.
In baptism he (she) died with Christ:
may he (she) also share his resurrection,
when Christ will raise our mortal bodies
and make them like his own in glory.
Welcome into your kingdom our departed brothers and sisters,
and all who have left this world in your friendship.
There we hope to share in your glory
when every tear will be wiped away.
On that day we shall see you, our God, as you
   are.
We shall become like you
and praise you for ever through Christ our Lord,
from whom all good things come.
Through him, etc., *as above.*

EUCHARISTIC PRAYER No. 4

(This Eucharistic Prayer may be used in Masses that have no proper Preface)

Priest: The Lord be with you.

People: **And with your spirit.**

Priest: Lift up your hearts.

People: **We have lifted them up to the Lord.**

Priest: Let us give thanks to the Lord our God.

People: **It is right and just.** [*Preface*]

Father in heaven, it is right that we should give you thanks and glory:

you alone are God, living and true.

Through all eternity you live in unapproachable light.

Source of life and goodness, you have created all things, to fill your creatures with every blessing

and lead all men to the joyful vision of your light.

Countless hosts of angels stand before you to do your will;

they look upon your splendor

and praise you, night and day.

United with them, and in the name of every creature under heaven,

we too praise your glory as we sing (say):

[*First Acclamation of the People*]

People: **Holy, holy, holy Lord God of hosts. ***

Heaven and earth are filled with your glory. *

Hosanna in the highest. *

Blessed is he who comes in the name of the Lord, *

Hosanna in the highest.

[*Praise to the Father*]

Father, we acknowledge your greatness:
all your actions show your wisdom and love.

You formed man in your own likeness
and set him over the whole world
to serve you, his creator,
and to rule over all creatures.

Even when he disobeyed you and lost your friendship
you did not abandon him to the power of death,
but helped all men to seek and find you.

Again and again you offered a covenant to man,
and through the prophets taught him to hope for salvation.

Father, you so loved the world
that in the fullness of time you sent your only
Son to be our Savior.

He was conceived through the power of the Holy
Spirit, and born of the Virgin Mary,
a man like us in all things but sin.

To the poor he proclaimed the good news of salvation,

to prisoners, freedom,
and to those in sorrow, joy.

In fulfillment of your will
he gave himself up to death;
but by rising from the dead,
he destroyed death and restored life.

And that we might live no longer for ourselves
but for him,
he sent the Holy Spirit from you, Father,
as his first gift to those who believe,
to complete his work on earth
and bring us the fullness of grace.

[*Invocation of the Holy Spirit*]

Father, may this Holy Spirit sanctify these offer-
    ings.

Let them become the body and blood of Jesus
    Christ our Lord

as we celebrate the great mystery

which he left us as an everlasting covenant.

[*The Lord's Supper*]

He always loved those who were his own in the
    world.

When the time came for him to be glorified by
    you, his heavenly Father,

he showed the depth of his love.

While they were at supper,

he took bread, said the blessing, broke the bread

and gave it to his disciples, saying:

Take this, all of you, and eat it:

this is my body which will be given up for you.

In the same way, he took the cup, filled with
    wine.

He gave you thanks, and giving the cup to his
    disciples, said:

Take this, all of you, and drink from it:

this is the cup of my blood,

the blood of the new and everlasting covenant.

It will be shed for you and for all men

so that sins may be forgiven.

Do this in memory of me.

Priest: Let us proclaim the mystery of faith:

People: [*Memorial Acclamation of the People*]

Christ has died. Christ is—ris-en. Christ will come a-gain.

For other acclamations, see p. 446

[The Memorial Prayer]

Father, we now celebrate this memorial of our redemption.

We recall Christ's death, his descent among the dead,

his resurrection, and his ascension to your right hand;

and, looking forward to his coming in glory, we offer you his body and blood,

the acceptable sacrifice which brings salvation to the whole world.

Lord, look upon this sacrifice which you have given to your Church;

and by your Holy Spirit, gather all who share this bread and wine

into the one body of Christ, a living sacrifice of praise.

[Intercessions: For the Church]

Lord, remember those for whom we offer this sacrifice,

especially N. our Pope,

N. our bishop, and bishops and clergy everywhere.

Remember those who take part in this offering,

those here present and all your people,

and all who seek you with a sincere heart.

[For the Dead]

Remember those who have died in the peace of Christ

and all the dead whose faith is known to you alone.

[In Communion with the Saints]

Father, in your mercy grant also to us, your children,

to enter into our heavenly inheritance

in the company of the Virgin Mary, the Mother
    of God,
and your apostles and saints.
Then, in your kingdom, freed from the corruption
    of sin and death,
we shall sing your glory with every creature
    through Christ our Lord,
through whom you give us everything that is
    good.

[Concluding Doxology]

Through him,
with him,
in him,
in the unity of the Holy Spirit,
all glory and honor is yours,
almighty Father,
for ever and ever.

All reply: **Amen.**

NEW PREFACES

Advent Preface I

(From the First Sunday of Advent to December 16)

Father, all-powerful and ever-living God,
we do well always and everywhere to give you
    thanks
through Jesus Christ our Lord.
When he humbled himself to come among us as a
    man,
he fulfilled the plan you formed long ago
and opened for us the way to salvation.
Now we watch for the day

hoping that the salvation promised will be ours
when Christ our Lord will come again in his glory.
And so, with all the multitude of angels in the
    heavenly courts,
we proclaim your glory as we join in their un-
    ending hymn: Holy, holy, holy, etc.

Advent Preface II

(From December 17 to December 24)

Father, all-powerful and ever-living God,
we do well always and everywhere to give you
    thanks
through Jesus Christ our Lord.
His future coming was proclaimed by all the
    prophets.
The Virgin Mother bore him in her womb with
    love beyond all telling.
John the Baptist was his herald
and made him known when at last he came.
In his love he has filled us with joy
as we prepare to celebrate his birth,
so that when he comes he may find us watching
    in prayer,
our hearts filled with wonder and praise.
And so, with all the multitude of angels in the
    heavenly courts,
we proclaim your glory as we join in their un-
    ending hymn: Holy, holy, holy, etc.

Preface for Sundays of Lent

(Used as a proper Preface on all Sundays of Lent

Father, all-powerful and ever-living God,
we do well always and everywhere to give you
    thanks

through Jesus Christ our Lord.

You bid your faithful people cleanse their hearts
and prepare with joy for the paschal feast.

More fervent in prayer,

more generous in works of charity,

more eager in celebrating the mysteries by which
we are reborn

may we come to the fullness of grace

that belongs to the sons of God.

And so, with all the multitude of angels in the
heavenly courts,

we proclaim your glory as we join in their unending hymn: Holy, holy, holy, etc.

Preface for Sundays of the Year I

(For Sundays after Epiphany and after Pentecost)

Father, all-powerful and ever-living God,

we do well always and everywhere to give you
thanks

through Jesus Christ our Lord.

Through his cross and resurrection

he freed us from sin and death

and called us to the glory that has made us

a chosen race, a royal priesthood,

a holy nation, a people set apart.

Everywhere we proclaim your mighty works

for you have called us out of darkness

into your own wonderful light.

And so, with all the multitude of angels in the
heavenly courts,

we proclaim your glory as we join in their unending hymn: Holy, holy, holy, etc.

Preface for Sundays of the Year II

(For Sundays after Epiphany and after Pentecost)

Father, all-powerful and ever-living God,
we do well always and everywhere to give you
    thanks
through Jesus Christ our Lord.
Out of love for sinful man,
he humbled himself to be born of the Virgin.
By suffering on the cross
he freed us from unending death,
and by rising from the dead
he gave us eternal life.
And so, with all the multitude of angels in the
    heavenly courts,
we proclaim your glory as we join in their un-
    ending hymn: Holy, holy, holy, etc.

Preface of the Eucharist

(For Holy Thursday and Masses of the Holy Eucharist)

Father, all-powerful and ever-living God,
we do well always and everywhere to give you
    thanks
through Jesus Christ our Lord.
He is the true and eternal priest
who established this unending sacrifice.
He offered himself as victim for our deliverance
and taught us to make this offering in his mem-
    ory,
so that by eating the bread of life in a holy meal
we might proclaim his death until he comes.
And so, with all the multitude of angels in the
    heavenly courts,
we proclaim your glory as we join in their un-
    ending hymn: Holy, holy, holy, etc.

Common Preface I

(For Masses that do not have a proper Preface)

Father, all-powerful and ever-living God,
we do well always and everywhere to give you
  thanks
through Jesus Christ our Lord.
In him you have renewed all things
and you have given us all a share in his riches.
Though his nature was divine,
he stripped himself of glory
and by shedding his blood on the cross
he brought his peace to the world.
Therefore he was exalted above all creation
and became the source of eternal life
to all who serve him.
And so, with all the multitude of angels in the
  heavenly courts,
we proclaim your glory as we join in their unending hymn: Holy, holy, holy, etc.

Common Preface II

(For Masses that do not have a proper Preface)

Father, all-powerful and ever-living God,
we do well always and everywhere to give you
  thanks
through Jesus Christ our Lord.
In love you created man,
in justice you condemned him,
but in mercy you redeemed him.
Through Christ the multitude of angels and all
  the powers of heaven
praise and worship the greatness of your glory.
May our voices blend with theirs as we join in
  their unending hymn: Holy, holy, holy, etc.

TREASURY OF PRAYERS

THE great prayer is the Mass. But there is another important prayer in the Church, "The Divine Office," which forms a circle of prayer around the Mass. All through the day and night priests, sisters, monks, and many lay people stop their other works and join the Angels and Saints in heaven in a hymn of praise to the great God.

We are likely not able to say all of the Office but these prayers are taken from it. They are shorter and more simple, but the ideas are the same as in the Divine Office. So we will be praying with the same wonderful thoughts as the Church. Notice how often we will say "we" and "us" because we are praying with the rest of the Church and for all her members.

These prayers may be used as a family prayer, said in unison, or preferably with the Father leading and the others responding alternately.

MORNING PRAYERS

℣. O God, ✠ come to my assistance. *
℞. O Lord, hurry to be my help.
　　Glory be, etc.

Psalm 94 — Call to Christian Prayer and Work

COME, let us sing joyfully to the Lord;
　let us acclaim the Rock of our salvation.

* Were we find ✠, we make the Sign of the Cross.

2 Let us greet Him with thanksgiving;
    let us joyfully sing psalms to Him

3 For the Lord is a great God,
    and a great King above all gods;

4 In His hands are the depths of the earth,
    and the tops of the mountains are His.

5 His is the sea, for He has made it,
    and the dry land, which His hands have formed.

6 Come, let us bow down in worship;
    let us kneel before the Lord Who made us.

7 For He is our God,
    and we are the people He shepherds, the flock
      He guides.

Oh, that today you would hear His voice:

8   "Harden not your hearts as at Meriba,
    as in the day of Massa in the desert,

9 Where your fathers tempted Me;
    they tested Me though they had seen My
      works.

10 Forty years I loathed that generation,
    and I said: They are a people of erring heart,
    and they know not My ways.

11 Therefore I swore in My anger:
    They shall not enter into My rest.

Psalm 8 — Man, God's Masterpiece

O LORD, our Lord,
    how glorious is Your Name over all the earth!
      You have exalted Your Majesty above the
      heavens.

3 Out of the mouths of babes and sucklings
      You have fashioned praise because of Your
      foes,
      to silence the hostile and the vengeful.

4 When I behold Your heavens, the work of Your
      fingers,

the moon and the stars which You set in
place—

5 What is man that You should be mindful of him,
or the son of man that You should care for
him?

6 You have made him little less than the Angels,
and crowned him with glory and honor.

7 You have given him rule over the works of Your
hands,
putting all things under his feet:

8 All sheep and oxen,
yes, and the beasts of the field,

9 The birds of the air, the fishes of the sea,
and whatever swims the paths of the seas.

10 O Lord, our Lord,
how glorious is Your Name over all the earth!

Prayer for Divine Guidance through the Day

LET us pray. Lord God most powerful, You have
brought us to the start of this new day. Let Your
strength redeem us more completely today, keep us
from any fault, grant that all our words, thoughts,
and works may be guided by the law of Christian
Love. Through Christ, our Lord. Amen.

Prayer for the Sanctification of the Day

LORD God, ruler of heaven and earth, please direct and make holy this day. Guide and regulate
our hearts and bodies, our thoughts, words, and
deeds according to Your law and teachings.

Thus with Your great aid we will find salvation
both today and in the life to come. O Redeemer of
all creation, Who live and reign always. Amen.

Short Lesson for the Day's Work

"Bear one another's burdens and so you will fulfill the Law of Christ" (Gal. 6, 2).

Final Blessing

MAY our Lord bless us, ✠ preserve us from evil, and lead us to eternal life. And may the souls of all our dead, especially . . . . . . , rest in peace through God's mercy. Amen.

EVENING PRAYERS

May the Lord Almighty ✠ grant us a restful night and a holy death.

Short Exhortation

"Brethren: Be sober and watchful, for your adversary the devil goes about seeking someone to devour. Resist him steadfast in the faith" (1 Pet. 5, 8-9). **Thanks be to God.**

(Here we make a short review of our service of Christ today, recalling our failings and sins. We then tell God we are sorry for them.)

O MY God, You adopted me as Your child, You love me very much. Today I have disobeyed You and committed these faults which You did not want in my life. I am sorry before You, God my Father; You made me and take care of me every minute with so much love. I am sorry before You, Jesus, my God and Brother; You love me so much that you were ready to suffer on the Cross to make up for my sins. I am sorry before You, O Holy Spirit; You are close to me all the time, to help me live as God's holy child.

Psalm 4 — A Prayer for a Peaceful Rest

WHEN I call, answer me, O my just God,
    You Who relieve me when I am in distress;
    Have pity on me, and hear my prayer!

3 Men of rank, how long will you be dull of heart?
  Why do you love what is vain and seek after
      falsehood?

4 Know that the Lord does wonders for His faith-
      ful one;
  the Lord will hear me when I call upon Him.

5 Tremble, and sin not;
  reflect, upon your beds, in silence.

6 Offer just sacrifices,
  and trust in the Lord.

7 Many say, "Oh, that we might see better times!"
  O Lord, let the light of Your countenance
      shine upon us!

8 You put gladness into my heart,
  more than when grain and wine abound.

9 As soon as I lie down, I fall peacefully asleep,
  for You alone, O Lord,
      bring security to my dwelling.

Psalm 90 — God Will Protect Us

YOU who dwell in the shelter of the Most High,
  who abide in the shadow of the Almighty,

2 Say to the Lord, "My refuge and my fortress,
  my God, in Whom I trust."

3 For He will rescue you from the snare of the
      fowler,
  from the destroying pestilence.

4 With His pinions He will cover you,
  and under His wings you shall take refuge;
  His faithfulness is a buckler and a shield.

5 You shall not fear the terror of the night
  nor the arrow that flies by day;

6 Not the pestilence that roams in darkness
  nor the devastating plague at noon.

7 Though a thousand fall at your side,
  ten thousand at your right side,
      near you it shall not come.

8 Rather with your eyes shall you behold
and see the requital of the wicked,

9 Because you have the Lord for your refuge;
you have made the Most High your stronghold.

10 No evil shall befall you,
nor shall affliction come near your tent,

11 For to His Angels He has given command about
you,
that they guard you in all your ways.

12 Upon their hands they shall bear you up,
lest you dash your foot against a stone.

13 You shall tread upon the asp and the viper;
you shall trample down the lion and the
dragon.

14 Because he clings to Me, I will deliver him;
I will set him on high because he acknowledges
My Name.

15 He shall call upon Me, and I will answer him;
I will be with him in distress;
I will deliver him and glorify him;

16 with length of days I will gratify him
and will show him My salvation.

Short Lesson

You are in our midst, O Lord. Your Holy Name
has been invoked upon us. Do not abandon us, O
Lord our God (Jer. 14, 9).
Thanks be to God.

Prayer of Trust in God Our Father

℣. Into Your hands, O Lord, I entrust my spirit.

℟. **For You have saved us, Lord, God of Truth.**
Glory be, etc.

℣. Keep us, O Lord, as the apple of Your eye.

℟. **Protect us beneath the shadow of Your wings.**

Canticle of Simeon: Nunc Dimittis

NOW You dismiss Your servants, O Lord,
according to Your word, in peace,
Because my eyes have seen Your salvation
which You have provided in the sight of all
peoples:
A light of revelation for the Gentiles,
and the glory of Your people Israel.

Plea for Divine Help

Ant. Protect us, Lord, while we are awake, guard
us while we sleep, so that we will always serve
Christ and rest in His peace.

LET us pray. Lord please visit our home and drive
all the snares of evil far from it. May the Holy
Angels dwell here to keep us in Your peace. Let
Your blessing never leave us. Through the same
Christ, our Lord. Amen.

Concluding Blessing

May the great Lord of all mercy, Father, ✠ Son,
and Holy Spirit, bless and protect us. Amen.

THE SACRAMENT OF PENANCE

We must be careful to distinguish the confession of
our sins from the Sacrament of Penance. If a deaf-
mute wishes to receive this Sacrament, there must be
a sign of sorrow, but no confession is necessary. The
confessing of our sins is a normal part of the way we
receive the Sacrament, but it is not the Sacrament.

A Sacrament is an external sign of an interior
change that is brought about in the soul of a Christian. In this instance, however, the sign actually accomplishes the things it signifies. But we must know
too that every Sacrament is a personal meeting with

Christ; by means of them the Lord continues His presence among us. And so, we must understand the Sacrament of penance as a personal ecounter with Christ, not merely as a confession of sin, nor a magic washing away of sin. We recall how, in the parable of the Prodigal Son, the father warmly embraced and welcomed his repentant son. Our meeting with the Lord in this Sacrament is just as personal as that.

Since sin is social in its effects, Penance also. We became members of God's family by Baptism, intimately joined to Christ and so to all His members. By sin we turn our back upon the Lord and our fellow Christians too; like the prodigal son we leave our household and family to look for love and happiness elsewhere. The Sacrament of Penance, then, reconciles us with Christ and with the whole family of God. It is a cause of joy to all.

The Examination of Conscience

First, we should put ourselves in Christ's presence, by reflecting upon some word of His or incident in His life which tells us of His love, mercy and forgiveness. A brief meditation on our Lord's Passion would help us to understand sin as a personal offense against Him; His Resurrection is the source of our hope: that if we put sin to death, we will enjoy again our life in God. To aid us in our brief meditation, we should bring our Bible to Church. All this may be done at home before we come to church.

Our examination of conscience should concern itself especially with our particular vocation and how well we have served Christ in it. We should examine our relations with those about us, in our family, at our place of employment, and measure these relations against the example of our Lord. If we know of no serious rejection of God in our life since our previous confession, it is better to stress some special area of our daily life to discover where we have failed and how we can better serve and imitate the Lord in it, than to scatter our efforts. Our last visit to Him in this Sacrament should not be forgotten. What progress have we made in those matters about which our resolution centred at that time? Finally, opportunities to respond to God's love by doing good, which we may have neglected, are important, as well as positive wrong.

Contrition For Sin

Without genuine contrition, of course, there is no forgiveness. This is an essential element that we must bring to our meeting with Christ in the Sacrament of Penance.

Contrition is not discouragement at our own failure. Rather it springs from our awareness that sin is a personal rejection of Christ, a decision to put somebody or something before Him in our life; involved also is our awareness that sin alienates us from the people of God. Contrition, then, must be a genuine sorrow that we have turned away from Christ and our brothers and sisters in Christ, that we, like the Prodigal Son have left our father's household to go our own way. Now we look with longing and desire toward it again.

A firm resolve to be loyal to Christ, and to be a faithful member of God's people, easily flows from such sorrow. This resolve must be specific. It could centre upon the special area of our life which we looked to in our examination of conscience. Our sorrow should be evidenced by a definite plan of action to serve Christ better in those things in which we have failed Him.

Our sorrow, should be expressed before we enter the Confessional.

Helpful Suggestions for Confession

1. It is well to personalize our confession by identifying ourselves, e.g., "I am a married woman and have three children," or "I am a widower," or "I am a teacher," etc. This reveals us to the Celebrant as a real person, living in a real situation and serving God in a particular vocation. It helps the Celebrant to judge our service to Christ and to direct us in conforming ourselves to Him.

2. The Sacrament of Penance is a means of Christian perfection. We should use it in a manner that will help us to grow more like Christ. We could refer to the progress, or lack of it, that we think we have made since our last visit to this Sacrament, e.g., "In my last confession I resolved to love Christ more in the people with whom I work; since then, I have improved, but still I have failed many times." Again, this personalizes our confession and avoids the automatic listing of our sins.

3. Our sorrow and purpose of amendment should be expressed before we receive the Sacrament, and is evidenced by our "Amen" in response to the principal prayer of absolution. It can also be expressed in the very confession of our sins. For example, we could say "In the past month I was irritable many times with my wife and family, hurting the spirit of our home. This month I really want to correct this." Again, this manner of confessing avoids the harmful cataloguing of sins, and is a sign of our sincerity of purpose.

4. How often should I meet the Lord in this Sacrament? If we have consciously chosen against the Lord in our life, in some serious matter, we should promptly seek His mercy in this Sacrament, as long as we are truly repentant. If there is no question of a turning away from God in this way, Confession is not necessary for us, regardless of how long it may be since our last Confession. However, received with the proper dispositions, it will help us to grow in the Christian life. If we receive the Sacrament often, but without necessity, the burden is on us to receive it fruitfully. The Christian's life is one of constant conversion, of a continually renewed commitment. If our regular confession is made in that light, and with that purpose, the Lord's grace will effect things in our spiritual life.

The Penitent's Formula for the Sacrament of Penance

Penitent: Bless me Father, for I have sinned.

Celebrant: The Lord be on your lips and in your heart that you may properly confess all your sins, in the Name of the Father, ✠ and of the Son, and of the Holy Spirit.

✠ *Penitent makes the sign of the Cross over himself.*

Penitent: It is ...... since my last confession.

(The penitent confesses)

Penitent: For these and all my sins I am truly sorry.

(The Celebrant instructs and gives the penance to the Penitent)

Celebrant: *Now absolves the Penitent, who does not say the Act of Contrition but reverently listens, and answers "Amen" to the principal prayer of absolution. Our "Amen" is a sign of our acceptance of God's mercy, and an evidence of our sorrow.*

"May Our Lord Jesus Christ absolve you, and by His authority I absolve you, from every bond of excommunication and interdict to the extent of my power and your need. And finally, I absolve you from your sins, in the Name of the Father, ✠ and of the Son, and of the Holy Spirit.

Penitent: Amen.

COMMUNION PSALMS

For Private Thanksgiving after Mass

Psalm 22 — The Lord, Shepherd and Host

THE Lord is my shepherd, I shall not want.
  In verdant pastures He gives me repose;
Beside restful waters He leads me;

3   He refreshes my soul.
He guides me in right paths
    for His Name's sake.

4 Even though I walk in the dark valley
    I fear no evil; for You are at my side
With Your rod and Your staff
    that give me courage.

5 You spread the table before me
    in the sight of my foes;
  You anoint my head with oil;
    my cup overflows.

6 Only gloodness and kindness follow me
     all the`days of my life;
   And I shall dwell in the house of the Lord
     for years to come.

Psalm 33 — Praise of God, the Protector of the Just

I WILL bless the Lord at all times;
  His praise shall be ever in my mouth.
3 Let my soul glory in the Lord;
    the lowly will hear me and be glad.
4 Glorify the Lord with me,
    let us together extol His Name.
5 I sought the Lord, and He answered me
    and delivered me from all my fears.
6 Look to Him that you may be radiant with joy,
    and your faces may not blush with shame.
7 When the afflicted man called out, the Lord
     heard,
    and from all his distress He saved him.
8 The Angel of the Lord encamps
    around those who fear Him, and delivers them.
9 Taste and see how good the Lord is;
    happy the man who takes refuge in Him.
10 Fear the Lord, you His holy ones,
    for nought is lacking to those who fear Him.
11 The great grow poor and hungry;
    but those who seek the Lord want for no good
     thing.
12 Come, children, hear me;
    I will teach you the fear of the Lord.
13 Which of you desires life,
    and takes delight in prosperous days?
14 Keep your tongue from evil
    and your lips from speaking guile;
15 Turn from evil, and do good;
    seek peace, and follow after it.

16 The Lord has eyes for the just,
    and ears for their cry.

17 The Lord confronts the evildoers,
    to destroy remembrance of them from the
        earth.

18 When the just cry out, the Lord hears them,
    and from all their distress He rescues them.

19 The Lord is close to the brokenhearted;
    and those who are crushed in spirit He saves.

20 Many are the troubles of the just man,
    but out of them all the Lord delivers him;

21 He watches over all his bones;
    not one of them shall be broken.

22 Vice slays the wicked,
    and the enemies of the just pay for their guilt.

23 But the Lord redeems the lives of His servants;
    no one incurs guilt who takes refuge in Him.

Psalm 148 — Praise the Lord in Heaven and on Earth

PRAISE the Lord in His sanctuary,
    praise Him in the firmament of His strength.

2 Praise Him for His mighty deeds,
    praise Him for His sovereign Majesty.

3 Praise Him with the blast of the trumpet,
    praise Him with lyre and harp,

4 Praise Him with timbrel and dance,
    praise Him with strings and pipe.

5 Praise Him with sounding cymbals,
    praise Him with clanging cymbals.

6 Let everything that has breath
    praise the Lord! Alleluia.

THE STATIONS OF THE CROSS

The Stations of the Cross is a devotion in which we accompany, in spirit, our Blessed Lord in His sorrowful journey to Calvary, and devoutly meditate on His sufferings and death.

1. Jesus is Condemned to Death

O Jesus, help me to appreciate Your sanctifying grace more and more.

2. Jesus Bears His Cross

O Jesus, You chose to die for me. Help me to love You always with all my heart.

3. Jesus Falls the First Time

O Jesus, make me strong to conquer my wicked passions, and to rise quickly from sin.

4. Jesus Meets His Mother

O Jesus, grant me a tender love for Your Mother, who offered You for love of me.

5. Jesus is Helped by Simon

O Jesus, like Simon lead me ever closer to You through my daily crosses and trials.

6. Jesus and Veronica

O Jesus, imprint Your image on my heart that I may be faithful to You all my life.

7. Jesus Falls a Second Time

O Jesus, I repent for having offended You. Grant me forgiveness of all my sins.

8. Jesus Speaks to the Women

O Jesus, grant me tears of compassion for Your sufferings and of sorrow for my sins.

9. Jesus Falls a Third Time

O Jesus, let me never yield to despair. Let me come to You in hardship and spiritual distress.

10. He is Stripped of His Garments

O Jesus, let me sacrifice all my attachments rather than imperil the divine life of my soul.

11. Jesus is Nailed to the Cross

O Jesus, strengthen my faith and increase my love for You. Help me to accept my crosses.

12. Jesus Dies on the Cross

O Jesus, I thank You for making me a child of God. Help me to forgive others.

13. Jesus is Taken down from the Cross.

O Jesus, through the intercession of Your holy Mother, let me be pleasing to You.

14. Jesus is Laid in the Tomb.

O Jesus, strengthen my will to live for You on earth and bring me to eternal bliss in heaven.

THE HOLY ROSARY

The Rosary calls to mind the five Joyful, the five sorrowful, and the five Glorious Mysteries in the life of Christ and His Blessed Mother. It is composed of fifteen decades, each decade consisting of one "Our Father," ten "Hail Marys," and one "Glory be to the Father."

How to Say the Rosary

The Apostles' Creed *is said on the Crucifix; the* Our Father *is said on each of the Large Beads; the* Hail Mary *on each of the Small Beads; the* Glory be to the Father *after the three Hail Marys at the beginning of the Rosary, and after each group of Small Beads.*

The Joyful Mysteries

Mondays, Thursdays, the Sundays of Advent, and Sundays from Epiphany until Lent.

1. Annunciation *(Humility)*
2. Visitation *(Charity)*
3. Birth of our Lord *(Poverty)*
4. Presentation *(Obedience)*
5. Finding in the Temple *(Piety)*

The Sorrowful Mysteries

Tuesdays, Fridays, throughout the year; and daily from Ash Wednesday until Easter Sunday.

1. Agony in the Garden *(Contrition)*
2. Scourging at the Pillar *(Purity)*
3. Crowning with Thorns *(Courage)*
4. Carrying of the Cross *(Patience)*
5. The Crucifixion *(Self-denial)*

The Glorious Mysteries

Wednesdays, Saturdays, and the Sundays from Easter until Advent.

1. Resurrection of Christ *(Faith)*
2. Ascension of Christ *(Hope)*
3. Descent of the Holy Spirit *(Love)*
4. Assumption *(Eternal happiness)*
5. Crowning of B.V.M. *(Devotion to Mary)*

INDEX OF HYMNS

I. ALPHABETICAL INDEX

Page No.

A Child Is Born 400
Accept, Almighty Father 379
All Glory, Laud and Honor 402
All People That on Earth .. 391
Antiphons 434
As with Gladness Men of Old 401
At the Cross 403
At That First Eucharist 385
Be Joyful Mary 411
Come, Holy Ghost 413
Come, O Creator Spirit Blest 414
Come, O Divine Messiah 394
Come, Thou Long Expected 396
Crown Him with Many
   Crowns 377
Dear Maker of the Starry
   Skies 395
Down in Adoration Falling 374
Faith of Our Fathers 388
For All the Saints 423
For the Beauty of The Earth 428
Good Christian Men Rejoice 399
Great St. Joseph 421
Hail, Holy Joseph 422
Hail, Holy Queen 420
Hark! The Herald Angels .. 398
Holy God, We Praise Thy
   Name 392
Holy, Holy, Holy! 375
Holy Spirit, Lord of Light 412
How Bright Appears the
   Morning Star 397
Humbly We Adore Thee 382
Immaculate Mary 420
Incline Thine Ear, O Lord .. 405
Jesus Christ Is Risen Today 406
Let All Mortal Flesh Keep
   Silence 415

Page No.

Let Hymns of Joy to Grief
   Succeed 409
Lord, Accept the Gifts 380
Lord Who throughout these
   Forty Days 405
Masses 436
Now Thank We All Our God 386
O Come, All Ye Faithful 398
O Come, O Come, Emmanuel 393
O Food That Weary Pilgrims
   Love 384
O God, Almighty Father 389
O God of Lovliness 387
O God, Our Help 390
O Jesus, Joy of Loving Hearts 418
O King of Might 381
O Perfect Love 425
O Sacred Head Surrounded 404
O Saving Victim 417
O Sons and Daughters 407
O Worship the King 426
On This Day 378
Our Father 432
Out of the Depths 430
Praise God from Whom All
   Blessings Flow 391
Praise, My Soul 429
Praise the Lord, All You
   Nations (Ps. 116) 425
Praise the Lord, Ye Heavens 376
Praise to the Lord 372
Psalm 99 462
Silent Night 400
Sing My Tongue 416
Singers, Sing 408
Sing We Triumphant Hymns 411
Soul of My Savior 384

Page No.

That All Be One 424
The Advent of Our King 396
The Church's One Founda-
   tion 427
The First Noel 398
The God Whom Earth and
   Sea and Sky 419

Page No.

The Magi Kings 400
The Strife Is O'er 410
To Jesus Christ 392
To the Name 374
We Praise Thee, O God 373
Where Abideth Charity 431
Within Thy Sacred Heart ... 418

II. LITURGICAL INDEX (Suggested Use)

ENTRANCE

1. Praise to the Lord 372
2. We Praise Thee O God 373
3. To the Name 374
4. Holy, Holy, Holy 375
5. Praise the Lord Ye Heavens 376
6. Crown Him With Many
   Crowns 377
7. On This Day 378

OFFERTORY

8. Accept, Almighty Father 379
9. Lord, Accept the Gifts 380
10. O King of Might 381

COMMUNION

11. Humbly We Adore Thee 382
12. Soul of My Savior 384
13. O Food That Weary Pil-
   grims Love 384
14. At That First Eucharist 385

RECESSIONAL

15. Now Thank We All Our
   God 386
16. O God of Lovliness 387
17. Faith of Our Fathers 388
18. O God, Almighty Father 389
19. O God, Our Help in
   Ages Past 390
20. Praise God from Whom
   All Blessings Flow 391

20-A All People That On
   Earth Do Dwell 391
21. To Jesus Christ, Our
   Sovereign King 392
22. Holy God, We Praise
   Thy Name 392

ADVENT

23. O Come, O Come Em-
   manuel 393
24. Come, O Divine Messiah 394
25. Dear Maker of the Starry Skies 395

CHRISTMAS

26. The Advent of Our King 396
27. Come, Thou Long Ex-
   pected Savior 396
28. How Bright Appears the
   Morning Star 397
29. Hark! The Herald Angels 398
30. O Come, All Ye Faithful 398
31. The First Noel 398
32. Good Christian Men .. 399
33. A Child Is Born in
   Bethlehem 400
34. Silent Night 400

EPIPHANY

33-A The Magi Kings 400
35. As With Gladness Men
   of Old 401

Page No.

LENT

36. All Glory, Laud, and Honor 402
37. At The Cross 403
38. O Sacred Head 404
39. Incline Thine Ear 405
40. Lord Who throughout these Forty Days 405

EASTER

41. Jesus Christ Is Risen Today 406
42. O Sons and Daughters 407
43. Singers, Sing 408
44. Let Hymns of Joy to Grief Succeed 409
45. The Strife Is O'er 410
46. Be Joyful Mary 411

ASCENSION

47. Sing We Triumphant Hymns of Praise 411

PENTECOST

48. Holy Spirit, Lord of Light 412
49. Come, Holy Ghost 413
50. Come, O Creator Spirit 414

BLESSED SACRAMENT

3-A Down in Adoration Falling 374
51. Let All Mortal Flesh Keep Silence 415
52. Sing, My Tongue 416
53. O Saving Victim 417

SACRED HEART

54. Within Thy Sacred Heart 418
55. O Jesus, Joy of Loving Hearts 418

Page No.

BLESSED VIRGIN MARY

37. At the Cross 403
46. Be Joyful Mary 411
56. The God Whom Earth and Sea and Sky 419
57. Immaculate Mary 420
58. Hail, Holy Queen 420

MISCELLANEOUS

59. Great St. Joseph 421
60. Hail, Holy Joseph 422
61. For All the Saints 423
62. That All Be One 424
63. Praise the Lord, All You Nations (Ps. 116) 425
64. O Perfect Love 425
65. O Worship the King 426
66. The Church's One Foundation 427
67. For the Beauty of the Earth 428
68. Praise, My Soul, the King of Heaven 429
69. Out of the Depths 430
70. Where Abideth Charity 431
71. Our Father 432
72. Our Father 433
73-86 Antiphons 434
92. Psalm 99 462

BENEDICTION OF THE MOST BLESSED SACRAMENT

At the opening of Benediction any Eucharistic Hymn may be sung.

Hymn: **Down in adoration falling,**
Lo! The sacred Host we hail;
Lo! O'er ancient forms departing
Newer rites of grace prevail;
Faith for all defects supplying
Where the feeble senses fail.

To the everlasting Father
And the Son Who reigns on high,
With the Spirit blest proceeding
Forth from each eternally,
Be salvation, honor, blessing,
Might, and endless majesty. Amen.

℣. You have given them bread from heaven. (P.T. Alleluia.)

℞. Having all sweetness within it. **(P.T. Alleluia.)**

Celebrant: Let us pray: O God, Who in this wonderful sacrament left us a memorial of Your passion, grant, we implore You, that we may so venerate the sacred mysteries of Your Body and Blood as always to be conscious of the fruit of Your redemption. You Who live and reign with God the Father in the unity of the Holy Spirit, God, forever and ever. ℞. Amen.

The Divine Praises

Blessed be God. * Blessed be His Holy Name. * Blessed be Jesus Christ, true God and true man. * Blessed be the Name of Jesus. * Blessed be His Most Sacred Heart. * Blessed be His Most Precious Blood. * Blessed be Jesus in the Most Holy Sacrament of the Altar. * Blessed be the Holy Spirit, the Paraclete. * Blessed be the great Mother of God, Mary most holy. * Blessed be her holy and Immaculate Conception. * Blessed be her glorious Assumption. * Blessed be the name of Mary, Virgin and Mother. * Blessed be St. Joseph, her most chaste spouse. * Blessed be God in His angels and in His saints. Indulgence of 3 years

THANKSGIVING PRAYERS AFTER MASS

Ant. Let us sing the Canticle of the Three Youths which these Saints sang in the fiery furnace, giving praise to the Lord. (P.T. Alleluia.)

Canticle of the Three Youths
Dan. 3, 57-88.56

Bless the Lord, all you works of the Lord,
   praise and exalt Him above all forever.
Angels of the Lord, bless the Lord,
   you heavens, bless the Lord;
All you waters above the heavens bless the Lord.
   All you hosts of the Lord, bless the Lord;
Sun and moon, bless the Lord;
   stars of heaven, bless the Lord.

Every shower and dew, bless the Lord;
   all you winds, bless the Lord;
Fire and heat, bless the Lord;
   cold and chill, bless the Lord;
Dew and rain, bless the Lord;
   frost and cold, bless the Lord;
Ice and snow, bless the Lord;
   nights and days, bless the Lord;
Light and darkness, bless the Lord;
   lightnings and clouds, bless the Lord.

Let the earth, bless the Lord,
   praise and exalt Him above all forever.
Mountains and hills, bless the Lord;
   everything growing from the earth, bless the
     Lord;
You springs, bless the Lord;
   seas and rivers, bless the Lord;
You dolphins and all water creatures, bless the
     Lord;
   all you birds of the air, bless the Lord;